THE RECTIFIED SCOTTISH RITE

BY RÉMI BOYER

The Ways of Awakening Trilogy

Freemasonry as a Way of Awakening

*Mask Cloak Silence:
Martinism as a Way of Awakening*

*Beneath the Veil of Elias Artista
The Rose-Croix as a Way of Awakening:
An Oral Tradition*
(with Lima de Freitas and Manuel Gandra)

*The Rectified Scottish Rite:
From the Doctrine of Reintegration
to the* Imago Templi

WITH SYLVIE BOYER-CAMAX

*Letters to Friends of the Spirit:
Martinist Views & Others*

The Way Without Masters

THE RECTIFIED
SCOTTISH RITE

FROM THE DOCTRINE OF REINTEGRATION TO THE *IMAGO TEMPLI*

BY RÉMI BOYER

Prefaces by José Anes and Serge Caillet

Rose Circle Publications
Bayonne, NJ
2023

The Rectified Scottish Rite:
From the Doctrine of Reintegration to the *Imago Templi*

Copyright © 2023 Rémi Boyer
English translation copyright © by Michael Sanborn

ISBN: 978-1-947907-24-9
Library of Congress Control Number: 2023903678

Originally published in French as *Le Régime Écossais Rectifié, de la Doctrine de la Réintégration à l'Imago Templi* by Éditions de la Tarente, Marseille, 2015.

Cover painting: *Maria Madalena ou Sophia* by Carlos Barahona Possollo, oils on canvass and wood, 2008.

Book design and layout by Michael Sanborn, TextArc LLC. michael@textarc.net

All rights reserved. No part of this publication may be reproduced, distributed, or transmitted in any form or by any means, including photocopying, recording, or other electronic or mechanical methods, without the prior written permission of the publisher, except in the case of brief quotations embodied in critical reviews and certain other non-commercial uses permitted by copyright law. For permission requests, write to the publisher at the address below.

Rose Circle Publications
P.O. Box 854
Bayonne, NJ 07002, U.S.A.
www.rosecirclebooks.com

CONTENTS

	Preface by José Anes	vii
	Preface by Serge Caillet	ix
	Introduction	xix
I	**The Doctrine of Martinez de Pasqually: What the Doctrine Can Say**	1
	Three Paths to Reintegration	3
	A Science of Numbers	11
	From One to Many	17
	Three or Four Immensities	21
	The Central Fire Axis	27
	Emanation, Emancipation, and Creation	33
	The Primordial Cult, *la Chose,* and the Good Companion Spirit	41
	Beneficence and Freedom	47
	Interlude: A Letter on Sanctity	51
II	**The Doctrine of Reintegration within the Rectified Scottish Rite: What the Rituals Can Say**	59
	The Temple and the Temples	61
	Journey into the Rituals	69
	The Ternary	69
	The Good Companion Spirit	75
	The Quaternary	80
	What to Make of 2 and 5?	93
	And of Colors…	97
	Here End the Symbols	99
	The Temples and the Temple	105
	Interlude: Metaphysics and Initiation	109

III	The Rectified Scottish Rite as a Way of Awakening: What the Instructions of the Professed and Grand Professed Can Say	125
	The Profession and the Grand Profession	127
	The Instruction of the Professed	137
	The Instruction of the Grand Professed	153
	To Never End	177
	Selected Bibliography	189

PREFACE BY JOSÉ ANES

IN MEMORIAM LIMA DE FREITAS, ANTÓNIO TELMO,
AND JEAN-LOUIS LARROQUE

With his book *Freemasonry as a Way of Awakening*, Rémi Boyer has already given us valuable tools for a truly initiatory Masonry. He now brings us a set of keys to open the precious edifice of the RER (Rectified Scottish Rite or Regime[1]) of the Order of CBCS (Beneficent Knights of the Holy City), and to pass from chivalric templarism—so appreciated by many Freemasons and within the framework of which I organized in Tomar several ceremonies with a strong international presence of grand priories from other countries when I was the Grand Prior of the GPIL (Independent Grand Priory of Lusitania), from 1995 to 2000—to permanent Templarism or Templism, less accessible to ordinary Rectified Masons, but available to all those who want to work on themselves.

Based on the Doctrine of the Reintegration of Beings by Martinez de Pasqually, an Iberian Jew (possibly Portuguese) converted to Catholicism, as Catholic as was Jean-Baptiste Willermoz, who wrote the Rectified rituals, this Templism starts from its Judaic roots to reach the Christian dimension, transcending Judaism without denying it. Although the theurgic ritual operativity of the Order of Knight Masons Élus Coëns of the Universe, clearly Judeo-Christian, is absent from the Rectified Scottish Rite, the ideas and techniques are nevertheless present of a Reintegration that calls to the interior work of the Rectified Mason wishing to pass from form to essence and thus from the rituals and catechisms

---

[1] Jean-Baptiste Willermoz founded a "Regime" (an initiatory order in its own right, autonomous and independent of a Masonic obedience) composed of a structure, a rite, and a doctrine. When the RER is found among other Masonic rites, practiced within an obedience (the *Grande Loge Traditionnelle et Symbolique Opéra* or the *Grand Orient de France,* for example), it is no more than a "Rite," depending on the particular obedience. The original French text of this book uses the term "Regime" more often than not, but this translation uses "Rite" throughout, to conform with English usage.–Trans.

of Apprentice to the Instructions for the Professed and Grand Professed, the extension of the Rite or Regime today occulted.

When I received Rémi Boyer within the GPIL and into the Order of CBCS, it was with the sense that his initiatory contribution, that of a true instructor, would help to awaken its members—starting with myself—to the richness of a doctrine within our reach, and that it was imperative to discover and derive spiritual benefit from it. I remember in this regard, with gratitude, that in the operative field I was introduced by Rémi Boyer to the complex operativity of the Élus Coëns, who constitute a Réau-Croix as part of the resurgence initiated by Robert Ambelain and restored by Robert Amadou.

It is certain that the Independent Grand Priory of Lusitania had illustrious members to whom this initiatory world was known. I would only mention Lima de Freitas and António Telmo, whom I had the honor of receiving into Rectified Masonry (curious circumstance, that of a disciple initiating his Masters…), but as Grand Prior of the Rite in Portugal, I had wished that this treasure could be accessible to a greater number of Rectified Freemasons, as I now also wish that this book by Rémi Boyer could be useful to the Rectified Freemasons of other countries, so that "the Order prospers"!

Feast of the Assumption 2014

José Manuel Anes
Past Grand Prior and Past National Grand
Master of the GPIL of the Order of CBCS

PREFACE BY SERGE CAILLET

1

The Rectified Scottish Rite claims, sometimes with flash and sometimes with modesty, to be the flagship of traditional Freemasonry, even its perfection, just as Christianity seeks to be religion perfected, the perfect religion. It is true that the Rectified Scottish Rite is a Christian Masonic rite, which rectifies Anderson's Freemasonry by re-Christianizing it for the benefit of those Christians whom the Masonic way seduces. It goes without saying (so it is better to say it anyway) that "Christian," in this case, does not refer to any particular Christian denomination, as Rectified Masons seek to be faithful to Christ Jesus, Grand Architect of the Universe, apart from but without prejudice to their individual attachment to the constituted churches, Catholic, Reformed, or Orthodox.

However, for some time the Rectified Scottish Rite has flourished in French-speaking countries where it has essentially been confined since its origin—to its benefit, no doubt, and that of disoriented Christian Masons, and perhaps Christian Masons of desire; to its misfortune too, no doubt, against a backdrop of obsolete and antiquated quarrels.

Rectified literature, long limited to a few classics, today bears witness to this liveliness in diversity. Two essential authors of the history of events, Alice Joly and René Le Forestier, had long occupied the shelves of bookstores and libraries by themselves. In the 1960s, three Grand Professed joined them, unearthing essential texts: Jean Tourniac (Jean Granger) regarding tradition, and Jean Saunier (Ostabat) and Robert Amadou (Maharba), notably in the columns of *Le Symbolisme*, concerning the commented editions of order documents. In the 1970s and until today, the school of *Renaissance Traditionnelle*, under the direction of René Désaguliers (René Guilly), then of Roger Dachez, followed suit, while *Les Cahiers de Villard de Honnecourt* of the Grande Loge Nationale Française, and, even more so, *Les Cahiers verts* of the Grand Prieuré des Gaules, produced their own studies in which the writings of Jean-François Var stand out in particular. Recently, Jean-Marc Vivenza and Jean-Claude Sitbon, each in his own way, have added a substantial contribution to this literature.

This literary proliferation, however, is not always exempt from polemics, echoing the quarrels (whether of resources or formalities) which are customary in Western initiatory societies and which, after having been spared it for a long time, now also affect, as I had mentioned, the Rectified Scottish Rite.

This new book by Rémi Boyer, which I am very pleased to preface, could well, in turn and despite itself, excite the bile of some polemicist. No matter, since it maintains the straight line of his three previous works: *Freemasonry as a Way of Awakening* (2020), *Beneath the Veil of Elias Artista: the Rose-Croix as a Way of Awakening, an Oral Tradition* (2021), and *Mask Cloak Silence: Martinism as a Way of Awakening* (2021),[2] the present volume of which completes the triptych so that it transforms (unsurprisingly) into a happy quaternity.

2

The Rectified Scottish Rite reforms traditional Freemasonry. In the last quarter of the 18th century, a man, Jean-Baptiste Willermoz, was its artisan, after having long searched in the Illuminist Masonry of his time for something to satisfy his desires for an authentic gnosis, which he ended up discovering in a peculiar school, in 1767.

This school, the school of Bordeaux, as it is sometimes called, had been active for about ten years, and was named the Order of Knight Masons Élus Coëns of the Universe, also known as the Order of the Élus Coëns of Joshua. Its great sovereign in our lands presented himself in the guise of a certain Martinez de Pasqually, with changing first names and uncertain identity. This one, admitted Willermoz, who had initially been wary, I knew none to compare to him. Louis-Claude de Saint-Martin, his impeccable companion, echoed him: he is, said he, the only living man of my acquaintance of whom I have not been able to take the measure. Let us understand that Martinez de Pasqually was a master, whereas most of those who considered themselves as such were most often not even capable of being disciples. Were not or are not, time is irrelevant here.

In truth, Martinez illuminates Freemasonry with the lights of a very

---

2   Bayonne, NJ: Rose Circle Publications.–Trans.

ancient tradition (with him, there is no Jewish Kabbalah in the strict sense, nor even a reputedly Christian Kabbalah), which can be described as a Judeo-Christian Kabbalah (Robert Amadou) that links him spiritually to the Judeo-Christians of the first centuries, notably those gathered in the Church of Jerusalem. His school, which numbered at most two to three hundred brothers and ten sisters, was entirely oriented towards the practice of the virtues and prayer, in a new form that associated theurgic worship with a Masonic setting.

It was said that Willermoz, admitted to the pinnacle of the temple and ordained Réau-Croix in 1768, had failed in his theurgic labors, on the grounds that he had not benefited from sensible manifestations. But that omits the recollection that the confession of this apprentice theurgist, in a letter to Martinez in 1770, motivated explanations from the master, who imputed his lack of success to an illicit reception, supplemented shortly thereafter with a new ordination by Martinez himself. Of Willermoz's subsequent operations we know nothing.

For the rest, unless one misunderstands its nature and limits the breath of the Spirit, *la Chose* presents itself in many forms, as Saint-Martin himself explained in a little *Traité sur les communications*, recently edited and published by Catherine Amadou. Since the tree must always be judged by its fruits, the success of Willermoz's work must be assessed very seriously in the light of his masterpiece: the Rectified Scottish Rite, which clearly testifies to the efficacy of the practice of the Coën from Lyon. Is not the Rectified Scottish Rite the most beautiful and sensitive manifestation of the operations of its founder?

3

The Order of the Élus Coëns did not survive the first years of the 19th century, since its leader entered the circles of purification in 1774, prematurely leaving two direct successors and a few emulators unable to fully maintain the blaze of new fire.

A flame, however, remained with some, in Toulouse for example. And Jean-Baptiste Willermoz himself maintained the Coën heritage, as much as possible, in the temple of Lyon, alongside Louis-Claude de Saint-Martin and Jean-Jacques Du Roy d'Hauterive, who combined their efforts with his in order to offer to the Élus Coëns of Lyon lessons that recapitulate, through explication, the doctrine of Martinez. Other lessons, at the Coën temple in Versailles for example, are in the same vein.

After this Willermoz limited himself, for the lack of any better options, to individual transmissions, the last of which is attested in 1813.

In the meantime, he formed the foundation then encouraged the propagation of the Rectified Scottish Rite, which rectifies the supposedly "Templar" Strict Observance while at the same time preserving the full doctrine of the Coëns. This doctrine consists of propositions, nothing less, nothing more, whose origin, long ignored or underestimated, leaves no shadow of a doubt. A Convent of Gaul in 1778, and a general convent in 1782, gave to the rite its definitive form, necessary for the preservation of this living lineage within traditional Freemasonry.

The secrets of Rectified Freemasonry therefore consist of a doctrine and rites, which are inseparable. Except when proposing a watered-down version of it, the Rectified Scottish Rite, whose sources are now clearly identified, is therefore not situated on the margins of Christianity, as is still sometimes written, but at the very heart of the Judeo-Christian tradition that Jean-Baptiste Willermoz, in particular, endeavored to synthesize in rituals. Everything there is symbolism, charged with meaning, which "secret" instructions ultimately illuminate at the summit of the ladder. However, starting from the grade of Apprentice, everything is declared for those who have the eyes to see and the ears to hear.

4

Alice Joly portrayed Jean-Baptiste Willermoz as a *Lyonnaise Mystic*. "Lyonnaise" is understood, but "mystic" is abusive, except to take the word in an overly vague modern sense, which winds up emptying it of its content. Willermoz is above all a Gnostic, in which moreover one cannot dissociate him from Martinez de Pasqually, nor even from Louis-Claude de Saint-Martin, although the Theosopher from Tours no doubt showed himself to be closer to mysticism than the Lyonnaise Mason.

Not only is the Gnosis of Willermoz not opposed to faith, but also, according to the words of Clement of Alexandria, it sublimates and perfects it. Religious, traditional, initiatory, and universal (as per Robert Amadou), this same Gnosis is the marrow of Freemasonry (as per Albert Pike) and the common lot of the three Theosophers who are the great lights of Martinism. It therefore makes the Rectified Scottish Rite a Gnostic rite, which rests on those two pillars of Gnosis that are Love and Knowledge.

Rémi Boyer shares this Gnostic approach with his readers today, in search of the Real. But the Real, he insists, is impossible to state; consequently, it is impossible to write. Text nonetheless remains one of the most useful tools, as are initiatory societies, to bring us closer to our Principle, or the Real, which is the essence of initiation.

Still, it is necessary to understand, and who wishes to understand the Rectified rituals, argues Rémi Boyer, must first know the keys used by their writers. However, these keys are the symbols and the knowledge, the propositions (as we mentioned), among the Élus Coëns, whose coherent whole precisely forms a doctrine. Reading the Rectified instructions and rituals offered by Rémi Boyer invites us to understand what the doctrine and rituals can say.

But for rites and symbols to be effective, it is still necessary to not dissociate them from the cultural and religious universe in which they were imagined and initially experienced. And what does it matter whether the intention of the authors was always conscious in this instance? The catechism of the grade of Master Élu Coën, for example, contains forty-four pairs of requests and responses. Now, the number 44 corresponds, as we know, to the double divine power, or the doubly strong spirit, Hély, the Christ, great Élu recurrent and perfect, which the fourth Coën grade symbolizes precisely. Did the author of this catechism therefore consciously and deliberately choose to include in it a total of forty-four questions and answers? Nothing is less sure! What is certain, on the other hand, is that this symbolic reading, even if unconsciously induced, becomes effective and legitimate, since it does not betray the tradition of the writers.

5

Rémi Boyer unearths in the rituals and instructions of the Rectified Scottish Rite a language of numbers and an operative grammar. But this language and grammar cannot be freed from the rules that constitute them. Martinez once taught them to his emulators; the Unknown Philosopher, better than anyone, restored the essentials from his collection of personal notes in *Les nombres*,[3] and no one can understand the Rectified Scottish Rite today without knowing them.

This new book by Rémi Boyer will be an excellent help to those who

---

3 *Les nombres* by Louis-Claude de Saint-Martin, ed. Robert Amadou (Nice: Bélisane, 1983). Published in English as "On Numbers" in *The Numerical Theosophy of Saint-Martin & Papus* by Gérard Encausse and Louis-Claude de Saint-Martin, trans. Piers A. Vaughan (Bayonne, NJ: Rose Circle, 2020).–Trans.

are not altogether unaware of the specific arithmosophy of the Coën tradition. In the Rectified Scottish Rite the numbers are everywhere, implicitly: numbers as signs of the Real, "luggage tags" as Saint-Martin said so cleverly, ever so useful to discern, to comprehend, to read in all simplicity in the letter of the texts in which the Spirit is conveyed.

But beware: there are two ways of conceiving numbers. In the first, the right one, divine eternity dissociates nothing from the decad, not even the 2 or the 5, which are nevertheless reputed to be apocryphal. But, in the world of forms and time—and the Rectified Scottish Rite obviously belongs to this world—the second distinguishes each number of the decad, from the divine unity to the denary, the first image of the divine. In the end, however, 10 is reduced to 1, and unity is reestablished by anticipation, and it will be definitively reestablished for each one of us with individual rehabilitation, which will precede the general Reintegration to which the Masonic initiation beckons.

6

The initiation, as proposed by the Rectified Scottish Rite, is accomplished, like the six days of creation, in the form of six ostensible grades, four of which are symbolic and two chivalric. These grades, which constitute the visible structure of the Rectified Scottish Rite, themselves form a hexagram, that is to say a double triangle, which is already present in the seal and in many of the operational outlines of the Élus Coëns, recalling the jewel of the grade of Scottish Master of Saint Andrew. This image is broken down into two triangles, one pointing up, the other pointing down, sometimes symbolizing respectively fire and water (which themselves form the sky), and sometimes symbolizing the Earth and the body of humans, among others.

Yet, all triangles rest on a center, invisible by nature, because 3 is a peripheral number and 4 a central number. The quaternary will therefore be the perfect number of the symbolic grades of the construction of the Temple, culminating in the revelation of the Scottish Master of Saint Andrew.

After which, the Squire-Novice and the Beneficent Knight of the Holy City, empowered practitioners of charity in the received truth, will complete the hexadic construction of a double triangle, of which 6 is the peripheral number. But the invisible point of the double triangle without a center, which is to 6 what 4 is to 3, that is the heptad. Such a symbol is this double center, manifested by 4 in the triangle and by 7 in the double triangle! A number, however, is missing, because "3 is to 4 as 7 is to 8," as Saint-Martin notes in his *Livre rouge*. And, a little further on: "The heptad is a state of constraint, and rest is only in the number 8." Another center, the last and the first, is therefore hidden behind 4 and 7, and it is the 8 which ultimately frees from all constraint and form. This invisible double center of the six visible grades can be identified with the seventh and eighth grades: the Profession and the Grand Profession.

Regarding this double secret class, placed at the heart of the rite much more than at its summit, what nonsense and widespread fantasies there are! We can never say it enough: the Profession and the Grand Profession in no way consist of some unguessable pseudo-ordination, while they preserve, beyond the forms, the doctrine of the Rite, in the silence that has always suited them, because, according to the saying of Saint-Martin, noise does no good and good does not make noise.

Today, after so many published and commented texts (to which this book contributes excellently), the double secret class is perhaps no longer formally essential, but its dual function of watchfulness and guardianship remains relevant, Rémi Boyer writes. Watchmen, in fact, are more necessary than ever for disoriented initiatory societies.

7

Watchman among watchmen, Jean-Baptiste Willermoz, the Gnostic from Lyon, came to seek, or even verify, from the Church Fathers what, in some way, could be in conformity with the teachings received from Martinez de Pasqually and more generally in the Coën Order.

The theology of Irenaeus, a Greek from Smyrna, a disciple of Polycarp, himself a disciple of John the Evangelist, who came to settle in Lyon where he succeeded Bishop Pothinus (martyred in 177 CE), marks in particular the fundamental themes of the Rectified Scottish Rite. Admittedly, sixteen centuries separate the patriarch of Rectified Masonry from one of the very first links in the apostolic chain of Lyon. From one to the other, however, a tradition of Gnostic essence, a spiritual filiation, emerges which in turn endows, in a certain way, the Rectified Scottish Rite.

With the Greek Fathers in particular, Irenaeus reminds us of the glorious state of man, created in the image and likeness of God. To man, who enjoyed immortality and relative perfection, God proposed becoming by grace what He is by nature: divine. For Irenaeus, the divine likeness of man takes the form of the spirit, while the composite soul-body participates in created nature. For Clement of Alexandria, as with Origen and Gregory of Nyssa, who scarcely distinguish the natural from the supernatural, the image is the desire for the supernatural and its germ in man, while the natural is in some way already implicitly contained in this same image.

Faithful to the Greek patristic tradition, Origen, Athanasius, and Basil the Great consider that this image, received in creation as the seed of our divinization, is absolutely indestructible. And Basil goes even further, for whom man was commanded to become God.

But, Origen insists, since the fall, the divine image does not exclude the presence of artificial images that accumulate in man: images of Satan or of Caesar, animal images that only hide the divine image of fallen man, for whom a real work of restoration is essential. In this process of initiation, the body of the embodied man therefore plays an ambiguous role, friend and enemy at the same time, as recalls John Climacus.

In line with Irenaeus, John Cassian emphasizes that the image is not destroyed by sin, but man, he says, is alienated, now subject to a master who is Satan. Like the image, the freedom of the degraded man is also not destroyed, but it is hampered, because man is a prisoner of the world and of its prince.

The present space where human freedom is exercised is therefore that of a fallen world, subject to suffering and death, this corruption caused (according to the Fathers) by the prevarication of the angels, and aggravated by that of our first temporal father. Martinez and Willermoz after him say nothing more.

But Christ frees man from the Evil One; he calls degraded man to cooperate freely with God in a loving union, of personal and reciprocal love, in restored freedom. To cooperate or to operate.

8

"So let's operate!" urged Saint-Martin to the Élus Coëns of Lyon. Yes, "let's operate!" added Robert Amadou, for other Élus Coëns, shortly before his call to God. In their own fashion Rectified Masons operate, Rémi Boyer insists today, because the exercise of benevolence and beneficence are theurgic acts and the specific operations of the Rectified Masons.

But where to operate if not in the temple? By renouncing the chimeras of an artificial Templar revival, Willermoz and his cohort have rediscovered the true Temple, where the Holy Order is periodically incarnated. Here, there is no ceremonial theurgic practice, as with the Élus Coëns, since the vocation of the Rectified Scottish Rite is quite different. But the body of man, the earth, and the universal creation are temples. And the temple is also in the heart of man where it must be built constantly by the search for knowledge in love since, the apostle John warns us, he who seeks the truth without loving his brother is in error.

Regarding the program of degraded man: find the divine resemblance, by the practice of the virtues and the guard of the thoughts. This deification of man, an unfathomable mystery according to John of Damascus, cannot be done without the grace of God who calls, in the words of Maximus the Confessor, "through love to reunite created nature with uncreated nature by making them appear in unity and identity through the acquisition of grace." This unity and this identity are those of the human person. The degraded man dies of hunger. But the Man of Desire finds his true nourishment by reversal, that is, by restoring things. His spirit feeds on God, his soul feeds on the spirit, and his body lives on his soul.

Christ, the new Adam, offers himself as food to fallen man. According to the formula of Irenaeus and Athanasius, unanimously taken up by the Fathers, God became man so that man could become God, thus opening the way to deification, which is the final end of man. Deification or Reintegration. The Rectified Scottish Rite offers nothing less.

Serge Caillet

INTRODUCTION

Let us follow Levinas. Rather than looking for what the texts mean, let's look at what they can say. First of all, it seems impossible to know what the author really means in a text that deals with the essence of things or the complexity of human experience. Does the author themself know? Whoever carefully examines the process of writing, this sublime trace, becomes aware that the mystery endures and how, on re-reading, every author feels the text escape them as soon as it is transcribed on the sheet. Words demand to come out, the better to escape. The texts are much freer than their authors.

What the text can say is often richer than what is intended or what might be intended, because the text is an exclusive space for the encounter of a spirit with itself through the thought of another. What matters, for us installed in the initiatory process, is what the text can say within the perspective of awakening, of liberation, of realization, or of Reintegration, with which we are concerned here. How does the text bring me closer to my principle, to my own nature, to my original and ultimate reality? How does it contribute to the deification of the human being? How does this text, delivered to the self, lead to the Self?

If we are here together in this place of the text, author and reader not separate, it is because we have the intuition, the sense of our original, ultimate, and absolute reality. Stuck in duality, the echo of our nondual nature, intrinsically free, resonates even in the cascade of vulgar words.

Today we would have to rethink an initiatory curriculum. This curriculum should be accompanied by a utopia, because only utopia can approach the Real. We have to define what an initiate is, an initiated woman or initiated man, commensurate with the absolute Freedom of the Real (of God, of the Lord, of the Self, etc.). We have to refuse to lower the threshold of initiation, as occurred in the slow initiatory erosion of a 20th century under the influence of the merchant caste. Initiation begins with the silence in which unfolds—unique, singular, and unexpected like the Spirit—the initiatory way. Let us never accept that initiation is lost in rumor, in dualistic rumor.

The dualistic error (but a salutary error if it is not accompanied by indifference) must be thought about. "To think greatly is to err greatly," said Heidegger. Every true thought engenders its negation. The dualistic play of antinomies symbolized by the mosaic pavement, if accepted in its permanent dialectic, does not allow one to freeze in a single posture. It thus leads to the silence of being, by abandonment. If, within this infinite dialectic of initiation, we tirelessly seek for the next step, we end up falling into the interval, the void and its fullness. What Montaigne calls the undulating, the undulating of doubt, turns out to be discontinuous, full of opportunities to access the Real. The self renounces its imposture and agrees to dwell in the luminous shadow of the Self.

Initiation consists in getting closer to oneself (or to the Self, which amounts to the same thing). There is only *Me*. There is only *Self*. In the original Consciousness, the Self and the me are identical as Silence and noise are one, as absolute freedom and dualistic imprisonment are one.

We do not have to let ourselves be caught up in the *accelerando* of the self, which seeks to mask the discontinuity of appearance, the innumerable passages towards the Real that it conceals. The creation of appearance makes it possible to veil being. Speed creates illusion.

Initiation in the Garden (oriented directly on Freedom) differs from initiation in the City[4] (oriented on the organization of the path to Freedom) because tragedy is absent. Founding and ruling a city is deeply tragic in ancient Greece. Any social foundation, and the initiatory society is one, is doomed to failure, a tragic failure. The initiation in the Garden—which made the choice of Festivity rather than Tragedy, of Joy rather than sadness (smiles and divine laughter are present in the arts as in mathematics, in a score by Erik Satie as in the DNA double helix), of astonishment and wonder rather than reason and analysis, of enjoyment rather than frustration, of liberty rather than constraint—frees itself from forms to let the paths unfold that have their source deep within us, within our own immaculate, unconditioned nature. The City must lead to the Garden. Poetry can bring life to the City.

At the point of Emptiness—in the experience of this Emptiness that sees the world being reabsorbed into the cutting edge of the Soul

---

4 Rémi Boyer, *Beneath the Veil of Elias Artista: The Rose-Croix as a Way of Awakening, An Oral Tradition* (Bayonne, NJ: Rose Circle, 2021).

according to Meister Eckhart, when we are the Place of God, the dual place where nondual Consciousness radiates, both God and his manifestation, both the Real and the free play of the Real in its infinite manifestations, so many fleeting realities, actualized or not in a tension of the consciousness that we call "I"—we grasp the first Intention of the Real or Absolute. The Absolute, to exercise its full Freedom, plays at forgetting itself and finding itself, in an infinity of modalities that constitute the continuum of Consciousness, from the divine to the vulgar, from the nondual to the dual. The distinction between subject and object, comparison, memory, language, replication, and temporality are synonymous and simultaneous consequences of the absolute will of the Real-One to get lost and find itself in multiplicity without ever ceasing to be this that it is, in the ecstasy of Itself.

If Silence is the father-mother of the Word that will be articulated in all languages (starting from the first Sound, A, which will be articulated all the way down to noise), then languages, sacred or otherwise, are fragments of the proto-language that all traditions have sought. But this proto-language cannot be uttered. It would then be the object of duality, perceived and implemented by a separate subject. It is not to be sought in Sanskrit, Hebrew, Portuguese, Chaldean, or Basque, languages that are nonetheless close to the Source. Nor is it the mother tongue even if it is, by privilege, the natural language of our magic and our poetry, the mastery of which allows the translation of reality on the way to the Real. It would rather be a melody of silence, whose music, like poetry, expresses the mystery. Language and time are identical: they build our reality, this tension of consciousness, this source of intensity in the divine game. There is a grammar of God, a sacred grammar, that language echoes when it itself becomes the mirror of nature. The name of God, Elohim, combines in a nondual and dual unity *Mi* and *Eloha*, the hidden subject and the hidden object.[5] We are in this name, in the heart of this name, in the palace of the Hidden King, of the Self. When Christ asks us to operate in His name, that is to say in the name of God, it is not about delegating any power or authority. It is rather for the sake of the heart of this palace where His name resounds, where the separation between subject and object becomes null, where the One celebrates Itself in the Intimate.

---

5   George Steiner, "Langage et gnose" in *Œuvres* (Paris: Quarto Gallimard, 2013).

Jean-Baptiste Willermoz wanted to preserve at the heart of the Rectified Scottish Rite a doctrine: that of his master, Martinez de Pasqually. He was helped in this by various collaborators including Louis-Claude de Saint-Martin, the Unknown Philosopher, another favorite disciple of Martinez.

The doctrine of Martinez de Pasqually, as presented in his *Treatise on the Reintegration of Beings into their First Property, Virtue, and Divine Spiritual Power*, is not marked by the councils; it is rather close to that of the first Christians. Robert Amadou sees in it a parallel current both to the Christianity of the Churches and to the Kabbalah. This doctrine is not dogmatic and has a fluidity and a sacred uncertainty that should not allow it to become fixed in beliefs. It invites to the experience of God.

What the text can express, and to each one in singular ways, is a path towards the experience of God, of the Absolute, of Freedom, of the Self, of the complete Man, whatever the first idea is that we hear through the word, a sense that guides us from the stream to the heights of the free spirit.

I will not go into the history, treated elsewhere by talented authors who you will find in the bibliography. I will not enter into the dogmatic debates that harm the practice and the silence essential to the work. Generally speaking, we lack an epistemology. When we make the effort to really identify what we know and how we know it, there remains little or nothing—indeed, plenty of nothing. I will simply indicate a few leads, uncertain as all initiatory leads are, for those magnificent adventurers of commitments and doubts that are individuals (not persons), women and men, engaged in an initiatory quest, whatever the borrowed traditional form.

The Origenist reader of the work of Martinez de Pasqually finds Origen as the source of the work. The Valentinian reader detects the mark of Valentinus there. The follower of Christian orthodoxy sees in the work a classic vehicle for the deification of the human being as proposed by the Orthodox churches. I could demonstrate to you that in the *Angéliques*[6] there is a series of drawings that accurately describe an internal alchemy of which, in all likelihood, Martinez de Pasqually knew nothing. The text can say it. That doesn't imply it means to. When a follower, on any current whatsoever, approaches his principle, he gives an account of this principle, which is none other than his divine nature. Being speaks to

---

6   Robert Amadou, *La Magie des Élus-Cohens: Angéliques* (Paris: Cariscript, 1984).

being. It tends towards the One. The self speaks to the self. It separates. Being does not speak to me. Being is without need. The self is only an assemblage of artificial needs. Who am I, reader of an inspired text, a text, sometimes clumsy, born from the experience of the divine, from the experience of the absolute freedom of the spirit? Am I able to give way to Being to approach the Being of Being?

There are only propositions and a number of contradictions here which remind us that language, even in a non-Aristotelian approach, cannot restore the Real. At best, it can awaken in us the sense of the Real.

To write this essay, I had of course to take up the texts, rituals, essays, and comments of the founders of the Martinezist and Martinist current, our "Masters of the Past" and those who studied them, in particular the "Companions of Hierophany."

I drew much from the shared operational experience of a college of researchers gathered, from 1992, around Robert Amadou, this eldest Brother, this Watcher, to whom I pay homage here on behalf of all those immersed in the so-called "Martinist" current in its four expressions, the Order of Knight Masons Élus Coëns of the Universe, the theosophy of Louis-Claude de Saint-Martin, the Rectified Scottish Rite, and finally the Martinist Order in its various branches. Of course, I particularly followed the works and oral teachings of Robert Amadou, with whom I worked closely for many years, such as the vast correspondence, nearly five hundred letters, that we exchanged over the years and events. I have also relied extensively on the *Cours de martinisme*,[7] so precious for its depth and clarity, established by Serge Caillet, courses that I invite you to study or reread now.

What is written here must however be understood as a simple singularity on the path, and not as any truth.

---

[7] To study Martinism, we can only insist on the excellence of the *Cours de Martinisme* by Serge Caillet, within the framework of the Eléazar Institute, as an essential basis for the work.

I

The Doctrine of Martinez de Pasqually

WHAT THE DOCTRINE CAN SAY

THREE PATHS TO REINTEGRATION

Initiation, according to Louis-Claude de Saint-Martin, consists in drawing us nearer to our principle, to our original and ultimate nature, or as we say today, to the Self. The desire of God and of Sophia, his Wisdom, directs the life of the quester, man or woman. All desire, even the most vile, points to the desire for God, for the Self, for the Absolute, for Freedom. The satisfaction of any desire is an expectation of completion through belonging, recognition, or realization. Initiation begins when the needs for realization manifest themselves and impose themselves against the needs for recognition or belonging, more typical of the movements of the ego and its need for adhesion or even adherence.

We often think that satisfaction arises from the attainment of the object of desire. Sustained attention allows us to grasp that this attainment gives access for a brief moment to the void, to the interval and its fullness, to being, to the Self. It is therefore not access to the object coveted by the Man of Desire that brings satisfaction. There is no satisfaction other than the tranquility of the Self. The New Man, according to Saint-Martin, finds himself within this discontinuity of desire, which is also a discontinuity of the self, in these luminous intervals of access to Being.

For Martinez de Pasqually, Louis-Claude de Saint-Martin, and Jean-Baptiste Willermoz, as for their friends, the initiate is a theosopher rather than a philosopher in the sense we understand it today. The initiate, on the contrary, is a philosopher in the ancient sense: "One is a philosopher who lives as a philosopher." It is an art of continually living the Wisdom of God, of uniting with Sophia.

Theurgy is the means of God and the means of that sacred and intimate union proposed by Martinez de Pasqually. According to the *Dictionnaire de Trévoux* of 1704,[8] theurgy would be "the power to do marvelous and

---

8   *Dictionnaire universel françois et latin* (Trévoux, Fr.: Ganeau, 1704), a.k.a. the *Dictionnaire de Trévoux*.

supernatural things by miraculous and lawful means, by invoking the help of God and his angels." Martinez de Pasqually calls on a hierarchy of entities, archangels, angels, and others, who are all self-conscious energies installed in a grand design, that of the Reintegration of beings into their original and ultimate plenitude.

Many authors who study our tradition—which, let us remember, is part of the vast current of Illuminism—distinguish (necessarily) or oppose (erroneously) the external way and the internal way. The external way designates the recourse to ceremonial theurgic practices, while the internal way designates a cardiac theurgy, in the locus of intimacy. Why do we say that the opposition between the external and the internal constitutes an error, a dualistic error more precisely, with regrettable consequences both from the theoretical and practical points of view? The "place" of the external and the "place" of the internal are the same. This is Consciousness. What the body can do, what the soul can do, and what the spirit can do is always installed (in whatever modality) within Consciousness. To operate externally or to operate internally is to operate within Consciousness. The problem is not to choose between the external and the internal but to be able to be situated, here and now, in a pure presence to what is. The "place" of the operation is the Land of Silence, beyond any identification with the "me," the ego, or the "person." This ability to reach the center, the heart, the middle chamber of the Freemasons, to extract oneself from the agitated peripheries of the self, is moreover represented in the fourth grade of the Rectified Scottish Rite by the first image presented to the candidate who asks to be received as a Scottish Master of Saint Andrew. The body is able, the soul is able, and the spirit is able, but only in this temple of Silence, where the word is creator. In the noise, in the agitated flow of sounds, the word is only one more noise; the word is lost, sterile. In silence, the word creates, the word constitutes, and the word receives.

In the *Instructions aux hommes de désir,*[9] Saint-Martin appeals to the virtues of humility, patience, and charity as preconditions. They are not qualities of the "person," of the "me." So we have to put the "person" at a distance, like a simple peripheral object. The humility of the "me," the patience of the "me," and the charity of the "me" are all diversions and

---

[9] Louis-Claude de Saint-Martin, "Instructions aux hommes de désir" I, *Documents martinistes,* no. 1, ed. Robert Amadou (Paris: Cariscript, 1979).

reappropriation of the path by the ego. What Saint-Martin tells us about are the natural qualities of the unconditioned and unseparated being.

The *Doctrine of the Reintegration of Beings* is not addressed to "persons" but to beings freed from personal considerations and dualistic identifications with the object, beings freed from dualistic gravity. A practical theosophy, a science of initiation, requires access to Silence as a beginning.

Louis-Claude de Saint-Martin's reference to a Society of Independents, which is reminiscent of the ideal society of the Rose-Croix or the unique inner Church of the Gnostics, does not evoke a human society or organization but a timeless and informal assembly of beings free from human contingencies.

For Martinez de Pasqually, the goal of the Order of Knight-Masons Elus Coëns of the Universe is "to bring man back to his glorious origin (...) by teaching him to know himself, to consider the relationship that exists between him and the entirety of nature, of which he had perforce been the center had he not fallen from this origin, and finally to recognize the Supreme Being from whom he emanated."[10]

According to Martinez de Pasqually, ceremonial magic imposes itself on us because, since the fall (the second fall, in reality), we are incapable of spiritual operations. In a Spinozist way, we could say that we can only intervene at the level of the first kind of knowledge, that of perceptions or forms, and sometimes at the level of the second kind of knowledge, that of causes, but no longer at the level of the third kind of knowledge, that of essences.

Let us recall the process of the double fall. God has always emanated the beings or free spirits who constitute his court, his celestial assembly. Some of them rebel against their Creator, whatever the reason for this rebellion. This rebellion also proves toxic for the spirits who remain faithful to the Eternal, which leads God to isolate the rebellious spirits in the material world, created for this purpose. Adam is a singular spirit, a member of a class of beings emanated by God in his likeness, that of man, to guard the material world but also to "educate the demons" that populate it. Adam will fail in his mission on the day when, fascinated by the prince of fallen spirits, he tries to generate a creature, Eve—a mistake. Eve is endowed with a body of darkness. Adam thus loses his

---

10 Vialetes d'Aignan, "Discours coëns," in Louis-Claude de Saint-Martin, *Théosophie et théologie. Documents martinistes*, no. 13, ed. Robert Amadou (Paris: Cariscript, 1980).

body of light and takes, like Eve, a dark body that keeps him a prisoner of matter. The jailer has become a prisoner of the world he had to guard.

This dramatic trial can be interpreted in different ways, all of which have operative consequences. Let us remember for the moment that Adam and we ourselves who are his descendants cannot henceforth escape either temporality or causality. We can only operate through perceptible forms, words, signs, signatures, symbols, sounds, notes, and figures in order to hope to regain our original place and power with the Eternal. To fully realize this Reintegration we can, according to Martinez de Pasqually, appeal to angelic intermediaries. For Martinez, it is much less a question of obtaining, even in a meritorious way, this initial place lost and sought after, than of celebrating, without expecting anything in return, a primordial Cult in complete freedom, as we would in essence never have ceased to do if we had avoided the process of falling, of drifting away from the center of everything. With ceremonial theurgy, we are not in a form of Promethean magic at the service of having and doing, but in the free play of grace and beauty. Martinez de Pasqually will not cease to insist on this priestly function which underlies the doctrine and the Order of Knight Masons Élus Coëns of the Universe, *coën* making explicit reference to this original priesthood.

Louis-Claude de Saint-Martin observes that the word *coën* comes from *coena*:[11] "The *coena* of Christ was the consummation of all sacrifices. This is why it had the same name as, and was made in the evening by allusion to, the total sacrifice that will be made in the great evening of the universe."[12]

Jean-Baptiste Willermoz, initiated into diverse Masonic rites, practiced the primordial cult within the Order of Knight Masons Élus Coëns of the Universe. As a received Réau-Croix, the culmination of the system implemented by Martinez de Pasqually, he made the choice at the death of his master to preserve the Doctrine of the Reintegration of Beings within a Masonic system. We can wonder about this choice. The initiatory model of Freemasonry (which we have analyzed elsewhere[13] as the model par excellence of the Initiation into the City that we distinguish from the

---

11   Latin: "supper."–Trans.
12   *Cahier des Langues* no. 43, quoted by Robert Amadou in *Les Angéliques*, vol. I, (Guérigny, Fr: CIREM, 2001).
13   Rémi Boyer, *Freemasonry as a Way of Awakening* (Bayonne, NJ: Rose Circle, 2021).

Initiation into the Garden), among other characteristics, has demonstrated its ability to endure within the vicissitudes of history. Freemasonry is a prime vehicle for traditions. Pythagoreanism, Hermeticism, and Rosicrucianism, among others, have penetrated Freemasonry in recent centuries to preserve their respective teachings. Martinez de Pasqually chose a Masonic structure to transmit a priestly tradition. It seems that the choice of Willermoz was therefore a strategic one. Time has proven him right: the Rectified Scottish Rite is flourishing and the doctrine is preserved.

On the other hand, there is with Willermoz, as with Martinez, this idea that Freemasonry is "apocryphal," to use Martinez de Pasqually's term, and must be reformed or rectified. This was still, a century later, the stated objective of Papus when he founded the Martinist Order. It is not a strange or outrageous idea. Within Freemasonry itself, there is this idea of necessary improvement. Jean-Baptiste Willermoz chose the Templar Strict Observance to preserve the Doctrine of Reintegration by means of a rectification that made it a new order: the Order of the Beneficent Knights of the Holy City. If Willermoz and his fellows not only inscribed the doctrine within the Rectified Scottish Rite but made it its invigorating axis, they also put aside theurgic practice. Within the RER, it is Beneficence that has the function of realization equivalent to theurgy among the Élus Cöens. It is appropriate to inquire about the nature of this Beneficence carrying such a power of restoration.

Jean-Baptiste Willermoz and his companions achieved, in a way that few are really aware of, an exceptional work of initiatory coherence by establishing the RER. The Doctrine of Reintegration is installed as theory within the rituals of the RER in a gradualist way, from the symbolism of the grade of Apprentice to the secret class of the Professed and Grand Professed, which offers an explicit synthesis of the teaching until then reserved for the Réau-Croix. This growth in the power of the Doctrine all along the eight grades or degrees of the Regime (Apprentice, Companion, Master, and Scottish Master of Saint Andrew in the symbolic class, Squire-Novice and Beneficent Knight of the Holy City in the inner order, and finally the Professed and Grand Professed) is accompanied by a de-masonization, a stripping away around an axiality that is maintained in the principles of a Christian chivalry. We go from Initiation in the City to Initiation in the Garden, from form to essence, from organization to freedom. Note that this chivalry of Templar origin, resulting from the Templar Strict Observance, becomes spiritualized and traverses historical forms to merge with the virtues of the primordial Christian, of the "living" in Christ and by Christ.

If Louis-Claude de Saint-Martin, to build his teaching, internalized the theurgy of the Élus Coëns, after having realized in essence what is installed in the form and energy of the Coëns operations, Jean-Baptiste Willermoz opted for the Masonic installation. Both succeeded brilliantly, and no doubt beyond their expectations, in preserving the old traditional current transmitted by a master, Martinez de Pasqually, whom neither of them denied, contrary to what some would like to imply. On the other hand, their distinctly Martinezist initiatory journey led them to a spiritual maturity authorizing them to state, in their own integrity and style, an ancient tradition, with contours difficult to identify but whose principles coincide with those of the vast current of Illuminism. They invite us to do the same through theosophy, through gnosis, and through chivalry.

According to Louis-Claude de Saint-Martin, man must extract himself from the stream to become a Man of Desire: to cease to be lived, according to his conditionings and those of his environments, to recognize in each desire a desire for God and for freedom. Thus oriented in a higher sense, the Man of Desire can prepare the coming of the New Man, the Christ in us who alone is able to celebrate the cult of the Spirit-Man.

"Once and for all," says Robert Amadou,[14]

> the immutable Unknown Philosopher recalls the very traditional program, in the titles of his four works that include the word "man." Let us know our present state: *Ecce Homo;* let us know our lost state, to recover and better: *The Man of Desire;* let us be reborn from above and in spirit: *The New Man;* let us help the other and even the Other: *The Ministry of the Spirit-Man.* Each according to his vocation, in his situation.
>
> It is true that we are like gods—not gods as such, but similar enough to find us very remorseful. No solution but to become God. But in spirit and in truth, in the only possible way: with Sophia.
>
> And may the Reintegration be that of all beings.

According to Jean-Baptiste Willermoz, the New Man is represented by the Beneficent Knight of the Holy City. Christ is the mediator par excellence. The initiate must pass from the *imitation* of Christ to the *invention* of Christ within himself. This is indeed a path of the body of glory. Both

---

14 Robert Amadou, *Occident, Orient, parcours d'une tradition* (Paris: Cariscript, 1987).

invite us, directly in the case of Saint-Martin, gradually in the case of Willermoz, to free ourselves from forms, including traditional forms such as initiatory orders, rites, and rituals.

A SCIENCE OF NUMBERS

Numbers are at the heart of the traditions, like letters, musical notes, and basic geometric figures.[15] For Martinez de Pasqually, as for Louis-Claude de Saint-Martin, numbers operate—more clearly for Saint-Martin than for Martinez. Jean-Baptiste Willermoz relied on this science of numbers for the construction of the Rectified Scottish Rite. None of the three used the term "arithmosophy." The term appeared later, notably in the work of Sémélas[16] (Sémélas Démétrios Plato, 1884–1924) within the setting of his traditional organizations.[17] For Saint-Martin, numbers are a language capable of representing the ideas of God. We could say that they are not the essences but are able to account for them. In the same way that we must not confuse the word and the object designated by the word, following in these non-Aristotelian logics, we must distinguish the numbers from the principles that they represent. Arithmosophy is indeed a mathematics, but a qualitative, not quantitative, mathematics. Numbers signify at the level of Spinoza's first type of knowledge, that of perceptions, they agree at the level of the knowledge of causes, but disappear at the level of the knowledge of essences. They characterize a being or typify it, to use a term dear to Claude Bruley.[18] They are, according to Saint-Martin, "the expression of the value of beings, the sensitive and at the same time most intellectual sign that man can use to distinguish their classes and their functions in universal nature."[19]

---

15 Boyer, *Beneath the Veil of Elias Artista*.
16 Serge Caillet, "Sémélas, Papus et les frères d'Orient," in *L'Esprit des choses* nos. 10–11 (Guérigny, Fr: CIREM, 1995).
17 The Order of the Lily and the Eagle, the Rose-Croix d'Orient, and also a Martinist Order whose rituals were published by Robert Amadou in *L'Esprit des Choses* no. 12 (Guérigny, Fr: CIREM, 1995).
18 Claude Bruley, a prominent Swedenborgian specialist, author of *Le Grand Œuvre comme fondement d'une spiritualité laïque. Le chemin vers l'individuation* (Cordes-sur-Ciel, Fr: Rafael de Surtis, 2008).
19 Louis-Claude de Saint-Martin, Jean-Jacques Du Roy D'Hauterive, and Jean-Baptiste Willermoz, *Les Leçons de Lyon aux élus coëns. Un cours de martinisme au XVIIIe siècle*. Introduction and commentary by Robert Amadou and Catherine

Number typifies a being and accounts for the characteristics and qualities of this being in the existent. The modalities of the manifestation of a being in the existent are inscribed in the number. "Thus, in any spiritual being whatsoever, we can recognize: 1st the being, 2nd its number, 3rd its action, and 4th its operation" says Louis-Claude de Saint-Martin.[20] All beings represented by the same number belong to a particular type that Martinez de Pasqually calls a class of beings. The emanated beings therefore belong to classes characterized by properties shared by the members of this class without them being identical. Martinez, like Saint-Martin, teaches that entering temporality suggests a second number. The first number characterizes the emanation in the existent; the second number, the action of being. It is through the second number that beings operate in temporality. This is of great importance in establishing the theurgic operations by which the Élus Coëns contribute to Reintegration: their own, in their individuality, as well as those of humanity. It means, in other words, that the numbers possess an energy of their own (Martinez speaks of a "power") that can be implemented in and by a particular operation, with a view to a temporal or atemporal realization. Numbers are neither concepts nor beings, but each number is a living and creative energy that weakens as it moves away from its source, from periphery to periphery. On the other hand, the numbers gain in power by moving closer to their source and their original nature. Their handling is therefore delicate and requires knowledge of their nature and the rules that govern them.

Martinez de Pasqually retains only the numbers of the decad from 1 to 10, all inscribed within the circle of this decad. The combination of these numbers generates all the others. A few rules are put forward by Martinez: theosophical addition or reduction and multiplication, which generates, but only between numbers of the same nature. Martinez, who thus echoes Pythagoras, warns against an abuse of multiplication. He defines an alchemy of numbers. He separates, by theosophical reduction, the spirit of number from its "envelope" or its "terrestrialities" which thus form a *caput mortuum*. Martinez de Pasqually was not an alchemist. However, certain parts of his teaching can make sense in the field of alchemy, metallic as well as internal.

Amadou, first complete edition from the original manuscripts (Paris: Dervy, 1999).
20 *Les nombres* by Louis-Claude de Saint-Martin, first authentic edition of the autograph manuscript provided with an introduction and notes by Robert Amadou (Paris: Cariscript, 1983).

Louis-Claude de Saint-Martin in his book *Les nombres* greatly clarified the teaching of his master. This essay should be studied, and the best possible introduction remains the course of Serge Caillet,[21] on which we insist once again for its pedagogical and traditional value. We refer you to them both, to discover the rules and their sublime applications in order to focus on the universal picture that arises from this arithmosophy.

Martinez distinguishes three circles or regions: the divine region, the spiritual region, and the natural region, arranged, as Saint-Martin described, like "a great tree," which will evoke to some the kabbalistic tree. This tree takes root in the divine world, develops in the spiritual world, and manifests itself—branches, flowers, and fruits—in the natural world. This deployment obeys the increasingly complex operations of numbers.

Let us summarize and simplify in order to give some indications on the nature of the numbers of the decad:

1 is the number of God, the number of unity, the primary power and essence of all things. All operations are included within it. Nothing can come out of it. Unity brings about manifestations, always within the decad, 10, which sends us back to 1, to unity. No zero for Martinez: a sign of nothingness, zero is not a number. It can, however, represent or symbolize the material universe as an ephemeral appearance.

10, a divine number consequently, is the image of God, the first image, His immaculate reflection.

4 is the quadruple (or "quatriple," according to Martinez de Pasqually) divine essence. $1+2+3+4$ makes 10. This quaternary takes its source in the 10 and is therefore not separate from unity. This denary composed from the sum of the first four numbers should not be confused with the decad. It could be a second image of God within undifferentiated form, an image that will produce the multiplicity of differentiated forms, the appearance. It is also the perfect, complete man, not separate from his source.

7 is for Martinez de Pasqually the number of the "holy spirit belonging to the septenary spirits." It is the number of the emancipation of spirits from the divine region.

8 is "the doubly strong spirit belonging to Christ." Martinez is not Trinitarian, unlike Saint-Martin and Willermoz who will further

---

21 *A Course on Martinism, An Introduction to Martinesism*, "2. Numbers," by Serge Caillet, Institut Eléazar.

Christianize the teaching of their master. Christ is as singular and unique as the number 8 to which the theosophical reduction does not apply. 8 carries its own meaning, without further operation.

3 is an essential number for Martinez de Pasqually. Symbolically, it represents the three elements (and not four according to Martinez, air being rarefied water):[22] earth, water, and fire; the three principles that structure the universe: salt, sulfur and mercury; the three terrestrial regions: west, north, and south; and the three immensities: supercelestial, celestial, and terrestrial. The ternary, the schema of the production of forms, is a constant of operativity: "divine," human, and material. This is why we find it at each grade of the Rectified Scottish Rite.

6 is the number of matter. It refers to the six thoughts of God that gave rise to all forms of creation. It is represented in the current of Illuminism by the double triangle called the Seal of Solomon.

9, a demonic (and not daimonic) number, is the number of fragmentation, of separation in and by matter. It corrupts the perfect man, the 4, by adding the 5.

2, the number of evil, divides 10. For Martinez, it is the number of confusion that he attributes to women. This attribution must be placed in the Judeo-Christian context of the time. 2 is the number of the first separation.

5, another evil number, also divides the denary. It separates. It seduces. It is the number of the corrupt man, identified with appearances.

3, 6, and 9, powers of three, belong to matter. They represent its progressive fragmentation, its increasing opacity up to point of the obscuring duality of appearance.

4 and 7, essential powers, are part of the secondary powers, directly linked to the center, or axis.

1, 10, 8, and 7 belong to the divine.

1 is the essential root of 4, 10, and 7, because the sum of all numbers from 1 to any one of them reduces to 1. For Martinez, the essential root is the soul of a number. The three roots (essential, square, and cube) are significant for calculations in sacred arithmetic. The three roots correspond to the ternaries *life–existence–death* or *emanation–incarnation–reintegration.*

We have thus a language and a grammar of creation which it is advisable to appropriate in its subtle nuances to understand what presents

---

22   Louis-Claude de Saint-Martin, "Instructions aux hommes de désir" III, *Documents martinistes*, no. 4, ed. Robert Amadou (Paris: Cariscript, 1979).

itself and to distinguish the path of Reintegration. Louis-Claude de Saint-Martin and his two principal exegetes, Robert Amadou and Serge Caillet, explain this grammar to us in their respective works. It is not about whether we are right. The grammar works. This was proven by the operations of the Élus Coëns who were crowned with success in the past as in our time. This was also demonstrated in chess. However, the proven is not the true, neither in science nor in theosophy. The language of numbers and its grammar do not constitute a truth but a tool, perhaps not indispensable, but capable of great service.

FROM ONE TO MANY

Martinez de Pasqually is profoundly nondualistic. This affirmation may seem paradoxical regarding someone who speaks unequivocally of evil and invites us through theurgic operations to oppose evil powers, reduce their perverse effects, and even bring them to nothingness if possible. All authentic tradition is *ultimately* nondualistic, even if the form that it borrows, necessarily ephemeral, can present exacerbated dualistic aspects. This is the case with the Cathar doctrine and is sometimes the case with Martinez.

For Martinez de Pasqually, the Being of Beings, God, Is. The Eternal, the Creator, the Father, the Unity, the One, the Absolute Unity, and the Divinity are for Martinez synonymous with God, the formless, the timeless, the incorporeal, the infinite, the sublime, or (according to Jean-Baptiste Willermoz) the all-perfect: "God is pure Spirit, incorporeal, without any form or figure, Eternal and infinite, without beginning and without end. He is the Being of Beings. Existent by Himself for all eternity, He is the unique and absolute principle of all that exists. He is an immense focal point of Light, Glory, and Bliss, and an infinite abyss of Grandeur, Wisdom, Power, and all Perfections. Containing in Himself within His own immensity all that Exists or can Exist, He is the fruitful germ, the inexhaustible source of all divine production and emanation..."[23]

"God is one and indivisible in his essential nature," continues Jean-Baptiste Willermoz in the following paragraph of the same document, taking up the teaching of Martinez. If God is one and indivisible, the multiple is included in this divine unity. Nothing is ever outside of God. All separation is only appearance, from the limited point of view of the man corrupted by the 5. But, in reality, reoriented towards the center of all things, filled with God, the unity imposes itself on the human being freed from the 5. This unity can only be understood by itself, insists

---

[23] Jean-Baptiste Willermoz, *Rituels. Deux cahiers d'écrits martinézistes. De Dieu considéré dans son unité et dans la Trinité de ses puissances.* Manuscript FM4 (508), Bibliothèque Nationale de France.

Willermoz, but on the other hand, specifies Saint-Martin, we can let ourselves be seized by it, in silence, when all our faculties are quiet. This is not unlike Heidegger, who invites us to leave space for Being.

This is sufficient to place the doctrine of Martinez within the setting of the ways of awakening and to install it in this vast movement of the return to the original state, of the recognition of oneself as God, of the recollection of one's own divinity, in which are included thinkers as different and as similar as Spinoza, Rabelais, Nicholas of Cusa, Meister Eckhart, and many others who make up the nondualist current in the West. (Nondualism is not, contrary to a vulgar cliché, the privilege of Eastern philosophies.) We must then distinguish what comes from the path and what comes from Martinez, the cultural markers of his time, or the traditional lineage of his family. All linguistic expression conveys conditioning and idiosyncrasies that, if we are not careful, can pollute, disturb, or twist the initiatory process. The path must remain at the service of the quester with a view to ultimate liberation (Reintegration, in the works of Martinez) and not the other way around.

If numbers constitute a language, this language is obviously of a different scope than that of words, even if any number is also a word within duality. Each number should alert us. The number, bearer of knowledge, also warns us against the abusive interpretation of what is presented. Numbers are for Martinez de Pasqually co-eternal with God. "God being the necessary being existing by himself, he therefore contained from all eternity all number."[24] Number is timeless. Numbers thus constitute an eternal language, without however being the protolanguage sometimes sought through sacred languages such as Sanskrit or Hebrew. If numbers constitute a language, it could be the language of God, an *absolutely* creative language. They are for Saint-Martin, "the abridged translation or the concise language of the truths and laws whose text and ideas are in God, in man, and in Nature."[25] The study of numbers brings us closer to the Unity in which they operate. When numbers divide, and we divide operatively as in everyday life, we are in error. In the world of forms, the One appears multiple to us. The separate identification with one aspect of this multiplicity rather than another plunges us into the dualistic stream that takes us to the peripheries of time, far from our source and

---

24 Louis-Claude de Saint-Martin, "Instructions aux hommes de désir" I, *Documents martinistes*, no. 1, ed. Robert Amadou (Paris: Cariscript, 1979).

25 Saint-Martin, *Les nombres*.

our divine nature. Against this "malady," this "malediction," born of the function of comparison specific to language, only practice in the heart of silence allows us to find ourselves in the "essential," the essence of heaven, the divine essence.

Martinez de Pasqually precisely offers a singular notion of this divine essence. It is both "triple and quatriple," which raises the question of the relationship between ternary and quaternary. The divine essence, one, presents itself within appearance sometimes as triple and sometimes as quatriple.

We refer you to the course of Serge Caillet and his sources, specifically Saint-Martinian, for the (certainly complex, but rigorous and logical) arithmosophical demonstration. We will retain here some points that interest us more particularly within the setting of our subject, the Rectified Scottish Rite.

The divine essence, one, acts in the spiritual world through the number 4. The essence is therefore power. The quatriple essence is also a quatriple power formed by 10, 7, 6, and 4. 10 is the image of God, the place where "the thinking imagination of God" prepares and conceives the creation. This evokes the "Eighth Climate" of Iranian Islam, what Henry Corbin, Gilbert Durand, and Lima de Freitas designate as the *imaginal.* 7 is the number of the emancipation of spirits from the divine immensity. The number 6 designates the operation by which God extracts from his thought an infinity of images of bodily forms that will manifest themselves in appearance. These are the "molds" of the forms we know from the six days of creation. 4, the number of man, is also that of the perfection of forms. We are always in the intention of God before it is released through a theophany.

This quatriple essence is projected, or precipitated (nearly in the chemical sense of the term), in a triple essence that, according to Martinez, refers to the three spirituous essences, three divine faculties which differ from the Father, the Son, and the Holy Spirit. These are divine intention, divine will, and divine action. Even if Martinez in certain texts uses the trinity Father, Son, and Holy Spirit, it is in a completely different sense than the modern meaning. The ambiguity is easy, especially since, while Martinez is not Trinitarian, Saint-Martin and Willermoz are. Jean-Baptiste Willermoz often used, while writing the rituals of the RER, a double reference, Masonic and Martinezist, which enabled him to embed the Doctrine of Reintegration within a Masonic framework. The key to this double reference is the passage from the ternary to the quaternary, from 3 to 4, a key inscribed in the symbol of the triangle pointed at its center.

Any equilateral triangle is inscribed in a circle whose center is the center of the triangle. Geometrically, the center of the equilateral triangle located at the intersection of the characteristic straight lines resulting from the vertices, bisectors, heights, perpendiculars, medians, all combined, is also the center of the circle inscribed in the triangle as of the circle drawn around it. The ternary divine operation, in the circle and through the circle, returns to the center. All action (of a ternary nature) ultimately indicates the center. It is because the 3 is a 4 that the path of Reintegration is always accessible, at the center of everything. The 3 is perfected by the 4. The triangle is perfected by the center.

Martinez de Pasqually makes the expected link between the triangle pointed at its center and the divine tetragrammaton, IHVH: "The Earth is triangular, and the triangle is the emblem of the real shape of the Earth, as God himself has given to Moses and Solomon as a frontispiece above the holy of holies; which they did by putting the Holy Name of God of four letters in a triangle; which proves that the name of God dwells in the center of the Earth. As the soul dwells in the center of the three material parts that make up the body of man, so God dwells in the center of the three terrestrial elements."[26]

God is inevitable.

---

26 *Carnet d'un élu coën,* No. 5, ed. Robert Amadou (Guérigny, Fr: CIREM, 2002).

THREE OR FOUR IMMENSITIES

In Martinezist doctrine, three immensities are defined: the divine immensity, the celestial immensity, and the terrestrial immensity. However, there appears in the texts and diagrams a supercelestial immensity, between the divine immensity and the celestial immensity. It is in the Universal Figure, drawn by Louis-Claude de Saint-Martin and clearly commented on by Jean-Baptiste Willermoz,[27] that an explanation of the unfolding of the divine game can be approached.

For Martinez de Pasqually, God is divine immensity, a "place-state," the very place of God, inaccessible except to God Himself. However, if God *is* divine immensity, He also *has* divine immensity. This distinction between being and having, between the nature of God and the action of God, is fundamental because it indicates the passage from an elusive nonduality to an observable, thinkable, and accessible nonduality. This immensity is made up of beings emanated by God. This emanation of pure spirits is divine action, an act of love to be exact. Emanation characterizes observable nonduality while creation characterizes duality, observable by definition. Emanated beings are eternal in God, in whom they were present before their emanation, while created beings are installed in temporality and causality, the play of subject and object.

While Martinez sometimes uses the word "creation" for "emanation," in most cases the two terms should be distinguished. Emanation is without object and without objective. It is a celebration in joy of the glory, the beauty, and the freedom of God. Creation, on the other hand, obeys rules born of separation. It has a beginning and an end, while emanation is infinite. Creation has and is a story. Emanation is uneventful. Creation requires organization, while emanation is a natural order, a sublime harmony requiring neither intervention nor adjustment. Within emanation, differences do not allow comparison since they reveal unity and totality.

---

27 In the Jean-Baptiste Willermoz notebook "D9." See Saint-Martin et al., *Les Leçons de Lyon*.

Quite to the contrary, creation arouses comparison and hierarchization within multiplicity.

Jean-Baptiste Willermoz indicates that the divine immensity "is the abode of the eternal unity which fills it with its Splendor and its divine Light, which is the Center, the circumference, and the whole. It is from this incomprehensible center that God sees everything, knows everything, foresees everything, embraces everything, and directs and governs all things by His Will, by His Wisdom, by His Providence, and sovereignly commands by His almighty Word."[28]

Because of its dual character, creation can be apprehended, studied, probed, and represented. It is an object. Emanation, by its nondual nature, cannot be understood. Repetition can be exercised in creation but never in emanation, in which everything is pure invention. Creation concerns the multiple. Emanation is characterized by multiplicity within unity. This distinction within the undifferentiated is established by the virtues, the powers, and the names that determine the pure emanated spirits.

The divine immensity in its unity (the 1) coincides with the divine immensity in its multiplicity (the 10) while being different from it. We are thus going from the first unity to the last unity (which is not the ultimate unity, the latter merging with, without being differentiated from, the first unity).

For Martinez de Pasqually, the divine immensity (the divine and uncreated world) is separate from universal space and the created worlds. It is appropriate to question this separation since nothing can be outside the divine. It is a separation that does not oppose but distinguishes in order to promote unity. There is a paradox here that is essential to approach so as to avoid the errors of dualistic tensions. Saint Ephrem, so dear to Robert Amadou, invited us to not define God. To define is to circumscribe and therefore separate what is One. Let us try to distinguish without defining or separating or above all opposing.

The denary unit (and not the decad) is made up of four circles, four classes of spirits typified by a sigil, a name, and a number.[29] This typification is a key to the theurgic operations of the Élus Coëns:

---

28   René Désaguliers, "2e cayer," in "Les Cahiers A et G. Les cahiers D1 à D9. Découverte de deux textes inconnus de Jean-Baptiste Willermoz," *Renaissance Traditionnelle*, no. 80 (October 1989).

29   Saint-Martin, "Instructions aux hommes de désir."

All was 4, which is the true number of all divine spiritual emanation, coming from the universal center, 1, from the divine action and reaction, 2, and from 3. Indeed, the number 1 belongs to the thought that is attributed to the creative father; the number 2 to the will, or to the divine word that commands action, attributed to the son; the number 3 to the very action that directs the operation, attributed to the holy spirit; and finally the number 4 to the operation that is the spiritual birth and distinct emanation of all the spiritual beings that came out of the bosom of the Creator and that existed from all eternity within him...[30]

The ternary represented by a triangle is always pointed in its center, without which it would not be. The Martinezist ternary, thought – will – action, is manifested by an operation that produces by emanation a manifestation or an actualization of what remains in the divine. This 3 which is 4 will be a constant of the Rectified Scottish Rite willed by Jean-Baptiste Willermoz.

The four classes of spirits are: the denary circle of higher spirits (the thought of God), the circle of major octonary spirits (the will of God), the circle of lower septenary spirits (the action of God), and the circle of ternary minor spirits (agents of the quatriple divine essence who operate for the production of forms and thoughts, willed and acted by God). The numbers 10, 8, 7, and 3 characterize these four classes. For Jean-Baptiste Willermoz, these four classes are the angels, archangels, cherubim, and seraphim of the Christian Church.[31] These names given by man are not the primordial and operative names, or names of power, of these four classes. These four classes emanated from the Divine dwell within the original, nondual, and non-separate consciousness. They have knowledge of the divine without the need for representation. They are absolutely present to the divine and in the divine. There is as yet neither temporality, nor trouble, nor a lost word. They participate fully in celebration of the absolute freedom, the absolute love, and the absolute beauty of the divine. It is the primordial cult of which all cults constitute an echo, a memory, or a clumsy intuition.

The temporal universal creation was made necessary by the first fall, which Martinez de Pasqually calls prevarication. Emanated spirits, absolutely free, abused this freedom; we speak of a "rebellion" against God,

---

30   Saint-Martin et al., *Les Leçons de Lyon*, lesson 108.
31   Désaguliers, "2e cayer."

against their own nature and principle. What is the nature of this rebellion? It consists of the will to divide the quatriple divine essence by the process of thought – will – action – operation, following the example of God. But while God can "divide" without separating, emanated spirits have no power to do so. They failed in their operation and their division begat separation. Instead of dividing while maintaining the quaternary unit, they split the denary unit into 5 and 5. This is the birth of duality. We have here a reference to the *diabolos,* the one that divides and separates. Martinez speaks of the "leader of the demons." This principle of separation is the very principle of evil, a temporary principle, since by failing to divide while maintaining unity it only underlines unity's permanence. Louis-Claude de Saint-Martin speaks of the pride of these spirits characterized as perverse, but what pride are we talking about when it comes to free and co-eternal spirits? This word does not evoke the movements of the "me" that we designate as egotistic, as fruits of our conditionings, but rather a vain attempt to "denature" the divine, which is a lack of knowledge, a source of confusion. The perverse spirits (they have perverted their own freedom) have given birth to Appearance, an apparent unity which, according to Saint-Martin, is not the real unity.[32]

These rebellious angels are therefore condemned and locked in a temporality, a universal creation, temporal but also temporary.

The temporal universal creation is composed of three parts, three and not four, which indicates the apparent absence of the quaternary. In reality every ternary points in its center to the quaternary for those who know how to "see." There is no possible emanation in the temporal universal creation. Here again, the thought of God (1), the will of God (2), and the action of God (3) produced the universal creation. Martinez de Pasqually adds these three numbers to obtain the number 6, a reminder of the six thoughts of universal creation or the six days of creation, to which is added a seventh thought, a seventh day, by which God granted seven spiritual gifts and installed "seven principal spirits" in charge of this creation.

These three parts are: *1° the universe, which is an immense circumference in which are contained the general and the particular; 2° the earth, or the general part from which emanates all the nourishment necessary to substantiate*

---

32 Saint-Martin, *Les nombres,* §1.

the particular; and 3° the particular, which is composed of all the inhabitants of the celestial and terrestrial bodies.[33]

These three parts form two immensities: the celestial immensity and the terrestrial immensity. The celestial immensity constitutes an intermediary between the supercelestial immensity and the terrestrial immensity. What distinguishes these three immensities is the increasingly marked degree of temporality from the supercelestial to the terrestrial. Time itself appears as a continuum, an essential and nuanced dimension of this creation. The celestial immensity is pregnant by the central fiery axis. It is made up of seven celestial regions linked to the seven traditional planets of astrology but in an original order.[34] The seven planets are integrated into three circles: a rational circle for Saturn, a planet of the highest importance since *it contains within it the universal divine spiritual*,[35] a visual circle for the Sun, and a sensitive circle for the other five planets.

The overall or particular vision of Martinez de Pasqually differs notably from that of astronomy, just as it does from the various models that originate from Hermeticism. But there is for Martinez a particular connection between the central fiery axis, Saturn, and the Sun, which evokes certain ways of the body of glory found in Hermeticism.

The terrestrial immensity is the densest part of the unfolding, the one where the principle of separation is most active and where the particular reaches its maximum intensity. The Earth, both component and symbol of this terrestrial immensity, of this material, nourishes the particular, not only in the incarnation but in the process of individuation that is conducted from the terrestrial to the supercelestial. The equilateral triangle symbolizes both the terrestrial immensity and the Earth because both were conceived in the imagination of God (the *imaginal*, as Henry Corbin, Gilbert Durand, and Lima de Freitas would say). However, they were not emanated from God, because there is no longer any emanation beyond the quatriple divine essence, but rather creation and emancipation. It is the spirits of the central fire axis who created matter through the play of the production of the three fundamental spirit essences.

---

33 "Le cahier vert," II, *Carnet d'un élu coën,* No. 5, ed. Robert Amadou (Guérigny, Fr: CIREM, 2002).
34 Saturn, Sun, Mercury, Mars, Jupiter, Venus, and Moon.
35 Robert Amadou, ed., *La magie des élus coëns, Théurgie, Instruction secrète*. Le fonds Z: les manuscrits réservés du Philosophe inconnu (Paris, Cariscript, 1988).

The powers of matter, called third by Martinez de Pasqually (typified by the numbers 3, 6, and 9), do not have direct access to the divine but constitute the architecture of the ternary divine plane. The 3, along with its developments, is the vector of divine manifestation in the world of matter. The terrestrial immensity, represented by an equilateral triangle, has only three cardinal points, west, north and south, to which correspond three elements and not four.[36] The west is associated with solids and mercury, the south with liquids and sulfur, the north with ice and salt.[37] The three essences, produced by the ternary spirits of the central fire axis, have become denser, embodied in the terrestrial. The six divine thoughts, in act and in time, are installed in this ternary. This is particularly indicated by the theosophical addition of 3: $1+2+3=6$. The 9, a demonic number which, when multiplied, gives itself back, indicates the prison of the self, which replicates itself *ad infinitum* without leaving space for our principle.

With Martinez de Pasqually we are in the presence of a complex game of mirrors that allows the divine light to be reflected in the terrestrial immensity despite the opacities constituted by the two falls. These reflections are all mediators that attenuate the power and effect of the light. The spirits of the central fire axis, sometimes unpredictable, are thus tempered in their actions. This dualistic game appears in the antagonism between the powers that contribute to Reintegration (angelic forces) and the powers that contribute to degradation (fragmentation, disassociation, disunity, dispersion, multiplication, and disintegration), which are for Martinez the demonic forces, all the more active in the terrestrial regions. Demonic thought arises from rupture with divine intellect.

---

36 Martinez de Pasqually is not the only one to distinguish air from the three elements water, fire, and earth. For Paracelsus, air is the home of the other three elements.

37 Saint-Martin, "Instructions aux hommes de désir."

THE CENTRAL FIRE AXIS

The central fire axis remains an enigma in the system of Martinez de Pasqually, already complex and sometimes even confused, an enigma that only operative practice can solve. In general, the system proposed by Martinez de Pasqually has the primary function of serving theurgic operativity, not of providing an explanation of the world or worlds. The central fire axis, or uncreated fire axis, separates (at the same time as it unites) the supercelestial immensity and the celestial immensity. More than a "space," the central fire axis can be envisaged, and especially apprehended, as a network of relationships between the spirits that Martinez calls "the spirits of the central fire axis." Present from the beginning, emanating from God, they are the minor ternary spirits of the fourth circle of the divine immensity. After the first fall, or prevarication, they were emancipated across the supercelestial immensity to constitute the central fire axis. Their primary function is to contain: they weave the space that encloses the rebellious spirits. They also constitute time, whether time appears as a dimension of space (since Descartes and Newton), or whether time is revealed as a necessity for the actions of imprisonment or confinement of spirits. The spirits of the central fire axis operate temporally. This is essential data in order to understand the necessity for presence here and now, atemporally, for access to the way of Reintegration. These igneous spirits are the origin of creation. The three constituent spiritual essences of all material bodies indeed have their source in their igneous nature. It is by separation that the spirits of the central fire axis generate forms within the undifferentiated, the chaos, called the "philosophical matrass"[38] by Martinez, from the principles of the three essences. Since they are, according to Martinez de Pasqually, "the center of all movement," they remain, immutable, immobile yet the source of movement, perfect intervals between and in the heart of the forms, ensouled or unsouled, to which they give life.

---

38 Matrass: a long-necked spherical or ovoid vessel, used in alchemy; the bottom part of an alembic. –Trans.

Unlike the spirits of the supercelestial immensity, the spirits of the central fire axis have neither freedom, nor intelligence, nor imagination. They are "working" extensions of the higher minds. They "have in them each only one action, thus they can operate only one kind of form; they cannot even operate this single action and this single form without the immediate operation of a superior being who commands them and disposes of them at will and according to the will of the Creator."[39] The spirits of the central fire axis are therefore "acted" according to divine thought and strictly obey the divine script. This primordial and original script, this plan of creation, born in the *imaginal*, will be precipitated as a theophany into matter by the spirits of the central fire axis. The original image, archetype of the divine plan, which will replicate itself to the greatest density, is an equilateral triangle whose center is none other than the Word itself, whose number is 8, named by Martinez the "word of creation," which is also, in a particular way, "the doubly strong spirit of the creator."[40] The spirits of the central fire axis are not only the operative agents of the divine will, they are also the carriers of the three undifferentiated spiritual essences (3 in 1) in their igneous nature. It is in their fire nature that these three essences have slumbered since the first emanation of the spirits of the central fire axis. These aspects of Martinez de Pasqually's model of creation echo certain stages of the alchemical Great Work. We have a primordial seed whose separation will generate the universal ternary structure of all forms. The explosion of the philosophical matrass, effected by the withdrawal of the "doubly strong spirit of the creator," the containing spirit that maintained the forces in the state, in their potentiality, engendered creation and unfolded the celestial immensity and the terrestrial immensity.

Martinez de Pasqually names the three spirit essences Salt, Sulfur, and Mercury, but as with the ternary Father, Son, and Holy Spirit, he attributes to them a particular meaning that differs from the current traditional meaning. The three spirit essences are constantly animated by the fire of the spirits of the central fire axis. This fire, vehicle, or vector of the divine intention is "the soul of matter," the "supermaterial" for Martinez

---

39 Martinez de Pasqually, *Traité sur la Réintégration des êtres dans leur première propriété, vertu et puissance spirituelle divine*. First authentic edition from the manuscript of Louis-Claude de Saint-Martin, ed. Robert Amadou (Le Tremblay, Fr: Diffusion Rosicrucienne, 1995).

40 Saint-Martin, "Instructions aux hommes de désir."

who has, for the ternary Salt, Sulfur, and Mercury, a function analogous to the Word in the original ternary. Each ternary is both unified and vivified by its center. These centers with successive ternaries that unfold from the center of the first ternary constitute an axiality, that of the presence of the Word. So we see that despite the two falls, the two prevarications, there is never any real separation from God:

> God is so essentially essential to the duration of every being in this universe that a grain of sand can only have form as long as it is united with Him. The grain of sand contains the three essences and the vehicle, 6. Now, the vehicle itself can only have life as long as it is vivified. Yet vivification necessarily belongs to God, who constantly maintains the whole universe of beings, which forms the quaternary number: the essences, 1; form, 2; life, 3; and vivification, 4. Likewise, by dividing the three essences, 3, the life of the forms, 3, gives the senary number, 6.[41]

This 6 is represented by a double triangle, which will become the hexagram, the central symbol of the Martinist current. The hexagram pointed at its center conveys the septenary.

That in which we have being, life, and movement remains our own original and ultimate nature even in the depths of the opacity of appearance. This point is fundamental to grasping how an initiatory way with dualistic expression necessarily remains fundamentally nondualistic, not only in operative practice but also in its doctrine, for those who are attentive, who know how to "see."

Just so, Martinez de Pasqually invites us to experiment with the central fire axis in an exercise that is as simple to implement as it is complex in the developments that result from it. Here it is:

Experience to convince of the truth of the central fire axis, which is innate in us, and without the powerful assistance of which no elementary body can subsist and operate.

Place a lit blessed candle on the ground, between the north and south and east or orient, if possible, otherwise in the middle or the west, according to the position of the room where you will be in the greatest secrecy, windows and doors closed for this test, at night, as the most conducive to the thing.[42] Then you will stand over the candle, with your head bowed and

---

41   Saint-Martin, "Instructions aux hommes de désir."
42   Fr.: *"la chose."*–Trans.

your eyes fixed on the light, for the interval of a minute or two (what we call "catching fire"). After this operation, you will withdraw to 3 or 4 paces, and will stare fixedly in front of you at the wall, your eyes wide open, without lowering them, and without looking to the right or to the left. Then, you will distinctly see a globe of fire, purple in color, of a greater or smaller size, which will come to you, and will even pass over your head. Always maintain this position, until the wall presents you with a circle in which you will clearly distinguish the air, the earth, and the water, that is to say sulfur, mercury, and salt.

This must convince us that these four elements are innate in us and in the whole and that we could not subsist without their spirituous essences.

Care must be taken that the candle is not placed in any candlestick, as the spirit cannot support matter, but is only standing on the floor or tile.

Martinez de Pasqually's proposal is both traditional and unique. It is common to use the fixation of the flame of a candle as a support for meditation or vision. But, in this case, it is no more and no less a question of observing, of "seeing," the ternary principle of creation at work by the action of the spirits of the central fire axis. A "constructivist" relationship to perceived reality follows from this proposition. How do we contribute to the construction of our reality, which is not the Real, and according to what modalities? This experience makes it possible to understand that the model proposed by Martinez de Pasqually in his doctrine, synthesized in the "Universal Table" or "Universal Figure" that you will find below, is certainly a representation at the service of theurgic practice, that certainly it echoes other models of creation in its multiple dimensions, all incomplete and all carrying a sublime intuition, but that it was born from an experiment in theurgic practice.

Martinez de Pasqually repeatedly insists on Fire in his writings. Any operative practice is sterile without Fire. Robert Amadou would sometimes come out of a ritual, Élu Coën, Masonic, or Martinist, murmuring: "The Fire was absent." The operator and his assistants, for lack of presence, too far from the axis, had not known how, or had not been able, to put it to work.

The doctrine of Martinez de Pasqually is not there to justify theurgic practice or to affirm a truth, but to serve those who embark on the series of operations proposed by the Order of Knight Masons Élus Coëns of the Universe and who must give meaning to the results obtained from the exclusive perspective of Reintegration.

In the setting of the Rectified Scottish Rite, like that of the theosophy of Louis-Claude de Saint-Martin, this theurgy, which has become internal, cardiac, or in other words axial, generates the same intimate experience as the external theurgy, the same intimacy with the divine, which the doctrine cannot account for but which it can support in an expression specific to each one.

Studying the doctrine or judging the doctrine without practice is nonsense. But on the contrary, if the doctrine bothers you, do not hesitate to reject it but keep the practice that it provides, in appearance, externally or internally, because the experience proposed by Martinez, in its very simplicity, radically reduces the opposition between external and internal.

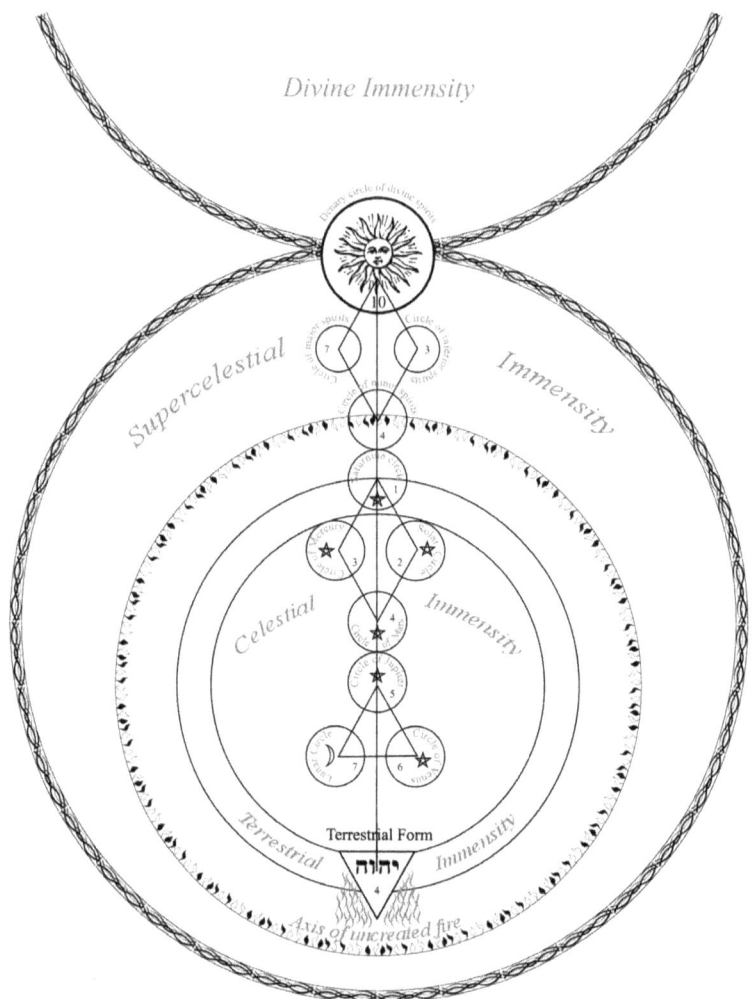

The Universal Table[43]

---

[43] According to information from Catherine Amadou, the representation of the Universal Table was executed for Van Rijnberk from the Kloss manuscript (library of the Grand Orient of the Netherlands) for the 1st volume of his book on Pasqually (1935, pp. 70–71). It was republished by Robert Amadou in l'*Initiation* (1969, No. 2, pp. 80–81) who also published it in 1974 in the *Treatise on the Reintegration*... published by Robert Dumas. A corrected version of the Table was included in the new edition of the *Treatise* published by Diffusion Rosicrucienne in 1999. This representation has been completely redrawn by Éditions de la Tarente. [Note to the French edition; graphic revised with English captions, 2021.]

EMANATION, EMANCIPATION, AND CREATION

It is appropriate to distinguish within the Martinezian doctrine between emanation, emancipation, and creation. This distinction is not only useful for understanding the system set out by Martinez de Pasqually and his emulators, but also allows us to understand some of the challenges of Reintegration.

Emanation is an absolutely free, non-causal act of the Supreme Being, the "Great Emanator." By the first ternary (divine thought, will, and action), beings are simultaneously emanated from it and absorbed in its immensity. The function of these beings emanating and not separated from the Supreme Being seems to be the celebration of the latter. The Absolute celebrates itself, celebrates its infinite freedom, for its "Glory." There is an initial Joy, source of all joy, an instasy, source of all ecstasies.

The emanated beings, not separated from their source, bathing in it, are endowed with the same powers and virtues as the Divinity but without the slightest personalization. Their "stretching" from the source produces an infinite gradation of the Love of the Supreme Being, a love that remains objectless, whose main characteristic is freedom. This is the primordial cult that resides in this movement of stretching and permanent reabsorption from the center to the periphery and from the periphery to the center, a generator of Joy.

The emanated beings, which are said to be "in the image and likeness of God," participate fully in His essence. They are characterized by the number 4, a perfect number, since it is also the quaternary of Divinity which is 1, of course, but also 3: thought, will, and action. These emanated beings, these pure spirits, are organized, as we have seen, into classes. One of the chiefs of these classes of pure spirits delights "in the eminent degree of his virtues and powers, desiring to equal himself to his principle, and to form for himself a unity opposed to His eternal unity."[44]

---

44   Saint-Martin et al., *Les Leçons de Lyon*.

Somehow this "chief of the demons" or "great prince of the demons," in Martinezist terminology, refused to allow himself to be reabsorbed into the source. Within the original and ultimate divine Consciousness, of nondual nature (or rather, neither dual nor nondual), appears the intention of duality, the intention of 2.

> Without this first prevarication, there would have been no change to the spiritual creation, there would have been no emancipation of spirits out of the vastness, there would have been no creation of divine boundary, neither supercelestial, celestial, nor terrestrial, nor any spirit sent to operate in the different parts of creation. You cannot doubt all this, since the ternary minor spirits would never have left the place they occupied in the divine immensity, to bring about the formation of a material universe.[45]

We are witnessing here the appearance of the principle of Evil, which is separation. This first separation inaugurates the fragmentation that will follow. According to the doctrine of Martinez de Pasqually, Evil "took its principle solely in the thought that the demonic leader, who was free, conceived of himself as opposed to the law, the precept, and the commandment of the Eternal; not that the demon is evil itself, since if he changed his evil thought today, his action would also change and, from that moment, there would be no question of evil in the whole extent of this universe. Evil, I repeat, originated only in the thought of the demon opposed to that of the Divinity, a thought which he conceived of his pure free will and by which he separated himself from the Divinity."[46]

We must consider that this act of separation, this act of pride according to Martinez, was born of the absolute freedom of the Divinity. Indeed, in this infinite freedom, the possibility was introduced of the abuse of this freedom of the emanated beings. Without this possibility, the original freedom would have been restricted and, therefore, not absolute. Martinez suggests that to allow complete freedom to the emanated pure spirits, God restricted His own freedom. If we accept this suggestion, we must go on to find that this chosen restriction is a higher act of freedom. The very principle of this freedom was exercised without any separation.

The initial "fault," already potentially inscribed in the exercise of this "freedom," resides (and this is the most important point) in a thought, a will, an action of division, orchestrated by a pure spirit:

---

45 Martinez de Pasqually, *Traité sur la Réintégration des êtres*.
46 Saint-Martin, "Instructions aux hommes de désir."

> The prevarication of the first spirits is to have wanted to divide and subdivide the quatriple divine essence by their own spiritual faculty. They conceived, by their sheer will, an intention and an act of thought contrary to the laws of action and operation which had been fixed for them by the Creator during their emanation; but, far from being able to effect this act with success, they were deceived, and very surprised, when they saw with certainty the impossibility that it was for them and for any spirit to remove from the Divinity the quatriple essence and the extraordinary denary number which were innate in it. They did not fully recognize this impossibility until they wanted to arrogate to themselves, each in particular, the product of the subdivision of this extraordinary quaternary number of emanation and of the divine and temporal spiritual creation, because their intention was to make this whole product into a single quaternary or denary unit. Far from that, they no longer found either the pure and simple quaternary unit or denary unit, but only two quinary numbers, instead of the divine denary that they wanted to put into their possession and power. It is by this that they were convinced of their atrocious and insane pride and of the impossibility of any divine spirit subdividing the quatriple divine essence, or its denary unity, this right only being able to belong to the Lord, who is alone and will never have an equal.[47]

Lucifer, whom Martinez de Pasqually never designates as such, the bearer of light, becomes Satan, the divider, the adversary, the one who opposes himself, the function of opposition, source of all duality.

The "founder" of this first prevarication, the "leader of the demons," brings with him a number of pure spirits. The others resist. There is therefore a partition, a partition that affects all beings emanating within the divine immensity by introducing the principle of duality within it in the form of a temporality. The first prevarication gives rise to a "before" and an "after" the event. But this temporality must be, according to Martinez de Pasqually, distinguished from time, which will only concern creation. Eternity becomes temporal for emanated beings. They are "spiritual-temporal" beings. Their consciousness, purely nondual, becomes nondual/dual. It is not the dual consciousness of created beings.

The prevaricating beings will be "emancipated" out of the divine immensity, into a "supercelestial immensity," in the likeness of the divine immensity and composed like it of four classes. Emancipation modifies

---

[47] Martinez de Pasqually, *Traité sur la Réintégration des êtres*.

the missions of the classes of superior spirits and the relationships they maintain among themselves both in the divine immensity and in the supercelestial immensity.

In the divine immensity, we find first of all the denary spirits which are for Martinez de Pasqually "the absolute unity of the divinity," the source of all divine thoughts at the origin of emanation, of emancipation, and then creation. They thus work in the temporal without being affected by time. The octonary spirits are sent out of the divine immensity, charged with a mission in the three immensities: supercelestial, celestial, and terrestrial. Part of the septenary spirits of the divine immensity will henceforth operate in the supercelestial immensity. The ternary spirits of the divine immensity were emancipated in the supercelestial immensity, to guard the prevaricating spirits. Within the divine immensity, they were replaced by Man. The correspondence of this particular class of the divine immensity within the supercelestial immensity is that of the divine spiritual minors, Man, endowed with a power of action and operation superior to all the other classes of the supercelestial immensity. Man, born of the divine ternary word, emanated after the first prevarication and therefore virgin of its toxic effects, who was immediately emancipated within the supercelestial immensity, with singular mission and responsibility, constitutes the only class of spirits possessing the quaternary power within the supercelestial world.

Adam is a special being within this general class of emancipated minors. Adam is the god-man, the scarlet, royal,[48] or red man. He is endowed with a body of glory, a body by virtue of the spirit, both ternary and quaternary, which is also his temple, both ternary (porch, temple, and sanctuary for the lower limbs, chest, and head) and quaternary (the holy of holies or upper chamber for the original and ultimate Consciousness, that which remains), independent of the entities of the central fire axis. Martinez tells us that in three operations, the Divine transmitted to Adam the law, the precept, and the commandment. "The law is: One God you shall worship, that is the support; the precept is: Thou shalt love thy neighbor as thyself, that is the guide; the commandment is: Thou shalt not take my name in vain, that is the advice,"[49] and indeed Adam commands both good and evil spirits. His main functions are the containment of evil spirits, the demons and their leader, but also

---

48 Fr.: "*réaux*," etymologically related to "royal" and "real."–Trans.
49 Robert Amadou, ed., *La magie des élus coëns, Théurgie, Instruction secrète*.

their instruction, which aims at the destruction of the very principle of Evil. Adam has four powers for success in his mission: an eternal soul, the sixth thought of God; spirit, always in connection with divinity, which will become the Good Companion Spirit after the second prevarication or fall; and intellect, the mediator between soul and spirit. Soul, intellect, and spirit form a ternary which then becomes a quaternary by the connection of spirit with divinity.

Martinez states in the *Treatise:* "The major good spirit has its immediate action from the Divinity. The soul has, therefore, its regular correspondence to the four divine powers, which we call quatriple essence, as follows: the minor soul, 1, is in spiritual correspondence with the intellect, 2; the intellect with the spirit, 3; and the spirit with the Divinity, 4. This is what the exact correspondence of every spiritual being with the eternal Creator proves to us."

Endowed with this triple power and this link with the quatriple divine essence, Adam will however also prevaricate, allowing himself to be seduced by the Prince of the demons over whom he must keep watch and thus replicating the first prevarication, the first "pride," out of weakness. From having been thinking, he becomes thought. Present to him are "good thoughts" emitted by the Good Companion Spirit, or "evil thoughts" produced by evil spirits. This time again, we must notice the application of the first principle of freedom, God allowing Adam to exercise this freedom even in the error produced by this "accidental" alliance of the Adversary and the scarlet man. Contrary to the first emancipated beings, Adam holds a total power of creation (but not of emanation); he can in particular replicate his own body of glory and thus constitute a divine posterity by a joint operation with God. Adam creates the form of glory (the act of creation) while God animates it from his quatriple divine essence (the act of emanation). Following the advice of the Adversary, Adam tries to create and emanate without the help of God. The result is a shadowy and soulless form.

This second prevarication entails a second fall into duality and temporality, which affects the supercelestial immensity but also, again, the divine immensity. All the immensities are reorganized around a new dispensation, the precipitation of Adam and his descendants among whom we are, in matter and time. This duality is twofold, it is "external" in the relationship maintained with the external object, and "internal":

> There exist in nature, principally for the minor-man, for the degraded and punished Adam, two very distinct lives which one can never confuse without falling into the greatest dangers. One is the active-spiritual life or the spirit, the other is the passive universal life which is that of matter.
>
> The life of the spirit is not created, but it emanates with the being who enjoys it, from the bosom of God where he drew it. It is immortal, indestructible, intelligent, and active; it thinks, wills, acts, and discerns, which constitutes it, the image and resemblance of its generative principle; it is strengthened in the exercise of Good, and can only be weakened and darkened in that of evil.
>
> Passive animal life, also called the universal soul of the created world, is only temporary, being emanated only for a time by the lower-spiritual beings, agents of the creator's senary power, who from the beginning received from him created things, the order and the powerful faculty of emanating from them and of producing by their own fire that general life that animates, maintains, and preserves for a determined time the whole mass of creation, all its parts, and each species of individuals destined to inhabit created space, for the duration of the centuries, who are moved in this space only by a vehicle of this general life which is inserted in them.[50]

In the *Treatise*, to which it is obviously necessary to return many times, Martinez de Pasqually describes at length all these stages, the consequences of the two falls, and the spiritual functions of the different classes of spirit and their evolution at each stage.

What interests us here is that this sequence: emanation, emancipation, creation, and fruit of the exercise of the absolute freedom of God, contains, by inversion, the process of Reintegration, a "decreation," an emancipation from matter and time, to allow oneself to again be absorbed into and emanated from the Consciousness-origin, God.

On the nature of this decreation, the practice of the theurgy of the Élus Coëns provides information. Jean-Baptiste Willermoz expresses himself as a Coën when he says:

> Man, after having passed through all the times of his purification and reconciliation, will himself only be perfectly reintegrated after having effected the

---

50 Jean-Baptiste Willermoz, notebook "D9," "Preliminary explanations serving as an introduction to the following chapters which contain the description of the spiritual facts concerning the creation of the physical, temporal Universe, and its principal parts..."

reintegration of the demons. That is what is represented by the reptiles on the corpses: one ceases only with the other.[51]

The reptilian powers are indeed threads in the fabric of creation. Oriented towards the peripheries, they are the substance of forms, they are the thread of time. Theurgic operations aim to release these reptilian energies from the peripheral forms to bring them back to the center and release them in a timeless and formless axialization. This "unweaving" of the fabric of creation participates in and inaugurates the Reintegration, which Robert Amadou has perfectly synthesized in a few words that we repeat insistently:

> Once and for all, the immutable Unknown Philosopher recalls the very traditional program, in the titles of his four works that include the word "man." Let us know our present state: *Ecce Homo;* let us know what is our lost state, to recover, and better: *The Man of Desire;* let us be reborn from above and in spirit: *The New Man;* let us help the other and even the Other: *The Ministry of the Spirit-Man.* Each according to his vocation, in his situation.
>
> It is true that we are like gods — not gods as such, but similar enough to find us very remorseful. No solution but to become God. But in spirit and in truth, in the only possible way: with Sophia.
>
> And may the Reintegration be that of all beings.[52]

---

51 Saint-Martin et al., *Les Leçons de Lyon.*
52 Robert Amadou, *Occident, Orient, parcours d'une tradition* (Paris: Cariscript, 1988).

THE PRIMORDIAL CULT, *LA CHOSE*, AND THE GOOD COMPANION SPIRIT

The Doctrine of Reintegration and its practice are based on three fundamental components: those of the Primordial Cult, that of *la Chose*, and that of the Good Companion Spirit. To address these three inseparable points, I will rely on an oral instruction given by Robert Amadou within the setting of the Marie de Gonzague Mother Lodge of the Order of Knight Masons Élus Coëns of the Universe on March 22, 1998 in Paris.

At the start of his speech, Robert Amadou announced:

> I would like to talk with you about *la Chose*. This Thing, whose notion and history may seem mythical, is of an extremely precise reality. I speak to you of it as an essential part of Wisdom, as it offers itself to those who seek it. Personally, I have found *la Chose* to be my entire path. It is the totality of the path of the Élu Coën.

La Chose is at the same time Order, which cannot be restricted to order as organization; the Cause, first, permanent, and ultimate (Robert Amadou evokes the phonetic proximity in Castilian of the words *cosa* and *causa*); the Way which leads to *la Chose* or the cause; and Sophia, Wisdom.

La Chose is for Martinez de Pasqually the purpose of theurgic worship, its justification, and its heart. It is Christ, he says. It is Wisdom, the Presence of God, absolutely autonomous, which gives itself or does not give itself according to Grace, but is also the universal spirit of the alchemists. This Wisdom, which is also Logos, will relate to the Son according to some, to the Holy Spirit according to others, or even to the Trinity, but it must be remembered that Martinez is not Trinitarian in the sense of the Councils, nor is he familiar with the doctrine of the incarnation. He is close to the Jewish mysticism of the 1st and 2nd centuries AD. For the Trinitarians, such as Louis-Claude de Saint-Martin and Jean-Baptiste Willermoz, wisdom is the divine energy common to the Father, the Son, and the Holy Spirit; this is not the case for Martinez de Pasqually. For the latter, *la Chose* could be (although it is rather vague) the Holy Spirit of Christ, present in all the prophets, an elusive figure that Martinez calls Hély or Rhély, who should be distinguished from the prophet Elijah.

On July 26, 1775, Jean-Jacques du Roy d'Hauterive and Louis-Claude de Saint-Martin raised the matter in a class of Coëns:

> Without Christ who came to stand between the Creator and man, the latter would have been but an object of justice, instead of becoming one of mercy by obtaining from this same Christ in the form of Rhély the means to perform his worship of expiation and reconciliation.[53]

La Chose is Rhély who is also the Holy Spirit, who is also the Christ— Martinez uses the Hebrew word *Messias*. Saint-Martin will go in the same direction by saying that *la Chose* is the Repairer, the Christ-Wisdom, mediator between God and the world.

During this instruction, Robert Amadou introduced the notion of the two Wisdoms: an uncreated, divine Wisdom and a created Wisdom, *la Chose* and the world that man must unite, passing from the dualism of Appearance to nonduality. Through theurgic operations with the Coëns and through Beneficence with the Rectified Scottish Rite, uncreated Wisdom manifests itself in the form of created Wisdom, a partial wisdom whose fullness is in the process of becoming. We can establish a correlation between the two Wisdoms and the two Natures, the *Natura naturans* and *Natura naturata* of Spinoza:

> By *Natura naturans* we understand a being that we conceive clearly and distinctly through itself, and without needing anything beside itself (like all the attributes which we have so far described), that is, God. The Thomists likewise understand God by it; but their *Natura naturans* was a being (so they called it) beyond all substances.
>
> The *Natura naturata* we shall divide into two, a general, and a particular. The *general* consists of all the modes which depend immediately on God, of which we shall treat in the following chapter; the *particular* consists of all the particular things which are produced by the general mode. So that *Natura naturata* requires some substance in order to be well understood.[54]

---

53   Saint-Martin et al., *Les Leçons de Lyon.*
54   Baruch Spinoza, *Short Treatise on God, Man, and His Well-Being,* Book I, p. 56, tr. A. Wolf (London: Adam and Charles Black, 1910).

For Martinez de Pasqually there is a correspondence, a mirror effect, between the (internal) deification of man and the (external) transfiguration of the world. The external, far from being opposed to the internal, is inseparable from it. It is a single operation in two dimensions, internal and external, following two Wisdoms, uncreated and created, which are one. Man rectifies the tragic consequences of the two falls, both internally and externally, by a formal theurgy that is internalized as an inner theurgy, or by a humanistic Beneficence that is internalized as a metaphysical Beneficence (and vice versa).

About the operation of the Body of Glory specific to the Élus Coëns, Robert Amadou speaks of an internal alchemy specific to this current, like other great traditional internal currents, a way of the Body of Glory, present in particular in the *Nouvelle instruction coën*,[55] a true treatise of resurrection. This alchemy[56] is an essential element of the Primordial Cult that can only be fully accomplished in the Body of Glory. Therein lies the real theurgy.

Divine Wisdom is Christ (Martinez does not use the name Jesus Christ) and created Wisdom is the Church, the Assembly, but also Mary, the immaculate, beyond all representation and concept, the transparent, which allows uncreated Wisdom to come about, and Robert Amadou to insist:

> Wisdom, person of God, is the presence of God in the sense that the rabbinical tradition, the Kabbalah, knows it. It is important to observe that *la chose* as Wisdom in man, as the Wisdom of Jesus Christ in man, as the Holy Spirit of Jesus Christ, is a feminine presence. But we must be careful, there is no sexuality in God. There is nothing of the tragic in God. This is an error of false gnosis. There is a feminine character of the Presence of God in the world, and there is, since the prevarication, a tragic character of the presence of God in the world.

The uncreated, fallen Wisdom, fallen into matter since the prevarication of Adam, is rehabilitated by the celebration of the Primordial Cult among the Coëns, by the implementation, in all its dimensions, physical and metaphysical, explicit and implicit, conspicuous and inconspicuous, of the Beneficence of the Beneficent Knights of the Holy City. This forfeiture

---

55 *Nouvelle instruction coën*, ed. Robert Amadou (Guérigny, Fr: CIREM, 1996), published internally.
56 The word "alchemy" is not used by Martinez de Pasqually.

and this rehabilitation, or rectification, are permanent. Every moment, I fall and I get up, until the final reconciliation and Reintegration.

For Robert Ambelain, the force at work in the theurgic operations of the Élus Coëns, this active power, is the fruit of the work of the Pleroma or the Communion of Saints.

"Insofar as Christ has the Pleroma of the Godhead," clarifies Robert Amadou, "we are his Pleroma. We have everything, fully, and we will end up being filled with the Fullness, with the Pleroma of the Godhead, since, being in Christ, we are in Him who has the Pleroma of the Godhead. From there, this idea of the Communion of Saints, of which Robert Ambelain spoke, appears in fact to be one of the consequences of this idea of the Pleroma. This Communion of Saints is the body of believers, of those, I would add, who belong to the inner Church as well as to the outer Church. Of these two Churches, it is Christ who is the chief, the head, while the entirety of the faithful constitutes the Body of Christ and the Church in the broadest sense."

The emulators of Martinez de Pasqually repeatedly came up against this question of the two Churches, of the conciliation of the two. This problem only exists from the standpoint of dual consciousness, which compares and contrasts forms. But, as soon as worship without worship and operation without operation are grasped, and the freedom consequently regained, this problem disappears without the need for formal solutions.

To return to the Good Companion Spirit: for Martinez, the Holy Spirit, the Holy Guardian Angel, and the Good Companion Spirit merge in practice, an essential practice, because only the Good Companion Spirit, since the prevarication, can help us to accomplish the adjustment necessary to Reintegration. Indeed, without the Good Companion Spirit, man can neither think, nor will, nor act. He can neither operate nor celebrate.

For Louis-Claude de Saint-Martin, faithful in this to his first master, Martinez de Pasqually, thoughts are not innate in man, nor are they the product of the senses.[57] Thoughts present themselves to us, offer themselves to a choice in which resides our free will, a freedom that has become very relative since the fall. Two spirits, according to the Martinezian doctrine, present us with thoughts, good thoughts by the Good Companion Spirit, bad thoughts by the Bad Companion Spirit. Here we have the

---

57   Louis-Claude de Saint-Martin. *Controverse avec Garat, précédé d'autres textes philosophiques,* ed. Robert Amadou (Paris: Fayard, 1990).

essence of all dualism. The fall causes a split in consciousness. The Good Companion Spirit remembers its original nature as pure emanated spirit, having been born before the fall. The Evil Companion Spirit was born from the fall, from the betrayal of its own divine nature. The antinomies present themselves as an uninterrupted flow to man who, without an alliance with the Good Companion Spirit, paradoxically cannot exercise his freedom and is even restricted from choice. The thoughts presented by the Good Companion Spirit are seeds of knowledge. The others keep us in decay.

When Jean-Baptiste Willermoz (to whom *la Chose* did not respond as he expected during theurgic operations specific to the Elus Coëns) asked to be convinced, Martinez de Pasqually sent him back to his intimacy with *la Chose*. He reminded him that the body "says" and the body "can." The five fingers of each hand and each foot are "the emblems of Truth": "the five fingers symbolize, starting from the thumb: the minor, or the emanated soul; the Good Companion Spirit, or guardian angel; the good intellect, or the good thought proposed by the good spirit; the evil spirit; finally, the evil intellect, or the evil thought proposed by the evil spirit to the minor." Martinez advised Willermoz to not get attached to *la Chose*, to let go and not to look for answers in the phenomenal; they arrive when the time comes.

Intention is therefore paramount. If it is disturbed by the desire to obtain, to have, to do, *la Chose* and the Cause seem to distance themselves. If intention is free of all attachment and bond, they reveal themselves.

BENEFICENCE AND FREEDOM

One of the fundamental questions raised by our "affair" through the two prevarications, or falls, is the question of Freedom and our freedoms, from which arises the delicate question of Beneficence and our beneficences.

We have the sense that the treatment of these questions will present itself very differently depending on the level of intervention observed (explicit, implicit, essential or dual, dual/nondual, nondual), depending on whether we find ourselves, in a Spinozist manner, at the level of knowledge through relationship with external objects, at the level of knowledge of causes or essences (in other words, at the level of the subject/object relationship), at the level of non-differentiation between subject and object, or finally, in the recognition of neither-subject-nor-object. These levels do not oppose each other but form a continuum from substance to spirit.

Serge Caillet[58] perfectly presents the issue of freedom through a question and answer by Jean-Baptiste Willermoz, taken from the "2nd Cayer":[59]

Question from Willermoz: "But, it will be said, God who is all-powerful, who is filled with such a tender love, so perfect for his creatures, could he not create them unfree, to ensure their eternal happiness by preserving them from the possibility of abusing their freedom and losing themselves?"

Answer from the same Willermoz: "God is the only self-existent being: he exists by his own law, with which he is one. This Law is the Good, which is the principle of all perfection. God is good in essence, and it is no more possible for God, being good, to depart from it through any evil, than to cease to be God; if created beings could exist by their own

---

58 *A Course on Martinism, An Introduction to Martinesism*, "4. The Divine Immensity and the Emanation of the First Spirits," by Serge Caillet, Institut Eléazar.

59 "2nd Cayer," ed. René Désaguliers, "Les Cahiers A et G. Les cahiers D1 à D9. Découverte de deux textes inconnus de Jean-Baptiste Willermoz," *Renaissance Traditionnelle*, no. 80 (October 1989).

law, could be the Good, they would be independent and so many Gods; but on the contrary, their individual, distinct existence began when it pleased God to give it to them; he gave them his own Law through which he united them to himself and to the Good, and since this Law, a necessary consequence of their existence, is given to them, it places them under the dependence of the one who gives it, and since it is not their own, it necessarily follows that they are and must be free to observe it or to deviate from it, since they have a will of their own, distinct and independent from that of the Creator."

For God, nothing can be superior to Freedom. God is absolutely libertarian[60] and the question of Evil cannot be grasped if this primary divine value is not integrated. Freedom precipitated into duality shines through in our search for autonomy. All initiates want autonomy. They want to give themselves their own law, their own values, their own rules, and to not impose them on others. Confronted with the problems of Evil, most Christian thinkers become entangled in contradictions. Only a non-dualistic approach makes it possible to cross this fundamental Good/Evil antinomy. If God is God, nothing is foreign to Him and nothing, in essence, can be outside of Him, even if the appearing of the existent tells us the contrary.

God is Freedom, Absolute Freedom. This means a simultaneous infinity of possibilities; among its possibilities, the imprisonment of God. In the exercise of this absolute Freedom, the Lord could not exclude anything, except to limit the exercise of this freedom. Within the divine Game, the Lord offered Himself this possibility of forgetting Himself, of losing Himself in duality and the greatest opacity, of becoming man by two successive falls into causal heaviness, He, the without-cause, without ever ceasing to be Himself, in order to find Himself, to recognize Himself, and to reintegrate.

By emanating all these free beings within Himself, or from His extension, He could in no way restrict the celebration of this freedom in all its forms, contrary to those who challenge him or even deny him. This freedom, this game, this joy, are exercised in a movement of distancing from the axis, from the center, from the principle that is the Divinity. This distancing can go so far as to lose sight of the principle in an apparent separation.

---

60 Note that in French, the term "libertarian" carries different connotations than in English. As a political view, it is close to anarchism, supportive of equality and critical of capitalism.–Trans.

However, the being who believes himself the most separated from God, from his principle, in total hostility, nevertheless does not cease to be God. Reintegration is only a matter of time, or more exactly of the abolition of time, as the objects within consciousness are recognized as empty and consciousness appears in its true nature, full and yet immaculate.

We are there in Gnosis, which Robert Amadou (who invites us to distrust academic gnosis) tells us is perfect knowledge, religious knowledge, traditional knowledge, initiatory knowledge, universal knowledge, and ultimately theosophy:

> Gnosis, religious, traditional, initiatic, and universal knowledge—gnosis, perfect knowledge—is both science and wisdom, not in synthesis, but in symbiosis and in essence, and therefore by definition also.
>
> This sapiential science, this learned wisdom, is such only because of its origin, its summary object, and its end: God and his Wisdom. (But could gnosis be perfect if it were not of God?)
>
> To know God and his Wisdom—gnosis—is to know eternal life by conforming to God, by conforming one's will to it as one's desire tends to it. (But it is a question of knowing and not of believing.)
>
> It is therefore correct to also define gnosis, amorous speculation, as a speculative love.[61]

Knowledge is nondual in nature. It is not objective knowledge. It is not subjective knowledge. It emerges when the subject and the object merge to disappear more completely. This loving search is an echo or memory of the original Love. It is a Love without object and without subject, born of non-separation.

"Spiritual death," suggests Jean-Baptiste Willermoz in an instruction to the Élus Coëns from September 18, 1776, "is nothing other than the separation of the spiritual being from its principle, just as bodily death, which is a weak image of it, is the separation of the material body from the soul that governed it."[62]

To come closer to one's principle, to one's own Divinity, to what remains, is to be reborn through the recognition of oneself as God.

Knowledge is this transmuting and liberating Love. Beneficence is the radiance of this Love. We are in a metaphysical Beneficence that affects everything, as everything is included in consciousness.

---

61 Robert Amadou, "La Gnose," *Lettres de Prahecq,* second special issue (June 1994).
62 Saint-Martin et al., *Les Leçons de Lyon.*

True Beneficence, not limited by considerations and conditionings, arises from non-separation, from the Silence of being, and from the Gnosis that reigns in this Silence. Thus the thought, the will, and the divine action (the original ternary) are prolonged, in a perfectly adjusted way, in the intention, the word, and the operativity within the world. The thought is right (proper to the Good Companion Spirit), the word is right, and the gesture is right.

Far from our principle, we will need the rite, which brings us closer to it and enables the ethics (reflection of the knowledge of the Laws) born from within. Failing that, we will need morals and rules, an external reference.

There is a continuum of Beneficence (or Charity, according to Saint-Martin) from our divine nature to our most dualistic "unnature." Constantly, a dialectic whispers between the echoes of our immutable principle (murmured by the Good Companion Spirit) and their negation (peddled by the "evil intellects," the conditioned "schemes"). In this lies the temptation but also the doubt, so dear to Montaigne, that opens the passage from belief to knowledge. If we switch to a dialectic of exclusive rupture, Beneficence is impossible. Whenever our dialectic is inclusive, Beneficence is exercised naturally. We therefore see the operative nature of Beneficence, which is why Robert Amadou says that it is the equivalent of theurgy for the Rectified Scottish Rite.

True Beneficence comes from the thought, the will, and the action of our principle. Beneficence imitated can lead us to our principle if it is accompanied by vigilance. Indeed, an externally conditioned good, exercised out of freedom, is a product of the separate self-replicating ego. The lucid and cold observation of what motivates us, without holding back the action, is the first operative step of Beneficence. Step by step, the motivations of the ego will give way to the intention of the principle. This vigilance, this constant reminder to oneself, to our reality, allows us to move forward on the continuum of Beneficence towards this nondual Love, another name for true Sanctity, which is its source.

INTERLUDE
A Letter on Sanctity

SOUND, CINCHED, AND SAINTLY IS THE TEACHER

What can be the meaning of sanctity, at the beginning of the third millennium, for peoples situated in worlds philosophically and spiritually in ruins, born in the absolutely perverse ambiguity of the Second World War, a great celebration of all human aberrations?

The question of sanctity poses the problem of the sacred in a world where modernity and tradition clash, where education and initiation no longer form an alliance. The etymology of the word is paradoxical. *Sanctus* refers to sanction, *sanctio*, rather than to *sacer*, sacred. The two words, however, are associated in a "sacro-sanct" alliance. *Sanctus* is a dedication to the religious. *Religio* refers to the relationship of the human with the divine power. Sanctity and religion consecrate the separation of the human from the divine, a separation that should be reduced. We are installed there, fully and painfully, in the dualistic rumor that is based on the separation between the human and God, a separation that is not self-evident, that ignores the alpha and the omega that is the original and ultimate nature of being, that which remains, inseparable from God, from the Self, from the Great Real, the God beyond God of Meister Eckhart, who is also God before God and God through the gods of human desire.

Political sanctity is of no interest—except, of course, to the merchant caste. What is of interest are popular sanctity and initiatory sanctity, both of which, in their own styles and through various arts, evoke the "living." This is what the first Christians were called: the "living," those who are intensely present in life, in permanent prayer, in this body, in this world, conscious, truly conscious, "living" and not lived by the conditionings of the "person," of the "me," of the ego, that tool made by assembly that claims to be an entity.

The homonym is sometimes more revealing than the etymology. *Sound, sealed, breast,*[63] *cinched, saintly.*

SOUND

A sound mind[64] in a sound body. The Holy Spirit in a Holy Body. The Free Spirit in a free body. The sound mind in a sound body knows how to use and not use, according to the advice of Eliphas Levi. He conquered hunger by fasting, sexual desire by abstinence, and sleep by waking. He can do or not do, without suffering.

What would a body in Europe be today that was not Catholic? A body which, by rejection or adhesion, would not be conditioned by Catholic determinants, asserted by men who did not like women. A free body, free from beliefs, values, criteria, or political corruptions, particularly those that seek to constrain the bodies of women. Any religion of men seeks to control women (their bodies certainly; with the soul it is less clear). There is a pathological fear of women's freedom, of their creative power, and of their infinite possibility for enjoyment.

A sound body would be a revolutionary body, capable of enjoying or not enjoying, of fertilizing or reabsorbing, a body of giving to life, a conscious body, a celebrating, musical body, a sound body. And a sound mind. Body and mind are not separate, nor separable. Appearance is a continuum from flesh to spirit, from duality to nonduality.

SEALED

The sound body and mind, finally aware of perfect harmony and in search of its manifestation, can then affix a seal at the bottom of their actions. Before then the human, unsound, was lived: caught in the nets of the species, the lineage, the collective, a simple tension of consciousness telling itself a story, working towards an illusory personal legend, caught in the archaic triangle Power–Territory–Reproduction, the triangle of the separator.

Played until then, the sound one can finally become a player. Increasingly aware of the game of God who loses Himself in duality without ever ceasing to be what He is, they finally sign their actions. Born from silence, thoughts, words, and deeds are creative. Energy follows

---

63 Fr: *"sein,"* breast or bosom. The whole sequence of French homonyms is: *"sain, seing, sein, ceint, saint."* – Trans.

64 The French word *"esprit"* connotes both the English "spirit" and "mind."

thought, speech gives form, and deed sets the form. Under a private seal, at first, the "me" is still there, until this "New Man" grasps that God has given them a blank check forever. Many then renounce their responsibility and prefer to reason with themselves rather than let themselves be dreamt by God. The New Man accepts. They are the sole creator, producer, director, actor, and spectator of their own world.

BREAST

The Saint is alive within his or her breast. They are reanimated in themselves, in the depths of themselves: the cardiac way, the way of the heart, the way of the center. They opened the temple of being to all the winds of life by crossing the path of antinomies. They reabsorbed all the oppositions in the center, in the heart, in the breast of silence. Love and hate, peace and violence, intelligence and stupidity, beauty and ugliness, etc., have been reabsorbed into silence, into the non-time before speech. The saint first sought ugliness in beauty and beauty in ugliness, love in hate and hate in love, peace in violence and violence in peace, stupidity in intelligence and intelligence in stupidity, the vulgar in art and art in the vulgar, the sacred in the profane and the profane in the sacred… The ground finally gave way under their feet and, freed from forms, they experienced the emptiness and its fullness within them. They imitated Christ on the way of the cross of antinomies and they reinvented Christ by themselves passing from *imitatio* to *inventio*, the operative key of the initiatory quest. They reached "the little spark of the soul" of Meister Eckhart, the "Place of God" that sees the *nous* descending into the hearts of hesychasts as well as Saint-Martinians.[65] Because the saint is another Christ, because the saint is Christ, they can welcome everyone into their breast. The pilgrim who takes refuge in the breast of the saints takes refuge in the heart of Christ.

CINCHED

The saints (male and female) are cinched and pregnant with God. The cincture allows headlessness without losing one's head, as suggested by the episode in the Grail Quest that places Gawain in the presence of the Green Knight. When the spirit rests not on a disordered mind but on the base of the belly, in the ocean of energy, it can verticalize, fit into the axis of being, and escape the turbulence of doing and having. Cinched,

---

65 Referring to Louis-Claude de Saint-Martin and his theosophy.

he or she is firmly anchored to the earth and can turn their gaze to the heavens without fear of losing their balance. They can adjust to the world without wanting to change it. Supramundane without being on the margin of the world, they know how to take the world into their heart. They can receive it.

Cinched, they can allow themselves to be fertilized by the Free Spirit and become pregnant, bearer of the embryo of immortality, of incorporation into Christ. They can weave the Body of Glory by unraveling the serpentine and infinite threads of life imprisoned in the dual opacity of the world. They will unravel the worlds, the forms, including angels and archangels, who all live in them, through them, and whom they have nourished since the origin of the worlds. As they created the worlds, they can reabsorb them, in the most subtle theurgic coincidence, which makes their own breath the very breath of God. Inhale, exhale, life and death. At each moment, the saint is born, dies, and is reborn within their Glory.

SAINTLY

One is saintly who is without thought, is pure presence to oneself, in the purity of experience, without representation and without interpretation. In the immaculate conception of the present creation, a conception free from all calculation, from all compromise, from all reserve, from all prejudice, and from all conditioning. The saintly time is therefore a non-time, outside of causality. Conqueror of time, the saint, man or woman, immortal and eternal, is a pneumatophore. Bearer of the Spirit, they are an illuminator of the world, a restorer of Unity.

Sanctified, *christified*, witness to the God-man, the saint is a total human, true, accomplished, real, a recurring Christ and not a shadow or a specter of themselves. They have restored the natural state of their being, which is sound and saintly. They are a living answer to the question: How can I be God? In daily accomplishment, everyone has a vocation to sanctity and is the unconscious bearer of a Christ-knowledge, of a Christ-gnosis, of a primary wisdom that is forever accessible.

It is all creation that is sanctity, life itself. Sanctity is not something reserved, it is the natural state of the human that is found in adjustment to Christ. This adjustment, this orthopraxy, is not an action but a non-action in the Spirit. The communion of saints is the conscious experience of the permanence of the One, of the impossibility of separation, of the inevitability of Union.

The revelation of sanctity, *Recognition* rather than bypassing, is the secret of conception, the intimate secret. In the loving relationship between a man and a woman is concealed the mystery of the sanctity of the people as the place of God. In the Bible, the same word, *echad*, designates the couple and God.[66] The saint recognizes the divine resemblance of all beings, the identity between the gross and most subtle emanations. Nature, *naturans* and *naturata*, makes all things equal because it participates in the reciprocity of God.

In silence, every act becomes liturgical, a celebration of divine freedom. The act conveys the hand of God. The saints (male and female) are then the temple of the Shekinah.

WHAT TO MAKE OF ALL THESE SAINTS?

Some damn them to all the devils. It must be said that the judicialization of sanctity orchestrated by a papacy drifting on the twists and turns of politicians is irritating. It was not always thus. It was only relatively recently that the papacy sought to control sanctification. In the Middle Ages, the popes were often local, "elected," chosen by the people from among the mediators between man and God, blessed intercessors, both mirrors of Christ and mirrors of man, able to present the good, to share it with those who lack it. The faces of sanctity are many. They are not organized into categories and do not follow criteria. They do not respect protocols, as evidenced by the worship of unknown saints. The life of the saints, this true prayer, this journey, chaotic in appearance, serpentine in operativity, vertical in the Real, that goes from shadow to light, from Mary Magdalene the penitent to Mary Magdalene in ecstasy and from Christ of the Passion to Christ Pantocrator, is like an encyclopedia of awakening to the Clear Light, a garland of asceses, metanoias, and ways of divinization.

Benevolence and beneficence are theurgic acts. The sanctified and the sanctifier are one. The saint is out of the ordinary; sanctity is near to madness. Sanctity is madness oriented in a higher sense, at the apex of oneself, the Self, the Absolute, God beyond God. Of course, not all saints were saints. Let us forget the political saints coming from the Vatican strategy. Some, sometimes "people of blame," were and remain true teachers, awakened ones, and awakeners: Saint Charbel and Saint Paraskeva, to name but two. But all of them can be integrated as aspects of ourselves, mirrors, sometimes very incomplete, but mirrors all the

---

66   Carlo Suarès, *The Song of Songs* (Berkeley: Shambhala, 1974).

same, reflecting our own divinity and illuminating life with an ineffable light. This integration is then operative, it is a power of change and liberation. The saint themself is nothing, the relationship with the saint is everything. If we grasp them as "living" within our consciousness and not as an external object on which we project our own vain desires, the saint can, for a time, bring us closer to ourselves, until we grasp that every being who presents themselves in the field of consciousness is the Teacher, who comes to tell us of our own sanctity. If sanctity is the very nature of God, of the Self, of the One, since nothing can be outside the One, sanctity is indeed my own nature, whether I know it or not, in light as in darkness, as "living" or as "postponed corpse." Awakening, sanctity, is the ultimate cure, which gives a singular meaning to the temporal and a temporary recourse to holy healers. Each malignity indicates a departure from this holy nature. Each act of caring restores the soundness prefiguring the saint. Care is reconciliation. It is a grace offered to all, available in an infinity of possibilities. Sanctity, the art of the ineffable, never ceases to amaze with its freedom of expression. Canons and rules can neither contain nor define it.

In the stripping away of conditionings, in the nakedness of being, the man and the woman in sanctity are what they have never ceased to be, conscious of the theophanies that unfold from the nondual to the dual, from pure clarity to the thickest darkness, without ever losing the container of the original message under the seal of the Absolute. Freed from the shackles of ego, the naked saint (male and female) sends back to the individual, to the indivisible, through the distorting mask of the person, an image of one's own reality, a reminder of oneself that also wants to appeal to the Beauty that remains. Sanctity is the fruit of a process, gradual or sudden, by the action or the grace of the eternally free Spirit. The saint wants to teach us to "see." It is the same world but not the same view. Against the substituted view, the saint interposes the radiant view of Fire. As alchemical salt, the saint advances the sacerdotal process towards the Great Work.

HYMN TO THE UNKNOWN SAINTS

All you, saints of oblivion
Anonymous by erasure
Or adepts of the shadow
Who preferred the hidden to the light
In order to accomplish the work without noise
Unknown saints
Unknown silents
Unknown superiors
Who preferred blame
To the recognition of men
You nameless
Who watch over the masterless
The casteless and other untouchables
You who solicit neither gilding nor powers
Neither prayers nor sacrifices
To guard the Holy City
To introduce the pilgrims
Without discrimination
Beneficent knights
Who renounced the sword
Armor and shield
But not the psychopomp horse
In order to connect the black earth
To the red sun
And take root in Heaven
All you, without churches
Who have the world as a temple
Saints of the simple and the banal
Prophets of unknown peoples
To the human senses
I salute you
I ask nothing of you
I know that where I am, you are
That where you are, I am
That we are, together
The ones we dream of
To better *Remember* us.

II

The Doctrine of Reintegration within the Rectified Scottish Rite

WHAT THE RITUALS CAN SAY

THE TEMPLE AND THE TEMPLES

The Rectified Scottish Rite must be studied through a double symbolic reference, that of Freemasonry in general and that, so singular, of the doctrine of the *Reintegration of beings into their first property, virtue and divine spiritual power,* the doctrine of Martinez de Pasqually who founded the operative practice of the members of the Order of Knight Masons Élus Coëns of the Universe, but also the more internal doctrine of the members of the Rectified Scottish Rite of Jean-Baptiste Willermoz.

"The Rectified Scottish Rite lives only by the doctrine of Reintegration and for Reintegration, like the Order of the Élus Coëns," asserts Robert Amadou.[67] The same doctrinal knowledge is shared by the followers of both orders. But if for the Coëns it is a question of "knowing in order to operate," for the members of the Rectified Scottish Rite it will be a question of "knowing in order to integrate and be integrated," knowing the origin, the mission, the spiritual function, and the ultimate destination of humanity.

On February 28, 1774, Louis-Claude de Saint-Martin broached before the Coëns of Lyon the theme of "three kinds of temples: that of Enoch, spiritual; that of Moses, spiritual-temporal, incorruptible from the wood of shittim; and that of Solomon, spiritual-temporal-corporeal."[68] These three temples can be related to the emanation of the divine immensity, the emancipation of the supercelestial immensity, and the creation. The spiritual is nondual. The spiritual-temporal is nondual/dual, nonduality within duality. The spiritual-temporal-corporeal is dual/nondual, duality oriented and orienting towards nonduality. It is this third temple, the Temple of Solomon, that is at the heart of the Rectified Scottish Rite and that unifies the two references, Masonic and Martinezist.

On Monday, January 17, 1774, Jean-Baptiste Willermoz had already developed the subject in a particularly relevant way:

---

67   Saint-Martin et al., *Les Leçons de Lyon.*
68   Ibid.

All beings from the creator are temples.

It is necessary to distinguish the different kinds of temple.

The material temple—the smallest atom of matter is one, since it has its vehicle that animates it.

The spiritual temple of beings who actuate and direct temporal creation without being subject to time, such as Adam was in his first principle.

The spiritual-temporal temples raised visibly on this surface for the duration of time, for reconciliation.

The main seven are that of Adam, Enoch, Melchizedek, Moses, Solomon, Zerubbabel, and Christ—the type of deliverance and reconciliation.

The others, like Noah, Abraham, etc., are different types.

The human body is a lodge, or temple, which is the recapitulation of the general, particular, and universal temple.

Masonry is the raising of buildings on their base. We are therefore spiritual masons.

The apocryphal Masonry derived from the Order calls its assemblies lodges while we call ours temples; they call themselves masons and we today, to distinguish ourselves, call ourselves Élus Coëns philosophers.

The Temple of Solomon, on which all Masonry is founded, holds a remarkable rank among the 7 principal spiritual-temporal temples for its infinite allusions to the universal creation.[69]

Several lessons, with consequences of the highest theoretical and practical interest, can be drawn from these different points. First of all, there is a continuum from the flesh to the spirit, which forms a temple, in the visible as in the invisible, in time as in non-time. It is necessary to distinguish between the different kinds of temples, or their degree of temporality and duality, in order for the operating mind to adapt to each environment, to each "place" or place-state of consciousness. This distinction should not obscure the continuum within consciousness. To actuate and lead temporal creation, to operate in the world, is possible for beings not subject to time. Here is what justifies, if it is still necessary to do so, the recall of oneself or recall to being, that prepares the Presence beyond time and place. Within time, reconciliation is based on spiritual-temporal temples, in other words, temporal sacred forms. There are seven great ways of reconciliation, or reintegration, deliverance, awakening, etc., represented by seven temples and their variants.

---

69   Saint-Martin et al., *Les Leçons de Lyon*.

These seven great ways evoke the seven fundamental practices of the Tradition that come in an infinity of variants according to the traditional and cultural trappings retrieved.

The human body is a temple in the image of the divine body, which evokes a way of the body of glory, built by theurgy among the Élus Coëns and by beneficence within the RER, thus these remarks by Willermoz are so valuable for the Élus Coëns to whom they are addressed and for the members of the Rite that he will found a few years later. The Temple of Solomon holds a privileged place in this way, both in the traditional framework of Freemasonry and in that of the Primordial Cult. It is therefore the key to the Rectified Scottish Rite, which is based on the two standards.

As Robert Amadou says, in the same tone as Willermoz:

> Everything is a temple provided that a spirit resides there, and every spirit proceeds from the Spirit—whether it has rebelled or has been created by an emanation—even though it is meant to be reintegrated, and particularly to be fortifying in its approach. This Presence installs the real presence, the Glory of God according to scripture, *Shekhina* according to tradition, that enters the temple through the eastern door and the dedication. The Temple of Solomon is the archetype of the Temple, and the numerical ratios of all temples are analogous to its own.
>
> This is why Masons must first study the Temple of Solomon, as urged by Jean-Baptiste Willermoz; the temple is a universal emblem for Freemasons, as well as for the Essenes and the Templars, and as it was for the most lucid Coëns. It is present by analogy, and in continuity (of what kind?), but with better intelligence, in the Rectified Scottish Rite.[70]

Let us examine some characteristics[71] of this particular and universal temple.

The Temple was prefigured by the Tabernacle that accompanied the Hebrews in their travels. It has the same sacred functions. The structure of the Tabernacle evokes, in a functional way, the three versions of the Temple of Solomon. The first Temple of Solomon, which was to

---

70 Robert Amadou, introduction to *Archives secrètes de la Franc-maçonnerie* by Steel-Maret, ed. Robert Amadou, with a study by Jean Saunier (Geneva: Slatkine, 2012).
71 Dov Levanoni, *The Temple: A description of the Second Temple according to the Rambam* (Lakewood, NJ: Israel Bookshop, 2004). This book offers a very useful translation of the *Michna Midot* or "Treatise on Measures."

replace the first fixed Tabernacle built at Shiloh, was built in Jerusalem and destroyed by Nebuchadnezzar.[72] It was rebuilt by the Jews on their return from exile. The third is known to us by Ezekiel's description of it.

The Tabernacle and the Temple have common elements: the Holy Ark, the Table made of acacia wood for receiving the loaves and incense, the golden altar on which the incense was burned, and the candelabra with seven branches (straight, not curved, rising diagonally).

The Temple is made up of four "places." Let us remember that they correspond to the structure of the spiritual body of Man, as well as to the "body" of God. These four places are the Court of the Women, the *Azarah* (which hosted the sacrifices), the *Ulam*, and the *Holy of Holies* or Sanctuary.

Twelve steps lead to the Court of the Women, the floor of which is a mosaic pavement. This pavement continues into the court for men and the *Azarah*. We pass from the Court of the Women to that of the men by fifteen steps that evoke the fifteen Songs of Degrees, present in the Psalms.

The *Azarah*, place of the sacrifices, corresponds to the courtyard of the Tabernacle. Its floor is made of precious stones. It presents seven doors whose names evoke the initiation process. Three to the North, the gates of the Spark, Sacrifice, and the Hearth; three to the South, the doors of Burning, the Firstborn, and Water; and one to the East, that of Nicanor, a character who can represent the sacrificial power and unconditionality of the way. The six other doors evoke stages of the path of the Body of Glory, once out of the zone of antinomies represented by the mosaic pavement. The *Azarah* has nine chambers: to the South, the Salt Chamber, the Fur Chamber for salting skins, and the Washing Chamber, connected by a spiral staircase; to the North, the Chamber of Hewn Stone, where the Great Sanhedrin sits, the Officers' Chamber, the Exiles' Chamber, the Chamber of the Clothier, responsible for making

---

72   King Nebuchadnezzar II and Babylonian troops destroyed Solomon's first Temple in 587 BC, driving the people of Israel into exile. This drama can be considered as the origin of a process leading to the monotheism of the three religions of the book. See Thomas Römer, *The Invention of God* (Cambridge, MA: Harvard University Press, 2015), but also the remarkable work of Israel Finkelstein, director of the Institute of Archeology at Tel Aviv University, *The Forgotten Kingdom: The archeology and history of Northern Israel* (Atlanta: Society of Biblical Literature, 2013). These works revolutionize the history of Israel and considerably modify our knowledge of the emergence of monotheism.

and keeping the sacerdotal vestments, and the Chamber of Offerings,[73] the room for preparing the aromatics for incense. Other chambers are located outside the *Azarah* such as the Spark Chamber and the Hearth Chamber. Each of these chambers can be related to a spiritual organ of the Body of Glory. More generally, the head evokes the Holy of Holies, the trunk corresponds to the sanctuary, and the sexual organs to the *Ulam*, with the feet resting on the courts. More specifically, the altar of burnt offerings or oaths corresponds to the heart, the Menorah evokes the seven organs of the colon, liver and gallbladder, spleen, pancreas, kidneys, stomach, and lungs. The Ark of the Covenant represents the brain.[74]

At the entrance to the *Ulam*, we find the two copper columns, so dear to Freemasonry, *Jachin* and *Boaz*. They are here surmounted by crowns. These columns are outside the Temple, *Jachin* to the right of the entrance door and *Boaz* to its left. Consequently the Lodge meets, not in the Temple, but outside of it, on the courts.

The *Ulam* has two floors. On the lower floor we find the lodges and, in the heart, the Sanctuary, the Holy of Holies. As we enter the Sanctuary, we can make out the candelabra with seven branches, the table which receives the twelve loaves of Shewbread, and the Altar of Incense in front of a curtain that conceals the sacred Ark. The Ark is gold in color and surmounted by two cherubs, also golden. Note that in the second Temple, this ark was not material. The officiating High Priest imagined it to himself.

The Temple of Solomon—whether under construction, constructed, destroyed, or reconstructed materially or spiritually—endures. It is the place-state of the encounter between God and the Man or Woman of Desire. It is the central point where all the initiatory paths converge, the Land of the Center, of the Heart, the Land of Silence, where all the prayers sail. Let us understand by prayers, the right thought, which is to say, the thought adjusted to our principle, the right word, the right act. The Temple of Solomon constitutes the prelude to the Heavenly Jerusalem. It is the place of all mediation, the place of all reconciliation that precedes Reintegration. It is in this Temple of Solomon that man is

---

73 Often referred to as the "Chamber of Avtinus," after a prominent family of spice makers.–Trans.

74 Xavier Tacchella, *Le Temple de Salomon*, collection Les Symboles Maçonniques (Paris: Maison de Vie, 2014).

raised up, a mirror-movement to the niche of God, the *Tzimtzum*, which leads from dual love to nondual Love, in Beauty, through Grace.

"The particular temples of the Rectified Order," Robert Amadou continues, "and of its Masons, convey, by right, the purest spirit of primordial Christianity. But this spirit is summed up in the commandment of love solely on the condition, not only of recognizing its double object (God and my neighbor); but also to not dissociate love and light. The RER has a doctrine: Judeo-Christianity, esoteric by definition; Christianity transcendent by construction."[75]

This Temple of Solomon, interiorized and deployed as a unity of Being, is the perfect celestial city that the Apocalypse of John invites us to join. What was external becomes internal through a transmutatory integration. Better, the distinction between internal and external fades until it disappears. By becoming the Temple itself, everything that presents itself to us within consciousness belongs to the Temple, conveying meaning and function. A detailed analysis of the different spaces of the Temple of Solomon and the transition from one to another allows us to understand how everything, every event, comes to fit perfectly into the plan and measurements of the Temple.

Two approaches to reconstructing the Temple can be seen in traditional culture. In one, after the destruction of the first Temple, the challenge is the reconstruction of the temple identically. We are in imitation, a proper function of the "Initiation in the City."[76] In the other approach, this phase of imitation is only a preparation, a way of learning the refinement that characterizes the art of the builders, but fundamentally, the Temple having been desecrated, any reconstruction will carry with it the same desecration. The challenge becomes quite different. It is necessary to "invent" the New Temple,[77] not from the ancient Temple of Solomon destroyed by ignorance but as a projection of the sole Temple of God, the Heavenly Jerusalem, the Temple of Presence that endures. We are then in the "Initiation in the Garden," free from human contingencies.

The initiatory and metaphysical process that takes the initiate from

---

75 Amadou, introduction to *Archives secrètes de la Franc-maçonnerie*.
76 For an approach to Initiation in the City and Initiation in the Garden, see Boyer, *Beneath the Veil of Elias Artista*.
77 The degree of Scottish Master of Saint Andrew explicitly marks the passage from the Old Testament to the New Testament, from the Old Covenant to the New Covenant, even from the Old Temple to the New Temple.

the City to the Garden can be broken down as follows: after the fall (the destruction of the Temple of Solomon) begins the exile. The wandering persists until the intuition of the Orient, which makes us recognize the world itself as the crypt of the Temple. It is in this world, that is to say in itself, since the world is a world-body, that the Temple seeks itself. This path to individuation leads to our indivisible aspect, the Temple of Light. Its recognition places exile at a distance from our principle and makes us see God as the only Temple in the world. After the destruction of the Temple, God replaces it as the center of the world. Then the remembrance of our origin, the Reintegration, a cosmic restoration, can begin. It is not merely individual, it is also communal. Therein lies the election. We reenter the Place of God at the same time that we "invent" ourselves as the Temple.

To conclude this chapter, let us give the floor to a renowned Beneficent Knight of the Holy City, Henry Corbin:

> I will say that the truth that we find and find again in our Temple is precisely, as such, the truth that we must forever continue to seek. Because to seek it is to attain without ceasing a new perception that transforms us. We know, of course, that the Temple of Solomon, the Temple of Zerubbabel, the Temple of the Grail, and the Heavenly Jerusalem exemplify the same archetype. We know that we are more than the heirs, by a material historical filiation, of those who built them and of those who were their visionaries. Or rather, we are their heirs in the true sense, because we are their continuators, by our resolute decision. But we only really find what we are looking for in the Temple by becoming what we are looking for, because the Temple is the symbol of the spiritual person who we are eternally, which our coming into this world has thrown into the darkness of ignorance and oblivion.
>
> So we are no longer just in the Temple; we are the place of the Temple; we are the Temple itself. Being such determines a mode of being that I would readily designate as hieratic, in the sense in which the Neoplatonists understood this word.[78]

Just like the Élu Coën, the Beneficent Knight of the Holy City officiates at the heart of the Temple of Solomon. As a Knight, they assume not only a martial function in the service of the greater good, but a royal function.

---

78 Conference delivered by the F∴ Henry CORBIN, speaker of the Resp∴ Lodge "Les Chevaliers du Temple de Saint-Jean," June 15, 1973. Published in *Les Cahiers Verts* 5 (1980).

They can sit at the King's table, which here evokes the Last Supper. As a Beneficent Knight, they assume a priestly function, like a Coën. They celebrate the kingship of Christ in the Holy of Holies. The Primordial Cult of Martinez de Pasqually becomes, within the Rectified Scottish Rite, the Primordial Order, particular to the divine immensity, of which all the initiatory orders are a shadow projected into the dualistic world.

JOURNEY INTO THE RITUALS

The rituals of the Rectified Scottish Rite can say a lot. They carry within them, in their symbolism, the Doctrine of Reintegration. However, what will be put forward here was not necessarily intended or thought out by Jean-Baptiste Willermoz. Indeed, the universal nature of symbols allows them to speak, independently of those who put them in place, in all traditional settings. They are initiatory operators of change and knowledge far more than indicators of rational meaning, as we too often believe. Their nature is mysterious.

The structure in three classes (one of which is described as "secret") of the Rectified Scottish Rite makes the grade of Scottish Master of Saint Andrew a hinge grade between the blue degrees and the inner order that encompasses the Squire-Novices and the Beneficent Knights of the Holy City, the place where "symbols end," according to Jean-Baptiste Willermoz.[79] This does not mean that operation ceases, quite the contrary. They operate in the symbolic class through an explicit order so that they may operate in the second class through an implicit order and in the final class through an essential order. We go from substance (in the Spinozist sense of the term) to energy and from energy to essence, according to the upward dynamic of the return or Reintegration. We find again this ternary which we must now revisit.

THE TERNARY

The ternary structures and vivifies all the operativity of the rite in all its classes. Let us observe that as soon as the Venerable Master enters the Blue Lodge (the Commander Deputy-Master in the grade of the Scottish Master of Saint Andrew, or the Prefect in the class of the Beneficent Knights of the Holy City), a reference to the Doctrine of Reintegration is indicated.

Indeed, the one who officiates in the East enters the Temple where the

---

[79] Letter from Jean-Baptiste Willermoz published by Pierre Chevalier in *Mémoires de la Société académique de l'Aube* 104 (1964–1966).

Brothers and the other officers of the Lodge await him, preceded by the candlestick of three branches, carried by a Brother. This candlestick is lit beforehand by the Venerable Master in the forecourt, outside the Temple. This ternary is placed in the East on the table of the Venerable Master. Of these three lights, the Venerable Master will take the middle one, and passing by the South, his sword pointing upwards in his left hand, silently lights the three Masonic torches placed around the Carpet of the Lodge. The Senior and Junior Wardens, as well as the Secretary, then move simultaneously, swords pointing downwards in their left hands, to light their respective candles from the three torches and bring them back to their posts.

This journey of the luminous ternary, which connects Heaven and Earth, according to the indication of the swords, goes from an elsewhere that evokes the divine immensity (on the square), to the East that represents the supercelestial immensity, then to the center of the Temple, around the Lodge Carpet and the three torches which thus represent the celestial immensity, and finally to the three posts of the Wardens and Secretary which represent the terrestrial immensity. The seven principal officers of the Lodge also correspond to the seven planets of the Universal Figure of Martinez de Pasqually. "But the planets could not communicate any influence to the earth, if they did not receive their virtues from the 7 spiritual agents who animate them and maintain their action, and these 7 agents in turn derive their virtues from their correspondence with the divine principle."[80]

We note the very subtle play of mirrors of this Universal Figure that allows the divine Light to be reflected even within the density. It is the principle of the replication of types that animates all of Martinez's metaphysics. Note that at the grade of Apprentice, the tracing board reverses the position of *Jachin* and *Boaz*. The tracing board is a mirror in which is reflected the door of the Temple and its two columns, just like the Moon, the Sun, and the Blazing Star. If the starry vault is visible, it is for the best that we are outside on the forecourt. The mirror mode of the tracing board typifies the function of the brazen sea in the Temple of Solomon,[81] the sea in which the heavens are reflected. This point is confirmed at

---

80 Saint-Martin et al., *Les Leçons de Lyon*, instruction of May 8, 1776, the author of which may be Jean-Baptiste Willermoz.

81 Although the brazen sea is not in the center of the court in the Temple of Solomon but in the southeast of the inner court.

the grade of Scottish Master of Saint Andrew when the second figure is revealed to the candidate. We discover the brazen sea in the axis of the inner temple. Jean-Marc Vivenza offers us some relevant leads in this regard:[82]

> Behind this altar of burnt offerings, prefiguring the Sacrifice of the God-Man, was the "brazen sea" which the Scottish Master of Saint Andrew discovers in his work that will take him beyond the veil of the Temple [...]
>
> This basin was placed between the altar of the holocausts and the tent of meeting, but a remarkable fact is to be noted: while all could approach the altar of the holocausts, on the contrary, access to the brazen sea was exclusively reserved for the priests of the temple, leading us here to think that the rectified brother is, by his initiation, admitted into the holy place as a descendant of the High Priest, that is to say as a member of the family of Aaron, enjoying a significant privilege in this capacity. [...]
>
> Let's not forget that the bronze which covered the basin came from a surprising source likely to provide us with a rich symbolic teaching. [...] At a time when the art of glass had not yet been mastered, women used polished brass mirrors to perfect their beauty. [...] But, surprisingly, in an impulse of the heart to respond to the request of the Eternal, the women of Israel agreed to melt down their instruments of narcissistic vanity to contribute to the construction of the tabernacle and allow the realization of the brazen sea.

They therefore sacrifice the mirror of the ego, or of the particular, to constitute the mirror of the Self, or of the Totality. On the forecourt, the Lodge tracing board of the Apprentice grade is not yet the brazen sea of the grade of Scottish Master of Saint Andrew in its full regenerative power. It is not yet, but is already; is in the making. The process of cutting the stone symbolically corresponds to the polishing of the mirror.

We must insist on this singular place, with the back to the columns of the Temple of Solomon and facing their reflection in the mirror. The initiate is in this in-between where, according to Henry Corbin, we can be touched by the *Imago Templi,* the Image of the Temple inscribed in the imaginal, at the "meeting-place of the two seas" according to Suhrawardi, in this Eighth Clime where time is abolished and the pure Ideas can cascade into duality:

---

82   Jean-Marc Vivenza, *Les élus coëns et le Régime Ecossais Rectifié* (Grenoble: Mercure Dauphinois, 2010).

> The whole task consists in purifying and liberating one's inner being so that the intelligible realities perceived on the *imaginal* level may be reflected in the mirror of the *sensorium* and be translated into visionary perception.[83]

All work in the Blue Lodge is a polishing of this mirror of perception. In the Middle Chamber, the heart of the Master reflects the Image of the Temple without alteration. He can then prepare his reconstruction.

If we consider that the Lodge meets in the forecourt and not in the Temple, the divine Light comes from the Temple itself to illuminate the forecourt, from the Holy of Holies, by a series of reflections that make this Light bearable for human vision.

There is a possible analogy between the play of mirrors in the Martinezian Universal Figure and the play of projected shadows in the operative Companionage, another Masonic reference. Indeed, in the geometry of the tracing, the stonemason Companions know that the projection of light on the volume of the cubic stone draws on the "merchant," the rough stone, the shadow of the pointed cubic stone. The subtleties of the perspective show how the divine Light stands out as a pointed cubic stone in a dialectic between cubic stone and rough stone. Only the divine Light reveals the hidden meaning of this dialectic, sterile if it remains in a binary framework.

The ternary comes in an infinity of combinations or alliances, triplets, at each level of manifestation.

At the level of the divine faculties, it is *Thought–Will–Action* (or *Speech*) or *Intention–Word–Operation* or even *Thought–Action–Will (Operation)*. In a Coën catechism, Martinez de Pasqually explains, "The V.M. designates the thought of the Creator; the Senior Warden, His action; and the Junior Warden, His operation."[84] Note that by taking the candle from the middle of the candlestick of the East, the Venerable Master indicates that it is by the *Word* that the Lodge is opened.

The ternary is also *Sulfur–Salt–Mercury* in the plane of luminous essences, *Fire–Water–Earth* in the plane of the elements, which correspond to the cardinal directions of *West, South* and *North. East* or *Orient* is absent. Is it because we can only view these planes from the East?

---

83   Henry Corbin, "The *Imago Templi* in Confrontation with Secular Norms," *Temple and Contemplation*, tr. Philip Sherrard (London: KPI, 1986), 266.
84   "Catéchisme de Maître particulier Élu Coën," in Papus, *Martines de Pasqually*, (Paris: Chamuel, 1895).

The Rectified Scottish Rite takes up a peculiarity of the doctrine of Martinez de Pasqually. We have not four elements but three. Air is considered to be rarefied water. This is not an invention of Martinez de Pasqually; we find this non-Aristotelian ternary in other traditional systems. Water, Earth, and Fire are composed of Mercury, Salt, and Sulfur in different proportions, and according to functions that differ from operative alchemy, Mercury balancing Sulfur and Salt. Salt dominates in Water, Sulfur in Fire, and Mercury in Earth. In the human body, we find Water, Fire, and Earth as well as Salt, Mercury, and Sulfur in varying proportions, depending on the organs and parts of the body. Sulfur corresponds to blood, Salt to flesh, and Mercury to bones, but they also correspond to other ternaries: *animal kingdom – vegetable kingdom – mineral kingdom* or *sap – bark – body* or *root – trunk – fruits*.

Let us remain at the level of the creation and function of Water.[85] The human physical body is predominantly aquatic. There is a continuum from the Saturnian body, from heavy matter, the densest and most opaque expression of dual consciousness, to the body of immortality. This continuum has water as its vehicle, the only vessel allowing the circulation of messages from one place-state of consciousness to another in the vast divine play of Consciousness and Energy. In the same way, around an identical abolition of the appearance that separates, there exists a *loving* continuum from the Flesh to the Spirit. Water, both ferryman between the peripheries and acrobat in the multiple dimensions of axiality, is the unique memory of Creation. In duality, water is the permanent element through which the nondual Consciousness-Origin manifests. The meditation that faces the Great Ocean tears us away from the accidental, the fragmented, the doctrinal. The aquatic body-world becomes one. The beauty and absolute freedom of immensity are revealed.

Water is inhabited by serpentine powers, original powers that weave and unweave ephemeral realities and times. The link, real or metaphorical, suggested by certain researchers between these powers and the DNA double helix, or even string theory, is relevant. The aquatic serpentine powers are at the same time bearers of the messages, of the codes of manifestation, and the creative agents of it.

Water, one of the three most common elements in the physical

---

85 During the Second Temple period, the Water Festival at the Well of Libations was considered the greatest festivity. It took place at the end of the first sacred day of the Feast of Tabernacles.

Universe, plays an essential role in the birth of stars to prevent them from bursting. Its balance with fire allows the birth of that star whose particles are constitutive of our bodies. We are made of stardust.

From the traditional point of view, Water, the Glory of God, the *Shekinah*, Knowledge, and Gnosis merge. The return of water to the Temple marks the return of the *Shekinah*, the Presence of God. In Ezekiel (47:1) it is said: "there was water, flowing from under the threshold of the temple toward the east, for the front of the temple faced east; the water was flowing from under the right side of the temple, south of the altar." This Water of Life restores the temple to its original function. Without it, the rebuilt Temple is just a dead form.

While remembering that Martinez de Pasqually is not Trinitarian but that Jean-Baptiste Willermoz is, let us consider that the ternary *Father–Son–Holy Spirit* manifests, in the relationship of God to man, the ternary *God–Double Power–Good Companion Spirit*, and in the relationship of man to God, the ternary *Man–Good Companion Spirit–Major Spirit of Double Power*. This double power is characterized by the number 8, the number of Christ, while the Holy Spirit manifests himself as Spirit, at number 7, in the function of the Spirit, a good companion, the one who leads to Christ.

In the *Traité sur les communications* by Louis-Claude de Saint-Martin,[86] other ternaries are proposed to us. "The natural law given to the patriarchs, the moral law given to the prophets, and the spiritual law manifested by Christ and by the apostles" are continued in the law given to Abraham by the ministry of the angels "in the infancy of the world," and the law given to Moses on Sinai "at a time when the different nations, devoid of moral knowledge, needed to be enlightened in that regard." The law "given by divinity itself" was brought by Christ in "the middle of time." "It is entirely spiritual," Saint-Martin points out, "and in this, superior to the two others."

This triple macrocosmic manifestation has microcosmic correspondences: the natural law is received by human beings "from the age of reason until 25 years old, from there they pass to the moral law until 50, and from 50 until the end to the spiritual law." Natural law expresses itself in the material body, moral law through the soul, and spiritual

---

86 Catherine Amadou, "Deux essais pour l'instruction des élus coëns. Manuscrit Prunelle de Lierre: Sur l'âme suivi du Traité sur les communications par Louis-Claude de Saint-Martin," *Renaissance Traditionnelle*, no. 170–171 (May–June 2013).

law through the spirit. We find the ternary Body–Soul–Spirit associated with the ternary Water–Earth–Fire, Mercury–Sulfur–Salt, and terrestrial world–celestial world–supercelestial world.

THE GOOD COMPANION SPIRIT

The Good Companion Spirit is represented in the initiations by the one who guides the candidates. The rituals of the first three grades of the Rectified Scottish Rite have the same structure on which are grafted the specificities of the grade.[87] At the grades of Apprentice and Companion, the candidate or recipient is guided, led, or accompanied in his three or five journeys. This leader, the Brother Introducer or Brother Junior Warden, represents the Good Companion Spirit who will help him find his way in the darkness.

"Since this man entrusts himself entirely to us, lead him yourselves, under the eyes of his first guide, in the painful and mysterious journeys which will procure him light if he sincerely seeks it," says the Worshipful Master to the Junior Warden in the Apprentice ritual before advising the candidate:

> He who, being in darkness, wants to direct himself and walk without a guide, goes astray and gets lost. Don't forget then that, in the state you are in, you can only protect yourself from error as long as, with full confidence in the Order and an unshakable will, you employ your forces to follow those who should guide you on the road you are about to take.

With this remark, the Venerable Master establishes the function of the Good Companion Spirit. The candidate must learn to listen to the thoughts of the Good Companion Spirit and to recognize them in the midst of those of the Bad Companion Spirit. The initiatory process therefore begins with an "imitation" of the guides until the candidate, who has become an initiate, demonstrates the necessary lucidity. The three journeys of the future Apprentice lead him to the three elements Fire, Water, and Earth as Seeking, Persevering, and Suffering, three states of consciousness that allow him, not to find the "right path"—he is unable to do so—but to be put on the right path by the Good Companion Spirit and to enter it with him:

---

87   Raymond E.F. Guillaume, *Structure des rituels maçonniques des trois premiers grades du rite écossais rectifié au XVIIIème siècle* (Toulouse: University of Toulouse–Le Mirail, Department of Modern History, 1993).

"...he is still weak. He has not had the courage to enter with you on the right path, he is still very far from it..." says the Venerable Master to the Junior Warden about the candidate, at the end of the first journey.

The candidate is asked on the first journey to not disfigure himself: "Man is the immortal image of God; but who can recognize it, if he disfigures it himself?" Thus in order to leave room for being, he must not substitute for the face that God gave him a mask, a "Person," an artificial assembly of heterogeneous elements, the "me."

On the second journey, he is washed and dried.

The Introducer teaches him that "It is by the dissolution of impure things that water washes and purifies; but it conceals their fatal influences and the principles of putrefaction." It is not enough to listen to the thoughts of the Good Companion Spirit; one must beware of those of the Bad Companion Spirit. Indeed any thought evokes, implicitly, the contrary thought, because we are in duality. After having discerned and heard the good thought, it is therefore advisable to enter into silence so as not to hear the echo of its opposite and in this way get out of the game of oppositions. It is an invitation to self-remembering, a prelude to Self-Remembering.

At the beginning of the third journey, the candidate is invited to conquer fear and informed that it is through compassion that fears, characteristic of duality, are kept at bay:

> The Mason whose heart does not open to the needs and misfortunes of other men is a monster in the society of the Brethren.

From this moment in the ritual of reception in the grade of Apprentice, some of the primary axes of the Rectified Scottish Rite are laid down: the will and courage that typify the chivalric axis, and the Beneficence that constitutes the operative axis of the Rite.

During the reception of the grade of Companion, it is no longer three trips but five that are offered to the Apprentice. We have here a remarkable example of the subtle interplay set up by Jean-Baptiste Willermoz between the traditional Masonic reference and the reference of the Martinezist Doctrine of Reintegration.

Why five trips? 5 is for Martinez de Pasqually, as we have seen, one of the numbers of Evil.[88] It is the number of the corrupted man, one

---

[88] Among the *Compagnons de la Tour*, if (as in Freemasonry) it is three assassins who attack Master Hiram according to the *Enfants de Salomon, Compagnons du Devoir*

of the numbers that divides the denary. This corruption passes through the metals that the candidate will discard, one by one, on each of his journeys: silver, bronze, and iron. The future Companion makes only three trips, but the Venerable Master "exempted him from the last two trips, in which perhaps he might have succumbed." We have in fact five journeys and five metals, corresponding to the number of Evil.[89] The recipient is not yet ready to confront the principle of Evil, the principle of separation that maintains consciousness in the opacity of duality. On the first journey, the Venerable Master recalls the need for meaning, the need to know where we come from and where we are going. It is the *Ecce Homo* of Louis-Claude de Saint-Martin. Knowledge of the lost original state is necessary for its pursuit and reconquest. It provides both the intention and the Orient. "The sage," continues the Venerable Master, "takes note of all his steps, because from these he knows [life's] importance and its end." From this simple sentence flows a true ascesis. It is a question of ceasing to be lived, tossed about by one's conditioning and idiosyncrasies, to truly live, in full consciousness. The recipient must, through the test of the mirror, see himself as he is. The Venerable Master

---

de Liberté, it is indeed five assassins who pierce Master Jacques with five daggers according to the *Compagnons du Devoir* and the *Saint Devoir de Dieu, Enfants de Maître Jacques*.

[89] An antidote to the five agents of corruption might reside in the five styles of architecture, of which Freemasonry, just as for the metals and the journeys, will retain only three. The five styles, which are five modes of proportion and decoration, indicate five modes of adjustment to axiality and five ornaments, which symbolizes on the initiatory level five praxes and five poieses. Remember that the Doric, Ionic, and Corinthian styles, inherited from ancient Greece, are preserved in Freemasonry just as among the stonemason Companions. The two Roman styles, Tuscan and Composite, are omitted. The Doric corresponds to the pillar of Strength, the Ionic to the pillar of Wisdom, and the Corinthian to the pillar of Beauty. In traditional architecture, the ground floor is in the Doric style, the first floor is in the Ionic style and the second floor is in the Corinthian style. The ground floor supports the building; it is the work of Strength. The first floor presents the rooms where Wisdom expresses itself. On the second floor are the rooms where the Beauty of Women is highlighted.

We have five metals in the grade of Companion, five among the seven metals that correspond to the seven planets in the Universal Figure of Martinez de Pasqually. These metals evoke the seven sins or demons typified by these planets, the seven thickenings, or bonds, or seals, of the second fall that Christ came to dissolve or break, but also the seven gifts of the Spirit that are inscribed in the jewel of the grade of Scottish Master of Saint Andrew, a true map that indicates the path or paths of Reintegration.

urges it thus: "Enter courageously into the recesses of your heart and probe into the depths of your soul to find there the knowledge of yourself. This work is painful, but it gives the key to all the mysteries and leads to true happiness."

The sage is at the level of Spinoza's knowledge of causes. He becomes a "Living One." It requires a high level of attention to what is here, the movements within consciousness, the causal weaving of life, which is to say, being. On the second journey, the original nature of man is recalled. He is "naturally good and compassionate," but pride, which caused the first fall, has degraded these virtues. "Why is man so often at odds with himself?" asks the Venerable Master. Why the antinomies? Why the duality? Again we are confronted with the two Companion Spirits, the Good and the Bad. The third journey points to perseverance as a means of resisting the inevitable corrosion induced by the Bad Companion Spirit. Master Philippe also gives a relevant indication of the functioning of the Bad Companion Spirit by evoking the "clichés" that correspond to the "bad thoughts" presented to the pensive man. According to Master Philippe, the "clichés" go by three times, and if we do not identify with a given "cliché" during these three passages, it does not express itself.

In the grade of Companion, "the introducing brother follows the candidate on each journey, not leaving him until he has worked on the cubic stone." Although having received the Light at the rank of Apprentice, the initiate still needs the Good Companion Spirit to avoid unfortunate missteps.

In the grade of Master, the Junior Warden represents the Good Companion Spirit who, once again, will guide the Companion on his three journeys, three journeys that end in the Orient. At the end of the first journey, which invites the future Master to think about death, the Venerable Master states this maxim: "He who travels in a foreign land is never nearer to going astray than when he sends away his guide, thinking he knows the way." It reaffirms the absolute necessity of alliance with the guide, with the Good Companion Spirit who represents the Holy Guardian Angel and "extends" in a way the Holy Spirit within the heart of duality. Here again, the recipient will make three trips instead of the nine announced in order to prepare to experience the death of Hiram. This 9 does not seem to be understood as 3×3 but rather as $5 + 4$ which for Martinez de Pasqually is "a demonic number belonging to matter," of which he says:

Join the quinary number with the quaternary number and you will find the ninth number, the number of the subdivision of the spiritual essences of matter and of the divine spiritual essences, and this by the junction of the quinary number, imperfect and corruptible, with the quaternary number, perfect and incorruptible.[90]

Through these three, five, and nine journeys, the Good Companion Spirit prepares the initiate for the discernment without which he could not claim to guide the Apprentices and Companions. This discernment requires confronting the dangers represented by each journey but also, through the death of Hiram, the abandonment of the "me," the "person," the mask that conceals the New Man who approaches, journey after journey. The operative function of the grade of Master, in the future perspective of the inner order, is actualized in the grade of Scottish Master of Saint Andrew, that pivotal grade of such importance. It is the Anastasis, the act of arising. After being raised as Hiram, in the Middle Chamber which is a Chamber of Silence, not occupied by the "person," the "me," which is only turmoil, the Master prepares for another elevation to the upper room. Alive, he quits the life of the psyche for the life of the Spirit. This H of Hiram which, as we will see later, evokes another major figure, is also found at the heart of the hexagram that adorns the Orient in the grade of Scottish Master of Saint Andrew.

The link between the Good Companion Spirit and the seven principal officers of the Lodge, in their respective planetary operative functions, appears in the Lessons of Lyon to the Élus Coëns:

> We may apply all this to man by regarding the heart as the terrestrial, the head as the celestial, and our spiritual guide as the supercelestial, since it does for the guidance of the minor the same work as the seven agents of creation do for the direction of the planets.[91]

The Good Companion Spirit, represented by the conductor in the initiations, is also represented by the principal officiating officers of the Lodge during ordinary work.

---

90   Saint-Martin et al., *Les Leçons de Lyon*.
91   Ibid., instruction of May 8, 1776.

THE QUATERNARY

If we examine an overhead view of the Temple of Solomon, its structure appears to be organized by the number 4. For Martinez de Pasqually, this number designates the "quatriple divine essence."

According to Robert Amadou,[92]

> The four powers included in the quatriple divine essence are:
> 1. Emanation, 10 $(=1+2+3+4=4)$;
> 2. Emancipation, 7 $(=3+4)$;
> 3. Creation, 6 $(=3+3)$;
> 4. Minor, 4 $(=1+3)$.
>
> Now, the first power is the quaternary itself in its entirety, God in His quatriple essence. Likewise the fourth is God Himself in Man, the God-Man, or god-man. The number opens itself and the cascade gushes forth, entering the number which then closes itself.

In reverse order, we have an indication of the path of Reintegration, which (appearing very dualistic in the cult of the Elus Coëns, but let's not let that stop us) is organized in the tetrad: atonement, purification, reconciliation, and sanctification; which, according to Jean-Baptiste Willermoz, can be expressed as the awareness of one's exiled state or alteration, the rectification by the spirit, the recognition of one's original state, and the realization of this original state.

The number 4 is perfect. It gives "10 by its addition to itself, presents to us the image of the unity from which it emanated, and thereby announces to us that its essence is eternal, since it is the same as that of God."[93] 4 perfectly engenders and structures all that is. The initiate approaches his principle through the number 4. "This is why it is in the quaternary number that man must learn to know all the numbers of the spiritual powers that are innate in him, since he had the misfortune of being deprived of this knowledge."[94]

The Rectified Scottish Rite proposes a quest for the 4. First of all, any ternary, represented by the triangle, carries within it a quaternary. Indeed, the geometry of the tracing board shows us how all triangles indicate a center. The quaternaries are thus present in the interlocking of

---

92   Robert Amadou, "Louis-Claude de Saint-Martin et le martinisme," (doctoral thesis, Paris-X, 1972).
93   Saint-Martin et al., *Les Leçons de Lyon*.
94   Martinez de Pasqually, *Traité sur la Réintégration des êtres*.

ternaries all the way up to the quatriple divine essence. For Louis-Claude de Saint-Martin, *"All visible and physical powers come from 4."*[95] This number is fundamental and foundational. It is in the grade of Scottish Master of Saint Andrew that it appears in all its symbolic exaltation but also in a sober operativity. In this degree, so important for the understanding of the Rite, Jean-Baptiste Willermoz inserts a Coën teaching: "It was further spoken of the quaternary of man and of 16 which is his power, as well as of the celestial quaternary by 22, and of its power, the septenary, by 49; which proves that the celestial is subject to man, since the numbers constituting the celestial and its power are further from unity than the number of man."[96] This closeness, this intimacy of man with God, is revealed in a particular way in the fourth grade of the RER. Man had received three powers before the fall. On the adversary's advice, he wished to exert his will on the fourth, which established the origin of the second fall. The whole of Reintegration can be seen as the restoration of a ternary relation adjusted to the quaternary.

This is not a lesson unique to Martinism. In its most encompassing sense, we find it, with nuances, in many of the great authors of tradition such as Trithemius (1462-1516):[97]

> The first principle consists in the One, not from which but through which all virtue of natural wonders is brought into effect. It is on this subject that we have said that the pure procession of the One is neither composed nor changed. From the Ternary and the Quaternary, the progression to the Monad is made, so that the Denary is completed, through which the numbers return to the One; simultaneously the descent into four and the ascent to the Monad. (...)
>
> The Quaternary is the Pythagorean number supported by the Ternary; if it observes its own rank and degree, being pure, purified in the One, it can operate in the wondrous and hidden nature of the Binary in the Ternary: this is the Quaternary, in whose measure the Ternary conjoined with the Binary does all things in the One, and does them wonderfully. For the Ternary number brought back to the Unity by insight contains all things in itself and can do whatever it wills.

---

95 Saint-Martin, *Les nombres*.
96 Saint-Martin et al., *Les Leçons de Lyon*, instruction of May 8, 1776.
97 Johannes Trithemius, *Ioannis Tritemii Abbatis Spanheymensis De Septem Secundeis: Id Est, Intelligentijs, siue Spiritibus Orbes post Deum mouentibus, reconditissimae scientiae & eruditionis Libellus* (Cologne: Johannes Birckmann, 1567), 91–95.

In a general and universal symbolism, the "Numeral of Four" or "Four of Numerals" evokes Totality. Sacred Number, Perfect Number, the series of Numbers stops with it since the arithmetical addition 1+2+3+4 gives 10. We have seen that the Doctrine of Reintegration differs from the Aristotelian doctrine of the four elements even if we are able to return to it in a certain sense. On the other hand, the Pythagorean approach to the Decad, the Holy Tetractys, echoes Martinez de Pasqually's Science of Numbers, as well as that of Louis-Claude de Saint-Martin.

We will discount the 4 as a square of 2. Indeed, if number is always a "power" according to Martinez de Pasqually, even "the expression of the powers of beings,"[98] and "the powers weaken as they move away from their primal source,"[99] nonetheless the 4 of the grade of Scottish Master of Saint Andrew, far from signifying a weakening, introduces an achievement by the passage from the ternary to the quaternary. Moreover, 2 is one of the numbers that divide the decad. Like 5, it is an evil number. "Consequently, they should never be squared or cubed, as is done with other roots, because they indeed lead to seductive results which are only good in appearance. Such is the privilege of iniquity."[100]

To better understand the function of the number 4, we can rely on the expositions of Louis-Claude de Saint-Martin, for whom each number has three powers: its root, designated as essential or integral (not to be confused with "root" in its ordinary mathematical sense), its square, and its cube. "By the essential root it has life or existence, by the square root it has progress, and by the cube root it has completion or consummation."[101] 10 is the essential root of 4. 1+2+3+4 gives 10 whose theosophical addition makes 1 (1+0), the return to the One. The theosophical addition of a number makes it possible to extract the spirit of a number from its materiality or even to grasp its nondual nature within duality itself. The 4 is here the very path of Reintegration.

Serge Caillet, invaluable as always, describes in a very clear fashion the way to find the essential root of a number:[102]

---

98 Saint-Martin et al., *Les Leçons de Lyon*, instruction of May 8, 1776.
99 Saint-Martin, *Les nombres*.
100 Ibid.
101 Ibid.
102 *A Course on Martinism, An Introduction to Martinesism*, "2. Numbers," by Serge Caillet, Institut Eléazar.

The essential roots proceed as a numerical series of nine digits, starting with 1, the first root, then with the following:

1 + 2 = 3
1 + 2 + 3 = 6
1 + 2 + 3 + 4 = 10 = 1
1 + 2 + 3 + 4 + 5 = 15 = 6
1 + 2 + 3 + 4 + 5 + 6 = 21 = 3
1 + 2 + 3 + 4 + 5 + 6 + 7 = 28 = 10 = 1
1 + 2 + 3 + 4 + 5 + 6 + 7 + 8 = 36 = 9
1 + 2 + 3 + 4 + 5 + 6 + 7 + 8 + 9 = 45 = 9

So we have the series of essential roots:

1, 3, 6, 1, 6, 3, 1, 9, 9.

From this numerical series, one can find in a simple way the essential root of any number. To do this, two rows of numbers are arranged horizontally: the first with the series of essential roots, the second with the arithmetic sequence of numbers from 1 to 9.

1, 3, 6, 1, 6, 3, 1, 9, 9.
1, 2, 3, 4, 5, 6, 7, 8, 9.

Next, take a number, for example 28. Reduce it theosophically: 2 + 8 = 10 = 1. Then put it in its place in the numerical order of the bottom line. The number that corresponds to it on the top line is its essential root, which is 1 in this case.

Now take the square of 4, 16. The theosophical addition is 7 (6 + 1), the spirit of 4. The septenary appears in the fourth grade of the RER on one of the charts presented to the recipient, the second chart illustrating the reconstructed Temple of Solomon, by way of the seven-branched candlestick.

Let us observe the illumination of the order of the Lodge at this grade:

"The walls of the chamber are lit on each of its four sides by four candles, placed in groups or separately, according to the layout of the room, sixteen in all. In addition, four candles are placed around the figure or carpet on the floor, one at each corner; finally, there are the three of the three-branched candlestick, on the Eastern Altar, and the two on the tables of the two Wardens. In all, twenty-five lights of the Order, not including the three lights which will illuminate, from the opening of the Lodge, the table of the symbol of the grade."[103] The manuscript also

---

103 Manuscript 5922/2 from the Bibliothèque de la ville de Lyon. This manuscript was written after the Convent of Wilhelmsbad in 1782.

specifies that "it is desirable that the four candlesticks are identical and square in shape."

We therefore have 4 square candlesticks around the figure of the Lodge and 16 candles arranged by 4 on the 4 sides of the Temple. 10 or 1 is the essential root of 4. 16, square of 4 whose spirit is 7, expresses the mean. The cube of 4, 4×4×4, is 64 whose spirit is 6+4=10 and/or 1, the promised fulfillment of this grade which announces the inner Order of the Beneficent Knights of the Holy City.

The 25 lights of the Order should not be understood as the square of 5, since 5 is a number that divides the decad and should not be squared or cubed. The 25 exists by the addition of lights and not by multiplication. The theosophical addition of 25 is again 7 which is indeed the operative key of this grade that the recipient must discover and implement in himself to rebuild the Temple. It is, according to the rituals of the fourth degree, in the first movement and seventh movement of the unveiling of the second figure illustrating the Temple of Solomon, that the septenary appears to the recipient. If we add to the 25 lights of the Order the three lights that illuminate the table of the symbol of the grade, we have 28 lights. 28, which is the product of 4 by 7, has as its spirit 10 by theosophical addition. The recipient will have to light up this septenary within himself, four times, in order to rebuild the Temple. Louis-Claude de Saint-Martin gave us this indication: "Man has to go through four septenaries to return to his original number, 28=1, in order to meditate on what they are."[104]

Let's take the path of the Numbers again from the grade of Apprentice. The 3 that signifies the grade of Apprentice expresses in potential all the ternaries to come. From an operative perspective, let us retain the ternary *Man–Good Companion Spirit–Major Spirit of Double Power* or 4, 7, 8 (twice 4); the New Man, the Spirit, the Christ. But this ternary must be released by the 4, already evoked in the grade of Companion by the cubic stone and its six faces. The 6, number of the Companion grade, evokes Martinez de Pasqually's six creative thoughts of God but is also the very life of the ternary because 1+2+3=6 which is thus the essential root of 3. The 9 of the Master grade is not the addition of 4 and 5, which would pervert the quaternary by adding the 5 (the 9 would then be demonic according to Martinez de Pasqually), but rather the square of 3. The 9

---

104 Saint-Martin et al., *Les Leçons de Lyon*, lesson 27 of June 1, 1774.

is the strengthening or perfecting of 3, but a strengthening or perfecting that is no more than appearance. Indeed, $3 \times 3 = 9$, $9 \times 3 = 27$, $7 + 2 = 9$, $9 \times 9 = 81^{105} = 9$, etc. These powers of 3 are sterile and cannot be extracted from matter or duality. Moreover, if we seek the spirit of a number by theosophical addition and remove the spirit from the number, the *caput mortuum* or "corpse" is always 9. Take 28 whose spirit is 10: $28 - 10 = 18 = 9$.

We come out of the replication of 9 only by an act of pure will that implies both an Intention and an Orient, both emerging and coinciding in the Middle Chamber, the Land of Silence, where the Master (let us insist on this point) is on the Axis, at midnight just as at noon. From the Intention to the Orient, undistorted echoes of the original thought of God, including a double Rectification, responses tailored to the two Falls, we find the original ternary according to Martinez de Pasqually, *Thought–Will–Action*, in line with the quatriple divine essence. This will, not of the conditioned person, but of the individual, the indivisible part of man (consequently his divine essence), encounters the divine Will in the form of Grace, without which installation in the Axis does not transmute into Presence.

It is only in the fourth degree, passing from the Middle Chamber to the Upper Chamber, by installation in a total axiality, that the quester will be able to extract himself from a cyclical pattern embedded in the inertia of matter. The number 4, which here is Man, is moreover halfway between 1 and 7, a mediator between the One and the sacred septenary, between Heaven and an illuminated Earth.

Masonic morality or ethics—dualistic, born from listening to conscience and choosing good thoughts from the Good Companion Spirit who *re-Orients*—is insufficient to liberate matter. It will be necessary to pass from a formal to a metaphysical Beneficence.

The batteries of the degrees provide the rhythm. This rhythm is love. It unites. It reminds of the self and the Self. In the unique context of the RER, it reminds us of what is indivisible within us and of Christ, of the Christ in us and of Christ the King. The batteries are the punctuation of the ceremony. They indicate the breath between the center and the

---

105 81 tears adorn the Lodge carpet at the grade of Master. In the grade of Master in the Rectified Scottish Rite, the fourth section of the *Instructions par demande et réponse* offers this clarification: "The tears designate the general mourning of the Masters, their number expresses the particular properties of the number nine which are found in its square."

peripheries. They have not only a symbolic function but an operative function. They bring us back to the center, to the silence from which thought can be creative because it is united with the thought of God. (It is always from the center that the initiate can think, will, and act.) They lead the ceremony towards the rite to which it strives, the central act of any ritual, inscribed in verticality, a sacred interval within the ritual progression that unites the assembly with the divine, most often through invocation. The batteries are signifiers of the working modality of consciousness. The three grades of Apprentice, Companion, and Master are governed by the ternary. By the repetition of 3, 6, and 9, the Apprentice who is perfectible matter, the Companion who installs the soul in the work of stone, and the Master who seals it with the spirit prepare themselves to escape the cycles of replication through the 4. At the grade of Scottish Master of Saint Andrew the battery is raised to a new paradigm. Its rhythm first evokes duality, then a third distinct point (the conscious witness of this duality), then a fourth point that represents the center. What was patiently prepared for in the blue degrees is enacted in the relationship of consciousness to the world, a consciousness that now tends permanently towards Unity, always dual but resolutely oriented towards the nondual.

How does 3 beget 4? Is it a begetting at all? How do we escape from the replication of the ternary within duality to reach the quaternary and implement the quatriple divine essence out of the dualistic temptation that caused the two Falls, according to the doctrine of Reintegration? The observation, even the contemplation, of the stated quaternaries can give us the sense of this passage without a door.

From a Trinitarian point of view (that of Jean-Baptiste Willermoz and Louis-Claude de Saint-Martin), the 4 can represent the union of the three Persons in a single being. Every ternary carries a center, visible or invisible, that leads to 4. For the Companions, the ternary and the quaternary are identical; it is a matter of the "point of view." If we raise the square, we get triangles.

The Tetragrammaton clearly indicates the passage from the ternary to the quaternary by the doubling of a Letter. The IHVH, Iod, Hé, Vau, Hé, includes a doubling of the Hé, just as INRI presents a doubling of the I. In Hebrew, the four letters I, N, R, I evoke water or the sea (*iam*), fire (*nur*), breath (*ruach*), and the salt of the earth (*iabasha*). In alchemy, the ternary *Sulfur–Salt–Mercury* calls another Mercury.

The ternary IVH, *Iod*, the Father, *Vau*, the Son and *Hé*, the Holy Spirit, becomes quaternary by the splitting of the Hé. Léon Bloy insisted in his time on the intimate link between the Holy Spirit, Lucifer as the bearer of Light, the Paraclete, and Woman. Hé splits to generate the feminine principle that will unite with Iod as the masculine principle. Hé constitutes the creative energy that is designated by the Celestial Virgin, the Mother of the World, Mary, or even ISIS, whose letters indicate the serpentine power enacting the creative potentiality of the Iod.

The Tetragrammaton includes in it three forms of the verb "to be," past, present, and future: HIHI, *He was*, HVH, *He is*, HIH, *He will be*, an operative key of the folding of time into a "here and now," a door of non-time and the "place" of the permanent actualization of the Works of God.

Vau keeps the past in the future, synthesizing the "already and not yet" to which we shall return, but it also reverses this vector in the sentence, "Let there be Light (IHI) and there was Light (IHHV)."[106] It is therefore by playing with the linearity of time, in the interval of Being and not in the given, that the Great Work is accomplished. Vau indicates that it is through inclusive power that the divine operation is accomplished. Vau is "unity" and "love."

"The Divine Name," Charles Mopsik tells us, "is a mirror with two faces and without reflection, where the form of Man and that of God coincide exactly. This is more than a meditation because it does not connect two separate ends. It is both simultaneously."[107] The Tetragrammaton carries within it the original nondual principle. The silent pronunciation of the Name restores this Consciousness-Origin. Theurgy is not a ceremonial operation but the reconstitution in ourselves of the Name of God whose letters have been separated. It is by putting exile (the locus of human life since the second fall) into exile that Being within man becomes present to itself again. God, who had "forgotten" Himself in His creation, becomes present to Himself again at the very heart of duality, the place of oblivion.

The letters that form the Tetragrammaton can also be represented by geometric figures. Two of these, the triangle and the square, do not have a concave or stellated aspect but the third, the pentagon, has a convex aspect and a stellated aspect.

If we superimpose the convex pentagon and the star pentagon, the

---

106 Virya [Georges Lahy], *L'Alphabet hébreu et ses symboles* (Roquevaire, Fr: Georges Lahy, 1997).
107 Charles Mopsik, *Les grands textes de la cabale* (Paris: Verdier, 1993).

five vertices being in common, and we draw a vertical from the apex, the symbol of the *axis mundi*, the figure presents 14 surfaces, symbol of the 14 pieces of Osiris gathered by Isis. But, in the Martinezist context, 14 is also attributed to Christ who, operatively, has the same function as Osiris.

Here is what Louis-Claude de Saint-Martin tells us in a lesson to the Elus Coëns on Wednesday March 6, 1776:

> The numbers of Man, 4 and 3, gave rise to an explanation of the Universal Reconciler, the Christ. He is at the same time corporeal man, spiritual man, and divine man. He came into the world on the 14th day of the March moon: this is to announce to us, by the number 14, that he is a double spirit, 2 times 7. Moreover, we see there the unity which comes united with the quaternary of Man; if we add to this number that of the principles of its form, 3, we will have 17, or 8, which always announces to us the being of double power.[108]

Iod (*Sol*) has the number 1; the first Hé (*Luna*) has the number 2; Vau (*Mercury*) has the number 3; the second Hé (*Venus*) has the number 4. $1+2+3+4=10$, i.e. the original and ultimate Unity, but also the creative Power, 1 and the matrix or chalice, 0. Analogously, the sound "I" (1) and the sound "O" (0) arise from a polarization of the primordial A that we find in the name of the two columns of the Temple of Solomon.

If we rotate the letters within the Tetragrammaton, IHVH, HIVH, HVIH, HHIV, HVHI, we keep the numerical total of 10. The rotation of the divine creative elements, their transposition, gives the same end result.

If we remove the Iod in the Name of God, there remains Hé, Vau, Hé, which is EVE, the Mother of the Living (by whom the living are incarnated) who lacks the supreme Will of the Iod. The Iod is the first ternary, *thought–will–action*, the ternary generator from top to bottom and from bottom to top, from the Light to the human body. Eve, in the absence of the Supreme Will, is the plaything of the serpentine generative powers. Mary reconquered her original state by trampling on the serpent, that is to say, by directing it to engender Christ, no longer by multiplying like Eve, but by sublimating.

The Great Work consists in sublimating the Earth into Water, Water into Air[109] (rarefied Water), and Air into Fire to bring it back to the state

---

108 Saint-Martin et al., *Les Leçons de Lyon*.
109 Thomas Vaughan writes in his *Anthroposophia Theomagica* (London, 1650): "The thing to be now spoken of is air. This is no element but a certain miraculous hermaphrodite, the cement of two worlds and a medley of extremes. It is Nature's

of Earth. The pure spirit, Fire, incarnates (Earth) after passing through two intermediate dimensions, Air and Water. In other words, the divine solar body only influences the densest saturnian body through the mirrors of the mercurial and lunar bodies. A perfect balance between the four bodies constitutes the Christ, or the Greek Hermes, or the Mercury of the Philosophers. Grace does not come from "outside" but from "inside," from within. By separating from matter, which is foreign to it,[110] the lunar body (Eve) becomes independent (Mary) and can unite with the mercurial body and its angelic principle (the Good Companion Spirit) in which the Sun is installed, the Holy Spirit or Paraclete. These four human bodies integrated in a perfect Christic modality correspond to the divine body represented by the Temple of Solomon.

This operation of separation is essential to Reintegration, whether by a theurgic modality or an alchemical modality. Louis-Claude de Saint-Martin explains:[111]

> Explanation of the numbers 4 and 3, which constitute the two natures of man in his present state; the number 4 being attributed to his spiritual soul and the number 3 being that of the principles that make up his bodily form. The first, giving us 10 by its addition to itself, presents to us the image of the unity from which it emanated and thereby announces to us that its essence is eternal, since it is the same as that of God; the second, having no unity or center or anything of its own, indicates to us that it is an assemblage which has begun and which must end. (...)
>
> It is necessary that ultimately the link that subjugates the one to the other is broken and that they continue to separate until the perfect reintegration of each one to its source, namely the particular bodies within the general body, the general body within the central fire axis, and the spiritual soul of Man within its divine principle.

---

commonplace, her index, where you may find all that ever she did or intends to do. This is the world's panegyric; the excursions of both globes meet here; and I may call it the rendezvous."

110   At the degree of Master in the RER, we encounter the inscription *Ternario formatus, novenario dissolvitur* or: "Formed by the ternary, it is dissolved by the novenary." The material body, formed by the action of the 3 spirit essences (*ternario formatus*), dissolves during the withdrawal of the soul, at the death of Hiram, after 9 journeys. This inscription is completed by a second, *Deponens aliena ascendit unus* or "Abandoning that which is foreign to him, one rises up."

111   Saint-Martin et al., *Les Leçons de Lyon*, lesson of Wednesday March 6, 1776.

No one can return to the Holy City or Heavenly Jerusalem if they have not rebuilt or liberated (depending on the operative approach) this body of glory. This integration is present at the grade of Scottish Master of Saint Andrew in the hexagram, the double triangle of the Orient or Seal of Solomon, that brings together the four symbols of Water, Air, Fire, and Earth into one. In its center, the letter H represents not only Hiram but Hély (to be distinguished from the prophet Elijah) or, according to Martinez de Pasqually, Rhély, the mysterious figure of Christ, the only indispensable mediator, the spirit of God who animates all the Prophets, which includes the "historical" Christ, fully and absolutely, Wisdom being the feminine aspect of Rhély.

We must evoke this symbol, which adorns the jewel of the Scottish Master of Saint Andrew, in its relationship with the drawing of Louis-Claude de Saint-Martin that was the origin of the pantacle[112] chosen by Papus for his Martinist Order.

The three symbols are very similar and convey the same mystery, the key to the relationship between the ternary and the quaternary.

This symbol is inherited in particular from Coën doctrine. Indeed, according to Jean-Baptiste Willermoz, "The double triangle alludes by its six salient angles to the three spirituous essences and their mysterious extension: mercury, sulfur, and salt. The simple triangle alludes to Earth which is ternary by the number of its corporeal principles, triangular by its form, having only three horizons, West, North, and South, and the center, without true East. The second triangle represents the body of Man, which is ternary in its principles and division and even also triangular in its form. He is the small world, the recapitulation of the Earth and of the universal creation over which he was to command. This is represented by his position in the center of the six circles and the double triangle. His division, the head, chest, and belly, is figured in the Temple of Solomon by the porch, the temple, and the sanctuary."[113]

This powerful symbol of the operativity of Reintegration among the Élus Coëns is found developed in the fourth grade of the Rectified Scottish Rite.

Saint-Martin tells us, with this drawing by his hand which we reproduce:

---

112 From the Greek *panta*, "everything." The word designates any geometric figure tending to express a universal or absolute structure.

113 Saint-Martin et al., *Les Leçons de Lyon*, lesson 113.

All these truths are found written in the circle divided naturally into six parts. The natural circle was formed differently from the artificial circle of geometers. The center called to the upper and lower triangles which, responding to one another, manifested life. It was then that the quaternary man appeared. It would be absolutely impossible to find this quaternary in the circle without using wasted and superfluous lines, if we limited ourselves to the method of geometers. Nature loses nothing; she coordinates all the parts of her works, each for the others. Also, in the circle regularly traced by it, we see that the two triangles, by uniting, determine the emancipation of man in the universe and his place in regard to the divine center; we see that matter receives life only by reflections springing from the opposition that the true experiences on the part of the false, the light on the part of darkness, and that the life of this matter always depends on two actions; we see that the quaternary of man embraces the six regions of the universe and that these regions being linked two by two, the power of man exercises a triple quaternary in the abode of his glory.[114]

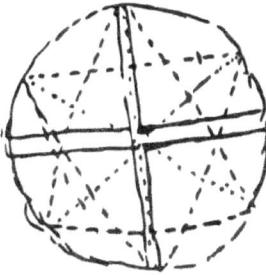

The seal of the Martinist Order presents a slightly different dynamic in its very clear outline. The symbolism remains, however.

---

114 Saint-Martin, *Les nombres*.

The six points of the hexagram evoke the six days or six thoughts of God inscribed in the circle of the divine eternity. The center manifests the immutable, the non-thought, that which remains. The two triangles inscribed in the circle also represent the duality between spirit and matter in the universal circle, a duality that comes in an infinity of oppositions that are reduced to the center.

The duality represented by two points of the triangle is balanced by a third principle but is reduced to the center, symbol of the Absolute. Mercury, the feminine principle, and Sulfur, the masculine principle, are balanced by Salt, the neutral principle. The three participate in the Great Work in the center. Dual consciousness creatively balances in nondual/dual consciousness, the remembrance of nondual permanence within duality, to ultimately merge into nondual consciousness.

The jewel of the Scottish Master of Saint Andrew combines, in the same symbol, obverse and reverse, the hexagram and the labarum or chrism evoked by the cross of Saint Andrew, both of which are crowned.

This is the path of the wise to the Christic crown. In the symbolic environment proposed by the decoration of the grade of Scottish Master of Saint Andrew, we discover another version of Martinez de Pasqually's Universal Figure. We in fact find the seven planets of the universal figure in a different arrangement: Saturn in the center (the natural habitat of Adam, from which he was excluded during the second fall) a Moon–Mercury–Sun triangle, and a Mars–Venus–Jupiter triangle. The observer is on Earth. Facing him are several possible paths to get closer to the center, inaccessible without the intervention of Christ or the Holy Spirit of Christ, Hély or Rhély.

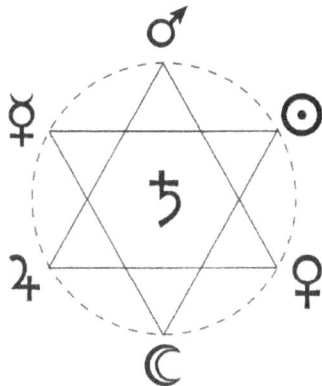

WHAT TO MAKE OF 2 AND 5?

In the Martinezist frame of reference, 5 is the number of evil. Like 2, it divides the decad. 5 and 5 symbolize the total duality with which we confront ourselves in the temporality carrying all antinomies.

The 2 and the 5 are part of the denary, as Serge Caillet reminds us in his preface. It is not a matter of ignoring them but of learning to operate with them. The 2 of course typifies duality through the two columns of brass that frame the door of the Temple. By traversing duality, appearance, the initiate is oriented towards the reintegration of the Holy of Holies where nonduality, the One, reigns. These two columns are made of metal. They evoke the five metals that the Companion must abandon on these journeys. 5 is the number of Evil according to Martinez de Pasqually. As we have mentioned, in other models it is also the number of the human. If we put Martinez de Pasqually's connotation and the "classical" Masonic model into dialogue, this human could be Louis-Claude de Saint-Martin's Man of the Stream, the plaything of appearances, carried away by his conditioning. Operationally, from 2 we must pass to 3 in order to take the path of Reintegration, the continuum of ternaries that leads to God. This 3 is constituted as soon as we observe duality.

The witness, the observer of duality, creates a new condition. We have duality and the witness of duality. This distancing of the 2 constitutes the 3. This observer posture influences the 5. It modifies in particular the relationship maintained with the five senses that, rather than tending to fragmentation and the partial and mosaic identifications that characterize Martinez de Pasqually's "Evil Companion Spirit," become integrated into silence. The initiate perceives the world before thinking it. They develop and master an ability to choose between perceptual and analytical thinking. This is self-remembering, a prelude to Presence. Establishing a renewed and unidentified relationship with the senses restores the relationship to essence. The 5 becomes 6 when silence emerges from the division of sensory attention between each of the senses, giving access to being. The pentagram generates the hexagram, the basis of the seal of the Rectified Scottish Rite, through which duality extends and fades, by the inclusion of nonduality. This is why, in the center of the seal made up of two entwined or interconnected triangles, the letter H indicates the New Man, Hiram, this other Christ. The 5 also becomes 4 when the view of the observer becomes a vision of the four divine essences. The New Man is a visionary who has recourse to the Imaginal, the place of theophanies. If the 2 and the 5, as operators of division, establish duality and maintain it by replication, they become, by reversing the relationship established in consciousness with duality and fragmentation, modal operators of new possibilities, those specific to Reintegration.

Another point of reference, that of Dante, brings another operative key likely to extract us from this division that borders on fragmentation and decay. Lima de Freitas (1927–1998), one of the great Portuguese painters and Hermetists of the second half of the 20th century (a Beneficent Knight of the Holy City under the name *Josephus Maria Eques a Quinque Stella* or Joseph Mary, Knight of the Five Stars), had the motto DXV EXPECTANS, which is "Waiting for the 515," that 515 that was at the heart of his quest and work and of which he is both the prophet-revelator and the guardian.

In *515, le lieu du miroir,* Lima de Freitas,[115] who continued the works of Fernando Pessoa and Agostinho da Silva, introduced us in a few words to the essential, that is, to nondual consciousness:

> As soon as man reaches the discernment of the position he occupies in the whole of creation as the "center of 4," in other words, as the consciousness of himself and of the world, resulting from the play of oppositions and fatalities against which he has tried to assert his will—the consciousness that ends up grasping the metaphysical unity which integrates it into the cosmic becoming and which, simultaneously, transforms the burning thirst to exist and

---

115 Lima de Freitas, *515, le lieu du miroir* (Paris: Albin Michel, 1993).

to live into a desire, no less ardent, for self-transcendence and ontological intensification — in other words, as soon as man arrives at the threshold of the science of good and evil and tastes celestial fire, everything is set in place for the ultimate mystery, which unfolds between pride and self-sacrifice. The infinite outcome of the drama leads consciousness to grasp itself as a mirror of God, the being finding itself not in the mirror, but in the Light that it reflects. Infinite, in short, because this ending opens onto a new, even more dazzling Light, which in turn calls for a sharper awareness, delighted in loving impatience to know the purer and more divine Light that is behind the Light.[116]

The pictorial work of Lima de Freitas constitutes a Johannine, Joachimite, Templarist, and Hermetist corpus, original in its form but of great classicism in substance. It reveals a precious operativity for those who know how to meditate on these works, a teaching concerning the final ways of the initiatic traditions. This operativity is organized around the mysterious number, 515. By studying the permutations of the numbers composing the 515, Lima de Freitas identified the three main types of paths of the body of glory. Also in *515, le lieu du miroir,* he wrote:

> Following the analogical and symbolic journey which has led us so far, we can read in this number 155, where all the elements of *515* are present but where unity, equivalent to divinity, still remains outside the 55 group, a numeric sign of the alchemical *rubificatio,* operated by "separation" and "reunification" (*solve et coagula*) of the number 927. In other words, we have there the number of the reconquered totality of the fallen man, or "first Adam," at the very level of the "lower waters," which is that of lived existence. 155 can therefore be contemplated as the completion of the figure of the Anthropos at the end of the successful alchemical transmutation, because, in fact, if we add to this *microcosmic* number that of the degrees in a circle, that is to say, the number of the *macrocosmic* totality, we obtain the Christic and paracletic number of the *Messo di Dio,* in other words, no longer that of the man *deified* by a long work of purification and perfection, but that of the divine incarnated within the man, an operation that depends on divine will alone; indeed, 155 + 360 = *515*.

He continues: "It should be noted that the position of the 1 in relation to the nucleus 55 cannot be arbitrary from the perspective of traditional

---

116 Lima de Freitas, *515, le lieu du miroir*.

numerology; therefore, 155 (similarly to 551) expresses, as we have just said, the exteriority of Unity in relation to the 55 group, symbolizing here the fusion of the 'sexes' — in the Hermetic Androgyne or *Rebis* — but which, despite its perfection, remains strictly *human*."

The 155 and the 551 therefore express two gradualist ways: the monastic way, 155, and a way of the couple with the 551, in a perspective that remains dualistic until the ultimate realization. Lima clarifies:

"The *opus alchimicus* could be symbolized by 55 + 1 not only as an arithmetical sum (the result of which would be 56) but as an incorporation, in the work of the adept of the Divine One (under the form of 155) as a result of a grace that can never be expected: it is this grace, crowning alchemical labor, that completes the transmutation." Grace, we are told, is necessary for the final realization of the Great Work: neither technique, nor science, nor art are sufficient.

> With permutation 515, we have a completely different situation, because the 1 is found inside the core of 55 itself, enclosed somehow within its body and made invisible, which denotes an essential divine nature, *ab origine*, to the very root of being: in a word, the divinity "made flesh," the Messenger of God *corpore vestitus*.

In a letter to Gilbert Durand, dated March 19, 1989, Lima de Freitas further wrote:

> My thoughts agree with what you said in your last letter about the Trinitarian Sign of the Cross, because the Annunciator — the *Veltro*, the 515, that is to say the star of the Magi, the *Messo di Dio* of Dante — merges into the angelic figure of Gabriel with the mercurial staff who greets Mary, our "femininity," who in us consents to transubstantiation (woe to us if, with the pride of a blind "male," we do not consent!) and who consequently performs the inversion of the inversion: from Eva to Ave. It is the mystery of Beauty — which while receiving, gives itself, effaces itself, to become a star, transmuting righteous vengeance into Life, and Life into a gift of love, passion, and resurrection: "Amen." Mary is thus a "mirror" between the left and the right, between the height and the depths. The divine light, according to the Saint of Siena, becomes the fire of hell for those who refuse it; therefore the fire of anger and punishment can also be metamorphosed into a consoling, "paracletian" light.

This is exactly what is proposed for the grade of Scottish Master of Saint Andrew. The initiate is at a crossroads. Three paths are available to him, two gradualist paths, represented by the 155 and the 551, and a direct path, that of Dante's *Messo di Dio,* represented by the 515. A fourth path, present by its absence, is that indicated by the number 151, also a direct path, requiring a double solarity.

AND OF COLORS...

A whole book would be needed to deal with colors in Freemasonry generally and within the Rectified Scottish Rite more particularly. Colors should be approached, not (as is generally the case) simply as conceptual symbols, but in the operative relationship that we have with them as an external object, a bearer of meaning. This relationship is unique to each person. It is also scalable. We will make here only a few remarks of partial, even partisan, scope.

From a reconciling perspective, the initiate can observe how and in what way the colors affect the soul, understood as the psyche, the intellectual and emotional systemic whole. We are here in the *therapia* of Greek antiquity, the reconciliation with oneself, the environment, and the gods. How do colors unfold in the "person"? How do they mobilize resources creatively?

From the perspective of Reintegration, the initiate observes how colors manifest to the spirit or respond to it. It is no longer the "person" that is concerned, but the individual, the indivisible portion, the being in itself. The colors, perceived in the *imaginal,* not the imagination, are no longer conditioned by the soul. They convey not just meaning but wisdom. Colors, like geometric shapes, are elements of an "imaginal language."

Within the Rectified Scottish Rite, several methods of the symbolic study of colors can be implemented. Black, Blue, Green, White, and Red dominate. If the alchemical sequence, Black–White–Red, is not part of the Willermozist repository, its application makes sense nonetheless because we are here on the basis of universals.

Jean-Baptiste Willermoz was influenced by the use of colors within the Order of Knight Masons Élus Coëns of the Universe. On November 11, 1775, Louis-Claude de Saint-Martin summed up the question before the Lyonnaise Coëns:[117]

> The color blue reminds us of the celestial color that was first seen by man at the time of his glorious emanation.

---

117   Saint-Martin et al., *Les Leçons de Lyon*, lesson 79.

The red color indicates to us that of blood, or the bodily principle of our form which has its seat in the blood.

The green color reminds us of that of water, which is the emblem of purification, since this element has always been used for all the ablutions practiced in the ceremonies of religion, both in the old and the new law.

White indicates to us the white color of the Sun, emblem of the unique first Being. White brings together all the colors and reflects them all to us, since it is only when we have the white light of the Sun on our horizon that we can perceive the colors and the dimensions of bodies.

Black reminds us of the night, or darkness, into which man was plunged when he ceased to be in view of the divine principle; just as when the Sun ceases to be on our horizon, we are in confusion and darkness, no longer seeing the colors, the distances, or the dimensions of bodies. However, in this state, we are left with the moon and the stars, which, by their dim light, preventing us from being in absolute darkness, perhaps indicate to us the good intellects that surround us so that we are not in absolute deprivation and so that, in the absence of our invisible Sun, they can reflect some rays of light and truth to us.

We see to what extent the words of Saint-Martin are applicable within the Rectified Scottish Rite, coinciding perfectly with the doctrine that Jean-Baptiste Willermoz wanted to preserve there. However, other contributions should not be neglected, in particular those, indispensable, of the specialist in heraldry, Michel Pastoureau.[118]

Michel Pastoureau demonstrates the cultural evolution of our relationship to colors, an evolution which is partly linked to technical innovations making it possible to manufacture one color or another but also to our ability to see these colors and their nuances. Socrates did not see colors in the same way as a modern city child.

Black, White, and Red are the three fundamental traditional colors. Black and White refer to the antinomies at play in duality. This opposition is both horizontal, indicating the infinite dual oppositions within creation, and vertical, opposing duality and nonduality, the multiple and the One. The Black, often associated with the principle of Evil or even the Devil, can have another meaning such as humility, which prepares us

---

118   And particularly the three superb volumes *Blue: The History of a Color, Black: The History of a Color,* and *Green: The History of a Color* (Princeton, NJ: Princeton University Press, 2001, 2008, and 2014, respectively).

for the purity of the White. Black and White no longer oppose each other but join in the initiatory process.

Black evokes the Chamber of Reflection, the cave where consciousness can turn towards being and watch for its sign. White generally evokes Christ, and Red, the Holy Spirit, in the classical Christian approach since the 12th century. This fundamental triad remains essential today in Western initiatory traditions even if blue bursts into the central Middle Ages to gradually become a recognized color that promotes the transition from three highly symbolic colors to six with green and yellow.

There is a dialectic between colors. These are questioned and answered bilaterally, trilaterally, and also, as far as we are concerned, quadrilaterally. The relational games between the Black–White–Red triad and Green within the Rectified Scottish Rite indeed reveal the functionality and purpose of the rite.

Michel Pastoureau draws our attention to these relations:

> Green is a middle color! This claim was not insignificant. Not only was green presented as the fourth color of Christian culture—from which yellow and blue were absent, let us note—but it was placed in the middle of a system (a triangle) for which white, red, and black served as the three poles.[119]

His statement coincides with the place of the Green within the degree scale of the Rectified Scottish Rite. Its "middle" positioning makes it both an indispensable regulator and a mediator in the elevation of the ternary. It also gives a more marked nondualistic orientation. At the same time, Green represents Nature. If the game of antinomies leads us for a time to be wary of Nature, of an "archaism" both beneficial for the human species but susceptible to all excesses, in the Center, in the Middle Chamber, then in the Upper Chamber, places of individuation, God and Nature are revealed as One. This reconciliation announces the Reintegration of all things into the Principle.

HERE END THE SYMBOLS

"Here end the symbols." The Scottish Master of Saint Andrew no longer needs symbols, which implies that what was separated is once again united. We have moved into nondual intuition, within duality itself, which intensifies from the grade of Apprentice to that of Master, to a nondual consciousness within duality. Therefore, the symbol is useless

---

119 Michel Pastoureau. *Green: The History of a Color*, 41.

since the initiate "sees." They contemplate the pure ideas within the imaginal and the theophanies that are part of the play of mirrors from emanation to creation. They prepare themself to contemplate the *Imago Templi* and to realize it in this world, individually and communally as a Beneficent Knight of the Holy City.

As we have seen, rebuilding the Temple physically is a business doomed to failure, as was the case for the second temple, that of Zerubbabel. It will be so until we grasp that this Temple is internal, that we must welcome the *Imago Templi*, present from the beginning, in our heart, our indivisibility or, more precisely, to recognize it because it is *jam et nondum*, as Henry Corbin insists,[120] "already and not yet," present but unmanifest. The contemplation of the Temple precedes its actualization *hic et nun*, here and now.

However, the Beneficent Knight of the Holy City is a Knight-Mason. They are able to rebuild the Temple physically but they abandon this project because they know its vanity and sterility. To physically rebuild the Temple is to give life to its enemies as well, according to the implacable law of balance within duality. The Knight renounces duality to join the nonduality of the Free Spirit. The divine plan does not require the material reconstruction of the Temple but awaits a Beneficent Knighthood established from Earth to Heaven, from the gross to the divine, in a continuum perceived as the unique radiance of God and His Freedom. The reconstruction of the Temple of Solomon is the constitution of the Knight's own body as a Temple, a body of Light, according to the operative plan established by the organization of the Temple of Solomon, archetype of the Body of Glory.

"If this famous Temple has become the fable of the world and a subject of ridicule for the common man, it was and always will be a useful example for the Masonic people, and the object of its deep meditations. Who does not know that it was said by Him who was the fulfillment of all prophecies: 'There shall not be left here one stone upon another, that shall not be thrown down' (Matthew 24:2)? But let us not imitate those Jewish people who mourn the loss; the veil is rent, and these words of the Gospel, 'Destroy this temple, and in three days I will raise it up' (John 2:19), are no longer obscure, we know that he was the figure of the

---

120 Henry Corbin, "The *Imago Templi* in Confrontation with Secular Norms," 324–326, 328–329, 333, 337, 365.

man, 'the temple of God, and that the Spirit of God dwelleth in you' (1 Corinthians 3:16–17)," says the instruction of the CBCS.

To destroy the Temple stone by stone is to undo all duality. To "break free from the empire of evil," according to the ritual, is to extract oneself from duality to unite with its principle. To rebuild the Temple in three days is to establish it in nonduality, to manifest it in consciousness-energy from the *imaginal*. It is to realize a hierophany of the *Imago Templi* within consciousness. The Beneficent Knight of the Holy City is released from their oaths. Indeed, oaths are necessary in duality, where the opposition between the thoughts of the Good Companion Spirit and those of the Bad Companion Spirit is polarized. The oaths are a relative rampart against the temptations of the second and an alliance, also relative, with the wisdom of the first. In nonduality, the individual consciousness is integrated into Christ consciousness at the same time as it integrates the latter. It no longer needs an oath: it has definitively actualized the promise of the oath.

The Beneficent Knight of the Holy City is in the truth, not a formal, enunciated, or enunciable truth, but in *Aletheia*. Truth in Greek is the exit from *lethe*, from oblivion, from dualistic lethargy. Lethe, daughter of Eris, likewise embodies oblivion. The river Lethe, in the underworld, is also called the river of oblivion. To extract oneself from oblivion is to remember oneself, to awaken. Truth is awakening and not concept, statement, certainty, or belief. Truth is Being in itself. To find the truth is to recognize oneself in its original and ultimate nature, its divine nature.

The Beneficent Knight of the Holy City becomes an Apprentice again, "but in another order of science, whose one true Master is in heaven," announces the ritual. Again, they are an Apprentice, but this time without the symbols they no longer need since, according to the etymology, everything is now put together. The signifier and the signified, the object and the subject, are no longer separated. The symbols no longer indicate, they no longer invite, they no longer teach—they operate naturally in and through the initiate. This is why the initiate learns another science, that of the divine emanation which they can access now that they are emancipated from matter, following in this way the process of Reintegration. They are an Apprentice but as a New Man. Born again, they still have to know but in another manner, without the distance between subject and object. They know because they are. This is what marks the battery of the grade of CBCS.

REGULA

EQUITUM BENEFICORUM
S. C.

A few words should be said about the Rule in Latin that is sometimes found annexed or joined to the General Code of the Order of the Holy City from 1778. The document is signed by Brother Jean de Turckheim, *Eques a Flumine*.

This rule is unfortunately little known or even ignored. It expresses the fundamental values of Chivalry and is particularly aimed at the Benevolent Knights of the Holy City, whom it places in the great traditional temporal chain of terrestrial Chivalry while directing them towards the principles of a timeless celestial Chivalry.

The reader may be surprised at the absence of a known translation of this text for two centuries, but the Latin of the rule is not classical and poses enormous translation problems, which may explain the absence of a French version.[121]

---

[121] CIREM, the International Center for Research and Traditional Studies, is currently working on a French version. It will be accessible via the CIREM blog when it is established (http://www.cirem-martinisme.blogspot.fr/). We especially thank Georges Courts who in particular devotes himself to this task.

Here is a provisional possible translation of the first words of article 1:

Vinculo arctae amicitiae et omnimodae aequalitatis aemuloche virtutis et veritatis amore conjuncti equites benefici civitatis sanctae, sub umbra et obsequio civilis imperii, eo omnes ingenii fortunaeque facultates steward ut humanae familiae commodis et praecipue pauperum necessitatibus bene consultant, et more sanctam Christiscepti religionem, bonosceptisquei religionem, bonosceptisquei religionem, et more sanctam Christisceptis religionem, bonosceptisquei exemplo omnibus quibuscumque sint Ordinis civibus commendent.

Friendship and love of truth, virtue and equality among all things, joint emulation of the obligations of the Knights is a blessing of the Holy City placed under the shadow of deference to royal authority, because all the capacities, the fate of the poor and in particular the interests, needs, and faculties of the human family as well as the intention to consult, in connection with the holy religion of Christ, good morals and the laws, are binding, following the example of all those who are citizens of the Order.

Traditional in style, the text evokes the great rules of the orders of chivalry in the Middle Ages. Article 2 recalls the operative values that underlie Beneficence: the religion of Christ, law and faith, charity and hope, support for the suffering and the weak, serenity and public peace, chivalrous wandering and compassion, wisdom, etc. The repeated reference to Christ in the rule makes it a call to the imitation of Christ.

What is to be done with chivalric rule and Chivalry at the beginning of the third millennium? How does this relate to the rule? What can the rule say to the Woman or Man of Desire?

Three relationships can be maintained with chivalric rule in particular, a tool in the service of the path, and with initiatory chivalry in general — relationships that determine a mode of spirituality.

The rule can be part of an augmentative spirituality. Chivalry comes to "increase" the spirituality of the quester, their religiosity, to fix the values that will be, more or less, implemented on a daily basis. The relationship to chivalric rule is exoteric.

The rule can appear as an alternative spirituality. Chivalry replaces the spiritual, religious, and cultural form in which it moves, to impose itself as a path in its own right whose religious expression is peripheral. The relationship to chivalric rule is mesoteric.

The rule can assert itself as the axis of a path of awakening. Chivalry then becomes the means of traversing formal and temporal spiritualities for a grasp of the essence of all tradition. This can be indicated by the universality of Chivalry, which presupposes a central core, indifferent to culture. The relationship to the rule is esoteric.

As part of an augmentative or alternative spirituality, Chivalry operates through personal development. It enriches the spirituality of the person.

As part of a path of awakening, Chivalry begins with a "counter-spirituality," a dissolution of affiliations, memberships, and societal recognitions claimed by the person, understood as the egoic assembly, in favor of traditional wandering service, freeing space for the individual, our indivisible portion, which remains, and which can only be God, the Absolute, or the Self, according to the terminology employed. The Sophia[122] is indispensable for this return to the essence of God, the Sophia, and the Holy Spirit or Free Spirit.

These three relationships to chivalric rule can be described as external, semi-internal, and internal.

The Latin rule of the Beneficent Knights of the Holy City can be understood in its three dimensions, which should not be arranged in a hierarchy. These are the three modalities that guarantee a fair articulation between the traditional functions of the warrior, the craftsman (or artist), and the priest, essential to the guardianship, the realization, and the influence of the Temple.

---

[122] See C.G. Jung, "Answer to Job," tr. R.F.C. Hull, *Psychology and Religion: The Collected Works of C.G. Jung*, vol. 11 (Princeton, 1973).

THE TEMPLES AND THE TEMPLE

The *Imago Templi* is present before time as the permanence of the Temple of God and of God as the Temple. It emerges from this that Templarism is clearly prior to Templar manifestations and is not a matter of history but of metahistory, which has only initiatory meaning.

In this Sacred Interval which we call the *imaginal*, the thought of God generated the *Imago Templi*, the image of the Temple of God which is also the Image of God that constitutes itself as Temple, prototype of all Temples and initiatory Orders that are its shadows projected into duality, necessarily deformed and sometimes corrupted.

This prototype of the *Imago Templi*, founding energy par excellence, prominently generated and nourished (in the case of our Western traditions) the construction of the Temple of Solomon, the foundation of the Order of the Temple, the Grail Cycle, and Emmanuel Swedenborg's New Church, but also those great operative initiatory myths of Portugal with universal vocation: the Hidden King, the Fifth Empire, and the Cult of the Holy Spirit.

The reference to the Order of the Temple, present in many Masonic rites and particularly in the Rectified Scottish Rite, is a matter of metahistory, of the timeless, and not of history and time. Unfortunately, many are those who get snared in the nets of the Templar illusion. We should salute the position of Jean-Baptiste Willermoz who quickly cut short the historical Templar temptation to turn to the realization of the *Imago Templi*.

During the Convent of Wilhelmsbad in 1782, he wrote an *Act of "Renunciation" for the restoration of the Order of the Temple* in these terms:

> *In the tenth session of July 29 of the Convent of Wilhelmsbad, returning to the questions raised by him during the eighth session of July 25, Jean-Baptiste Willermoz solemnly declared:*
>
> I conclude from all that I have put forward in this Brief on the first three questions which form part of my motion of the 25th or the 8th session:

I   That we have no interest in the restoration of the Order of the Templars with respect to the possessions & wealth that have been taken from it; but that as Masons desirous of participating in the scientific knowledge of which it appears to have been possessor, we have a great interest in establishing our affiliation with it.

II   That the System of filiation & restoration relative to the titles, wealth & any possessions of this Order is absurd, ridiculous & illicit; that we have not the slightest title to produce to support it.

III   That, even if this System were founded on indisputable titles, it would be imprudent, harmful to the progress of the Masonic Order, & even very dangerous for the said Order & the individuals who compose it, to confess, support & favor in any way the continuation of this System; that in the event that any particular Society, known or unknown, wishes to attempt to carry out in any way the System of effective restoration, we must take absolutely no part in it, & even that we must break any species of liaison with this Society if there had been one.

IV   That the General Convent of the Order will have to insert in its acts a declaration binding on all those who will be represented therein, clear & precise on this object.

V   That the filiation of the Masons with the Order of the T. relative to the scientific knowledge of Masonry being established by a constant & universal tradition, & proven by monuments & authentic testimonies, it is useful & necessary to preserve or establish an intimate connection between the Masonic Order & the Order of the T. in the manner most suitable & proper to promote the progress of Masons in their scientific aim, without giving any reasonable concern to political Governments.

VI   I beg the General Convent, in the name of the Grand Provincial Chapter of Auvergne, to grant me an act based upon my conclusions on the above three questions.

The position of Jean-Baptiste Willermoz remains totally topical and must be recalled to avoid new wanderings and new dramas and to not abandon the essentials. Just as the restoration of the Temple of Solomon should not be understood as a material restoration, any restoration of a formal Templar chivalry can only be doomed to failure. Robert Amadou also clarifies regarding the grade of Scottish Master of Saint Andrew: "The motto on which the ceremony ends more or less confirms that presently—which is to say, in the inner order—the veil of the symbols will be lifted: *Meliora praesumo* (which in 1778 certainly also meant, to Willermoz's mind, that there was more to be found in the Rectified Scottish Rite than the foolish project to restore the Order of the Temple)."[123]

Solomon's Temple was rebuilt and again destroyed. According to the principles of polarity at work in duality, any material reconstruction will similarly raise the enemies of the Temple. Rebuilding the Temple materially will result in further destruction. The Temple is not to be rebuilt. It is. We have to incarnate the *Imago Templi* in ourselves and by ourselves. The reference to the *Imago Templi* appears particularly in the degree of Master in the Rectified Scottish Rite, more precisely in the third section of the "Instructions by question and answer." To the question, "What are the essential virtues and qualities of a true Master?" it is answered, "Those which are designated by the three columns that support the mystical Temple of the Masons, namely: Wisdom, Strength, and Beauty." This mystical Temple evokes the *Imago Templi*. Note that the Temple, of a quaternary nature, is supported by a ternary.

"The Temple!" exclaims Robert Amadou. "Not the Temple of Jerusalem, at least not other than that of Solomon, which survived its dismantling and did not have to be aped by the service of an illicit priesthood. But the spiritual temple of the New Jerusalem, of the new heavens and the new earth (the Apocalypse of John describes no building assigned to worship in the City: it is all temple). And the temple of human stones made by the fraternity, which would come to enlarge the people of men. We are in full Essenism, we are in full Christianity, among the Hellenists and in the fourth gospel, in full Jewish gnosis, in full Christian gnosis which is first of all a Judeo-Christian gnosis; in full Christian esotericism. The cult of the internalized temple, the Temple and its retinue."[124]

The Knighthood of the Temple is not to be formally restored as a temporal organization, under penalty of experiencing the same avatars as the Templars of Jacques de Molay who saw their temporal works destroyed. The historical Order of the Temple had become a financial, political, and martial power much more than a spiritual power. Matter destroys matter. The Spirit does not destroy the spirit. It raises it.

Historical Templar claims are simply ridiculous and toxic except for

---

123 Robert Amadou, "Martinisme," *Documents martinistes*, no. 2 (Paris: Cariscript, 1979), 25.
124 Robert Amadou, introduction to *Archives secrètes de la Franc-maçonnerie*.

official successors like the Order of Christ in Portugal. Even if they were established by a few valid documents, their initiatory interest would remain very questionable. Indeed, the alleged esotericism of the Order of the Temple was never established, even if it is probable that individuals, members of the Order, showed an interest in the traditional sciences. These claims are above all typical of a great ignorance of the action of the *Imago Templi*. They constitute, and this is most serious, a lack of axiocracy and contemplation.

The destruction of the Temple, notes Henry Corbin, is the destruction of the man-temple. The challenge, the Divine Game, is not a physical and institutional reconstruction but the restoration, the rebuilding of man as a temple of God and the keeping of this space open to divine operations and contemplation.

As Henry Corbin asks:

> Might not the *Imago Templi* appear to us as "resolving," or *absolving* (in the sense that it sets us in the presence of an *absolutum*, an *absolute* because it *absolves* from the limits which block our world off from the horizon of the spiritual worlds) the horizon of the world beyond?[125]

This is the whole intention and direction of the Scottish Rectified Rite. It is not insignificant that the famous traditional seal of the Order of the Temple, depicting two knights on the same mount, is replaced in the Order of Beneficent Knights of the Holy City by the phoenix, symbol of resurrection, or the rebirth of beings, and the pelican, symbol of beneficence, both signifiers of immortality.

---

125 Henry Corbin, "The *Imago Templi* in Confrontation with Secular Norms," 386.

INTERLUDE
Metaphysics and Initiation

Let us recall an essential presupposition to address the question of Initiation and the Ways of Awakening: everything that will be stated on this subject will be false, or, more exactly, neither true nor false, the world of antinomies being foreign to that of Initiation and language being powerless to account for the Real. However, language, in its twilight dimension, its metaphors, its paradoxes, and its poetic power, can give us an intuition of the Real.

René Daumal,[126] in *Mount Analogue*, writes: "A knife is neither true nor false, but anyone who seizes it by the blade is in error."

The challenge is to acquire a global, integral, and inclusive tool that is not merely one more truth but a meta-framework in which to think the unthinkable, a metaphysics at the service of the individual on the quest and of the practice of silence implied by this quest.

The Ways of Awakening, all traditions combined, can be broken down into four modalities that determine four relationships to the Real[127] (see Figure 1, p. 122).

If the quester immediately grasps that they are the Absolute (the Absolute simultaneously grasping them), the quest is completed, here and now, forever. It never started. Everything is accomplished. The word "Absolute" can be replaced by the word "God": the ultimate personal pronoun. The Absolute is also the All, the One, the Great Real, or whatever word is used as long as we understand it as the Self.

The Absolute is first of all Absolute Freedom. The manifestation of this

---

126 René Daumal (1908–1944), poet, sanskritist, and indologist, played a paradoxical and decisive role within the avant-gardes. In 1928 he created, with Roger-Gilbert Lecomte, *Le Grand Jeu,* an ephemeral review and movement which have become legendary. *Mount Analogue* (Boston: Shambhala, 1992), unfinished, is however his most successful work.

127 Rémi Boyer. *Le Discours de Venise. Second manifeste incohériste* (Cordes-sur-Ciel, Fr: Rafael de Surtis, 2007).

Freedom leads the Absolute to forget itself in the multiplicity of forms it creates, to lose itself in order to better find itself, to recognize itself, to deny its own nature in the Great Game, the game of Consciousness and Energy.

If they do not grasp the Absolute, but perceive the Game of Consciousness and Energy, Shiva/Shakti, Absoluteness/Being, the quester is the player themself, the one who is played within duality, while behind the scenes never leaving the joy and bliss of nondual consciousness. They are simultaneously all pairs of opposites without ever being identified with either of the two terms of opposition.

If the Game of Consciousness and Energy remains foreign to the quester, then they respect the rites and rules (the absolute *Rule* being the absence of rules and infinite Freedom). They study its myths, symbols, and mysteries until they distinguish, behind the traditional forms, what appears to them as an absolute structure, an archetype of traditional forms, an energetic vessel sailing on the ocean of Consciousness. This absolute structure is then revealed as the memory trace of the Game of Energy and Consciousness, a trace left "hollow" in the Silence, which can be considered, metaphorically, as a virgin substance.

The traversal of dual forms and, among them, traditional forms, leads to the Land of Silence, of non-representation, to "Middle-Earth," to the "High Country of the Friends of God."

If the quester does not understand the rites, if the rites do not make sense to them, then they devote themself to Beneficence, which Robert Amadou called the equivalent of theurgy. They puts themself at the service of the other. They serve their neighbor whom they believe to be other, whereas the true "neighbor," the one who approaches, is the one who springs up, free from all hindrance, in themself, the Self.

The primary function of initiatory societies consists in accompanying the quester to the Zone of Silence where Being and nondual Consciousness unfold. It must help the quester find access to infinity, the Void Point of some traditions, which is reminiscent of the Sublime Point of André Breton and the Surrealists or the place of Being (the place of the Heart) of the Chevalier Andrew Michael Ramsay. It is also Meister Eckhart's "Fine Point of the Soul," the "Place of God" that sees the *nous* descending into the Heart of hesychasts as well as Saint-Martinians.[128] This "Place of

---

128   In reference to Louis-Claude de Saint-Martin and his theosophy.

God" within us is also the "Middle Room" of the Freemasons, the access to the "Upper Room." Indeed, at Noon, as at Midnight, the Master Mason is on the axis, outside personal representations, in the Silence of Being.

The Void Point, from the dual "point of view," becomes the Point of Enchantment, the Assemblage Point of realities or worlds, from the nondual "point of view." It is the Point from which unfolds temporality, judgment,[129] movement, and the increasingly dense peripheries of form, conditioning and alienating as the distance from the axis of Being increases, towards a raw and brutal duality. In dual Consciousness, creator of the limited worlds, "having" and "doing" reign. Forms are structured according to the permanent action of the archaic triangle Power–Territory–Reproduction. By "reproduction," we do not mean only sexual reproduction, nor the replication of forms, but above all the replication of the self, the ego, the "Person," in the identity.

This journey, which passes through the Land of Silence, Land of an "Immaculate Conception,"[130] to reach the Fifth Empire of the Lusitanian Tradition where reigns the Hidden King, the Self, Empire of the Holy Spirit, or Free Spirit, is indeed a return trip. It is the journey of Odysseus, prototype of the initiate, who returns to Ithaca. It is the Remembrance of Hermes, the Reintegration of Martinez de Pasqually, the Recognition of Abhinavagupta and of the nondual Shaivism of Kashmir.

To stop being tricked, the quester will have to become familiar with the archaic conditioning and conditioned powers by reversing them and installing them in a new verticality, which a number of traditional symbols evoke. This initiatory process will require going from *imitatio* to *inventio,* or even from Initiation in the City to Initiation in the Garden.[131]

Note that the distinction, constrained by language, that we seem to draw on either side of the Zone of Silence is of a dualistic nature and cannot account for reality.

In the Real, the Self and the "Person" merge—the simple and the hypercomplex, the One and the many, the Silence and the noise, the

---

129 Indeed, with temporality emerges judgment, that is to say, object comparison. From this point of view, the "last judgment" is the one that, grasping the empty nature of all objects, annihilates judgment. Master Eckhart insisted on "thinking of God as nothing because He is unnameable and creatures as nothing since they are creatures [...] Everything that must welcome and receive must necessarily be empty."
130 Consciousness without concept, without object or subject, and without causality.
131 Boyer, *Beneath the Veil of Elias Artista.*

infinite and the limited, immobility and movement, the nondual and the dual, are perfectly identical and are not.

The tetrad *Beneficence – Rites – Game of Consciousness and Energy – Absolute* can be illustrated through a few quotations. Here are some:

Regarding Beneficence, we could take any article of international human rights legislation and deepen it in its philosophical, ethical, and legal dimensions.

To discuss the issue and the necessity of traversing the Rites, let us hear Louis-Claude de Saint-Martin:

> People who have a penchant for philosophical establishments and societies, Masonic and others, when they derive some happy fruit from them, are most inclined to believe that they owe it to the ceremonies and all the pageantry that is in use in those circumstances. But before confirming that things are as they think they are, it would be necessary to have tried also to put into use the greatest simplicity and the entire abstraction of the form, and if then we enjoyed the same favors, would we not be justified in attributing this effect to another cause? and to remember that our Grand Master said: Wherever you are assembled in my name, I will be in the midst of you.

About the Void Point or Sublime Point, here is what André Breton has to say:

> Everything suggests that there is a point in the mind from which life and death, the real and the imaginary, the past and the future, the communicable and the incommunicable, the high and the low, cease to be perceived as contradictory.
>
> Now, it is futile to examine surrealist activity for any motive other than the hope of determining this point.

The Void Point also evokes the Bauhütte Point defined by a famous quatrain:

> A point that is placed in the circle
> That lies in the square and the triangle
> If you find the point
> You are saved
> Relieved of pain, anguish and danger..

The quatrain is sometimes summed up in this single companion sentence:

> If you know the point within the circle, the square, and the triangle, you will be saved.

Finally, nondual consciousness is perfectly approached by this quote from Abhinavagupta:

> From the start, situate yourself beyond spiritual progress,
> Beyond contemplation,
> Beyond skillful speech,
> Beyond the search,
> Beyond meditation on deities,
> Beyond concentration and the recitation of texts.
> Tell me, what is the absolute reality
> That leaves no room for doubt?
> Listen closely!
> Stop clinging to this or that,
> And, residing in your absolute true nature,
> Peacefully enjoy the reality of the world!

We have had the opportunity to develop in different ways the *Beneficence–Rites–Game of Consciousness and Energy–Absolute* tetrad, which should not be perceived as a ladder, despite the attached representation, but rather as a multidimensional and mutable labyrinth.

The tetrad can be expressed with other analogies:

With Louis-Claude de Saint-Martin, we will speak of the Man (or Woman) of the Stream, who becomes a Man of Desire, to engender the New Man and, finally, by a redeification, to manifest their original and ultimate nature of the Spirit-Man and assume their ultimate ministry.

Meister Eckhart developed, in the Christian West, a thought very close to that of Abhinavagupta, the great master of nondual Shaivism.[132] But, while the latter had total freedom of speech, Meister Eckhart needed to evade the suspicions of the Church that wound up condemning him in 1329 after his passing. From coarse duality to the nondual Void, filled by divine Bliss, Meister Eckhart distinguished six degrees that can be

---

132 Read on this subject the excellent work of Colette Poggi, *Les Œuvres de vie selon Maître Eckhart et Abhinavagupta* (Paris: Deux Océans, 2000).

grouped in four stages. First of all there is the imitation and tension regarding the Divine and His Wisdom. Then comes the time of detachment, of abandoning conditioning, of idiosyncrasies, of installation in the love of God, of autonomy. The seeker then accesses tranquility and peace, and bathes in the ineffable. And, in the ultimate degree, by definitively abandoning themselves, by stripping themself of themself, by renouncing the "Person," they attain the perfection of their own original nobility and remain in divine Bliss.

In Freemasonry, we will find the same functions in the four symbols of the rough ashlar, the mosaic pavement, the pointed cubic stone, and finally the pointed cubic stone surmounted by an axe.

Carlo Suarès, in *La Kabale des Kabales*,[133] proposes a relevant structure: the projections organized around the repose (or absence) of the divinity–the verdant Earth, support of the consciousness of Elohim-Man–the waters above and the waters below, dual-nondual consciousness–the Light.

It is the same tetrad that is represented in the Arthurian Tradition by the three Knighthoods of the Grail. The vulgar man (or woman) who, by dint of preparation and merit, becomes a Knight, is introduced into an earthly Knighthood, then into a spiritual Knighthood, and finally into a celestial Knighthood. To these three Knighthoods correspond three different alchemical contents of the Grail.[134]

Fernando Pessoa expresses the same ascent through three deaths and three exits from the tomb. The conditioned man, the lived man, the "postponed corpse," discovers the Law of Nature. He is Hiram, dead to the profane world, raised from the tomb by the discovery of the three assassins who represent the archaic triangle power–territory–reproduction.[135] Hiram goes in search of the Lost Word of which he has a premonition. He becomes Christian Rosenkreutz at the opening of his tomb, holding the *Book T.*, complement of *The Book of the World*. Christian Rosenkreutz knows the Word but only through its symbol. He has an intuition. This is the second death, death to the conditioned sacred world. A third tomb

---

[133] Carlo Suarès, *La Kabale des Kabales* (La Bégude de Mazenc, Fr: Arma Artis, 2009).

[134] See Claude Bruley, *L'Amour Courtois, les Cathares, le Graal* (Cordes-sur-Ciel, Fr: Rafael de Surtis and Soisy-sur-Seine, Fr: Editinter, 2006), and Claude Bruley, *Le Grand Œuvre comme fondement d'une spiritualité laïque. Le chemin vers l'individuation* (Cordes-sur-Ciel, Fr: Rafael de Surtis, 2008).

[135] Boyer, *Freemasonry as a Way of Awakening*.

then opens, this one empty. The quester, by divine marriage, becomes Christ. They *are* the Free Word.

Fernando Pessoa is part of the Joachimite heritage: the Time of Thorns, the Time of Roses, the Time of Lilies, and non-time, from the heaviest duality to absolute nonduality. Indeed, the Cistercian monk Joachim de Fiore announced the three ages that we find in the *Trovas* of the prophet Bandarra who orients the entire Lusitanian Tradition:[136]

- The era of the Old Testament, age of the Father, which begins with Abraham and ends with the birth of Christ.
- The era of the New Testament, age of the Son, the Time of Grace, which begins with the last king of Israel, Hosea (732–724 BC), and develops with Saint John the Baptist and Jesus.
- The era of the coming World, age of the Holy Spirit,[137] or the Time of Lilies, underlying the other two, but explicit with the return of the Prophet Elijah to continue until the Last Judgment.

These three ages become five times according to Antonio Vieira who, after the disappearance of King Sebastião,[138] revisited and revived, within the perspective of a Fifth Empire, the prophecies of Bandara from the dream of Nebuchadnezzar reported in the prophecy of Daniel. Father Vieira announced the advent of the Fifth and last Empire of a thousand years succeeding the Assyrian, Persian, Greek, and Roman (extending into the Holy Roman) empires. The Assyrian Empire is that of the Father, the Persian Empire is that of the Father and the Son, the Greek Empire that of the Son, the Roman Empire that of the Son and the Holy Spirit. The Portuguese or Lusitanian Empire marks the reign of the Spirit, represented by Sebastião who assumes a function of priest-king of Christ, similar to that of the mythical Prester John, whom certain missions in the Age of Discoveries sought in Africa and then in India.

Boris Mouravieff spoke of the Ego of the body, the personal Ego, the real (individual) Ego, and finally the universal Ego,[139] an integrative process that he likened to the work of Derzhavin who said: "I am a worm,"

---

136 Which will be brought to Portugal by the Order of Christ, by the Franciscans, and by the Jesuits.
137 Joachim de Flore had fixed this descent of the Holy Spirit in 1260.
138 In Alcácer-Quibir, in present-day Morocco, on August 4, 1578.
139 Boris Mouravieff, *Introduction à la Philosophie ésotérique d'après la Tradition de l'Orthodoxie orientale* (La Bégude de Mazenc, Fr: Arma Artis, 2010).

"I am a slave," "I am a King," "I am God." Deification indeed appears as the emancipation from all dual conditioning, a leap from gross duality to nonduality, an inclusive and non-exclusive leap.

With our dear François Rabelais, we will propose this tetrad: the Divine Bottle and the sacredness of ingestion – the Carnival of Fools – the alchemy of the lair of Saturn – the famous and immense nondual principle of the Abbey of Thelema, "Do what thou wilt."

In Buddhism, we would speak of form – symbol – method – Awakening.[140]

In the domain of therapy, we observe medication and surgery – spagyrics and herbal medicine – alchemy and energy therapy – Awakening, which is the ultimate healing.

In a more provocative way, we will distinguish the stupidity that is believing that one understands and acts, idiocy; the antidote to stupidity which consists in not understanding anything, the blocking of thought, the prelude to silence; then controlled madness, magnificently embodied by Don Quixote de la Mancha, another prototype of the initiate; and finally, Awakening. In any case, Liberty or Death.

We can also think in a completely different manner regarding this process that leads to a non-process. The human being is stuck in "conformism," which should be understood not in the ordinary sense but as all identification and adherence to form. Under the impulse of the Self, the human being revolts against alienation. This revolt leads him to enter into dissidence. We distinguish personal and horizontal dissidence from initiatory and vertical dissidence. The first operates a revolution within the "person": it remains "egoic" and temporal. The second operates a "devolution," or the exit from all evolution. Evolution is indeed another word for temporality. If the "egoic" revolution invariably leads to a new conformism and new identifications that recycle conditioning, devolution leads to the absolute freedom of being, to the realization of the Self.

Note that under these four modes there appear four levels of compassion, a fundamental value in all expressions of the Rose-Croix traditions. True compassion, the only compassion, is nondual. No separation, only the One. The very concept of "compassion," any concept, is absent from nondual consciousness. There is fullness. Neither object nor subject. Dual-nondual compassion is free, immediate, and unconditioned love, manifested without intention within a duality not experienced as such. There is knowing by the spirit and not knowing. Object and subject are

---

140 Or, perhaps, according to some practitioners: form – method – symbol – Awakening.

perceived within consciousness. Mindful dual compassion relies on the interplay of consciousness and energy. The vision of the energetic play of compensations within dual consciousness is clear and the root of suffering appears within the artificial relationship between subject and object. There is, however, the intention and adhesion of the "person." Finally, the most relative form of compassion resides in the dual consciousness identified with the object. This relative compassion arises from a "person" to another "person" and not from "Being" to "Being." It is societal and civic compassion.

Just as the tetrad determines four modalities of compassion, it indicates four relationships to the dragon, in whom we must recognize the angel of the turning. Philippe Lavastine considers that the spear of Saint George represents the solar ray, symbol of the divine ray of compassion.[141]

For the conditioned man, plaything of forces that exceed him, the dragon is the enemy, the evil. He projects on the dragon what is in him, ignorance and coarseness. He denies the goddess and, often, the male human being humiliates the woman to forbid her to be embodied. Her freedom frightens him. When desire becomes vertical, ceases to be mimetic, and tends towards the summit of itself, the dragon awakens and appears in its true incorruptible nature: neither good nor bad. But the dragon is nonetheless a dreaded other. It is only by acquiring the vision of the game of energy and consciousness that the dragon truly becomes an ally, an ally in itself that reveals the secret of ambrosia in the interval of nondual consciousness.

This metaphysics of the *Beneficence–Rites–Game of Consciousness and Energy–Absolute* tetrad can be discerned in all cultures, traditions, and arts. Neither true nor false, it makes it possible to recognize, by a quantum leap, a radical paradigm shift, the imposture of the "Person" as fully participating in the "posture" of the Self, imperfection as the "finishing" of perfection.

Wassily Kandinsky,[142] when he talks about his art, does he not speak of this nondual Consciousness that is inevitable whatever one does or doesn't do, which hides with pleasure in duality:

---

141 Tara Michael, *Des Védas au Christianisme* (Saint-Martin-de-Castillon, Fr: Signatura, 2009).
142 Wassily Kandinsky, *Du spirituel dans l'art, et dans la peinture en particulier* and *Point et ligne sur plan* (Paris: Denoël/Gallimard, Folio Essais, 1989 and 1991).

An empty canvas. In appearance: very empty, remaining silent, indifferent. Almost dazed. In truth: full of tension with a thousand low voices, full of suspense. A little afraid, since you can violate her. But docile. She willingly does what is wanted of her and asks for nothing. She can hold everything but cannot endure everything. She reinforces the just but also the false. And she mercilessly devours the face of the false. She amplifies the voice of the false to a high-pitched howl — impossible to bear —

Wonderful is the empty canvas — more beautiful than some paintings.

The simplest elements — straight line, straight and narrow surface: hard, unshakable, standing without regard, seemingly "self-evident" — like a destiny already lived — thus and not otherwise — curved, "free," vibrancy that dodges, that yields, "elastic," "indeterminate" in appearance — like the destiny that awaits us. It could turn out otherwise, but it won't. Hard and soft. Combinations of both — endless possibilities.

We now come to the question of practices, of the operations that the initiatory paths convey. Mystical, theurgic, alchemical, or other, complex or minimalist, the purpose of the operativities is not to obtain or conquer, but only to celebrate and actualize the Beauty and Freedom of the Absolute, here and now.

There is a practice common to many traditions, from the West or East, accessible to all and yet the most secret, which we will identify under the global name of "The Practice of the Letter A."[143] We have been able to identify it in certain forms of Buddhism, Shaivism, the Kabbalah, ancient Rosicrucianism, and Sufism, among others. It is present, symbolically, in Freemasonry. It is a meditation, simple and difficult, that works through chants, theurgies, and alchemies, or on the contrary condenses into an infinite bliss-filled Emptiness. It is said to be the meditation, art, and play of the Lord Himself through all that is and all that is not. "The Practice of the Letter A" constitutes both the origin and the end of the real ways. It also constitutes the origin and the end of the dual life, from the first inbreath, the first A, to the last outbreath, the last A. The Letter A, origin of all letters, of all sounds, but also of all numbers, is nondual in nature and merges with Consciousness, hence its importance, hence its permanence. It is said, in certain traditions, that the Letter A is not

---

143 A basic form of this practice was presented in Rémi Boyer, *Eveil et Incohérisme* (La Bégude de Mazenc, Fr: Arma Artis, 2005). Advanced elements can be found in *Eveil & Absolu* by the same author (La Bégude de Mazenc, Fr: Arma Artis, 2009).

practiced but that it is found in us, in the permanent meditator who is our intrinsic reality.

Figure 2 (p. 123) illustrates the infinite deployment of the Letter A and its withdrawal to the source of all manifestation. It tells, in a different manner, what the tetrad *Beneficence–Rites–Game of Consciousness and Energy–Absolute* wants to express.

Neither A nor non-A: Neither dual, nor nondual, nor (neither dual nor nondual)

The Absolute, being Absolute Freedom, in order to (or out of order to[144]) manifest this unlimited Freedom, plays at enjoying, at experiencing Itself even in loss and enchainment.

Nondual A:

For this, the Absolute creates an Interval in itself. It becomes aware of Itself, the initial Interval being the primordial mirror. The Absolute becomes Absoluteness and Beingness, the Great Nothing and its Fullness. The Interval constitutes and emphasizes nondual, integral, inclusive, and total Consciousness.

Nondual/Dual A:

Within Beingness, a second interval is created. Beingness becomes Being and Nonbeing. This first duality gives rise to Appearance by the movement between Being and Nonbeing (note that the Absolute is both Being and Nonbeing and not [Being and Nonbeing]). Nondual/Dual Consciousness is still only an ocean of Bliss, the dual movement within the nondual being immediate, without gap, and without time.

Dual A:

Appearance then unfurls through multiple separations. The multiplicity of intervals, which are so many mirrors in which the Absolute plays with Itself, generates in infinite fluidity the multiplicity of beings and forms in a single movement, the movement of Appearance, which is the infinite game of consciousness and energy.

---

144 There is neither subject nor object nor causation "there."

Dual A polarized, stretched into I and O:

The polarization of the game gives rise to an increasingly marked, fragmented, and contracted Dual Consciousness that is characterized by:
- The forgetting of its nondual origin.
- The loss of Bliss.
- The original fear of not finding one's unity.
- The original desire to return to its state of wholeness.
- The fascination with forms, identification with Fantasy, with the Spectacle of Appearance. Fixation on "the Work"; Doing and Having.
- The distinction between subject and object.
- Time, judgment, memory, and comparison.

Each parcel of Consciousness, immersed in duality, nonetheless does not cease to be, in essence, absolute Bliss and Freedom. Each part includes the Whole. But Consciousness plays at ignoring itself in order to better experience the intensity of Recognizing itself, Reintegrating itself, and Remembering itself as the Absolute, the Lord, the Self, the Great Nothing and its Fullness.

The extension of the A (represented in the Masonic Temple by the Venerable Master) towards its solar pole, the I (represented by the Senior Warden), and its lunar pole, the O (represented by the Junior Warden), the solar quality being able also to be attributed to O and the lunar quality to I, according to traditional cultures, generates time and space (the parentheses of sacred time and sacred space in which the Lodge meets). We find these three sounds, I, A, O, in multiple forms, from the Masonic lodge to the 515 of Dante.

A, generator of all sound:

The Absolute moves further and further away from Itself, until it loses Itself completely, frightens Itself, afraid of never finding this integrity that it nevertheless cannot lose. Ignorance emerges in Appearance, the ignorance of Its own original and ultimate nature.

All desire points to the Absolute, the Self.

All fear is only a derivative of the initial fear born of separation.

All contraction of Consciousness at any point of a periphery resulting from the dual/nondual axiality creates and constitutes a being, a more or less self-conscious form, which, once named, will never cease to replicate, to prolong itself in temporality.

The "I," the "Person," the ego, is an ephemeral contraction of Consciousness, a moment of play, that has been given a name.

All movement, all creation, is the repetition of this "Great Game" and tends to the Return.

All operative practice is a celebration of this Return, a Festival,[145] a time of Being. It does not contribute. The Return is indeed inevitable. It is the abandonment of the name, that is, Silence. It is the abandonment of the form, that is, Void.

The Return, the Reintegration, of course belongs to duality, to Appearance. In the Real, there is no distance, no separation, and no Return. Everything is accomplished.

---

145 A time for the cessation of work.

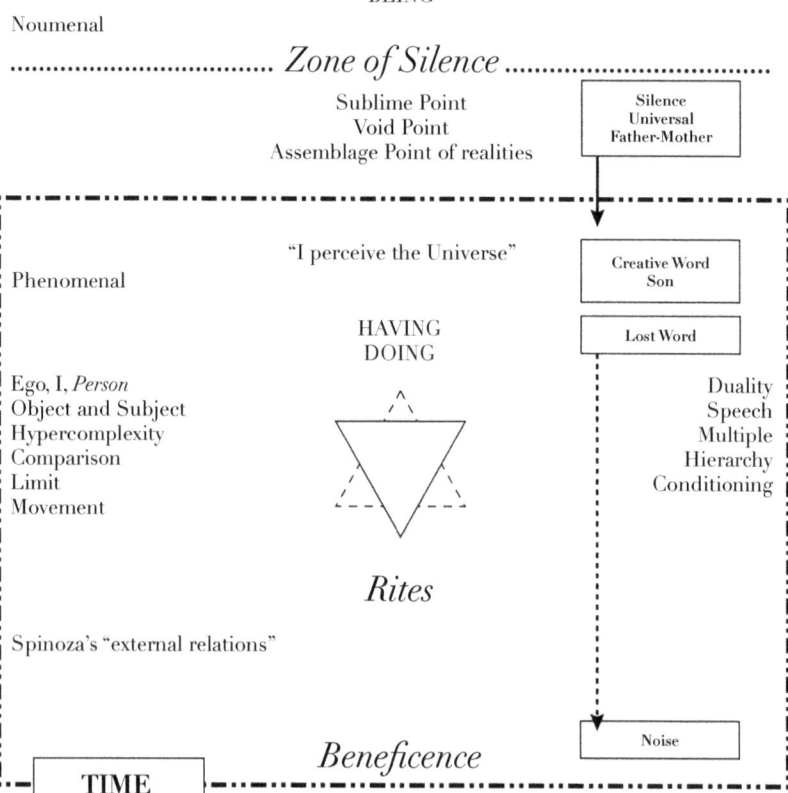

Figure 1

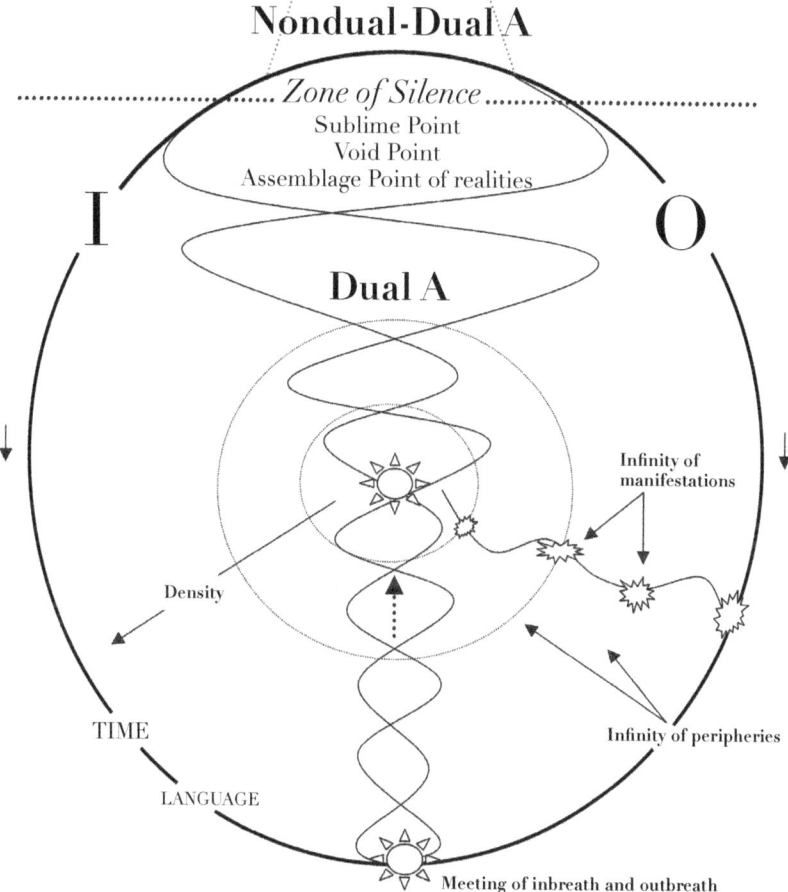

Figure 2

III

The Rectified Scottish Rite as a Way of Awakening

WHAT THE INSTRUCTIONS OF THE PROFESSED AND GRAND PROFESSED CAN SAY

THE PROFESSION AND THE GRAND PROFESSION

From Martinez de Pasqually to Jean-Baptiste Willermoz, we move from one initiatory modality to another, from "Knowing to operate" to "Knowing to integrate," propositions that are reversible in a significant way: "Operating to know" or "Integrating to know." This passage from one initiatory modality to another, from a theurgy going from the external to the internal, to a theurgy operating from the internal to the external, finds its expression in the synthesis of the Martinezian doctrine that Jean-Baptiste Willermoz achieved in the instructions to the Professed and Grand Professed, which come to complete, or crown, the initiatory work prepared in the Blue Lodge, elaborated up to the grade of Scottish Master of Saint Andrew, and fully installed in the Chivalry and Beneficence of the Holy City. The Profession and Grand Profession seek to confirm the accomplishment of Reintegration announced by the movement of the ternary of lights in the opening of the grade of Apprentice.

Does Jean-Baptiste Willermoz's Trinitarian view of the Doctrine of Reintegration affect it? Formally, yes, no doubt, but not essentially. Doctrine carries praxis and is itself praxis. Practice dissolves identifications and separations. It does not seem useful to focus too much on this point which will be erased, like everything else, in the presence. Distinctions are useful when they bring proximity to the One, but are sterile when they separate. Louis-Claude de Saint-Martin perceived the danger when he invited us to not wonder about the composition of Jesus Christ, unlike Jean-Baptiste Willermoz, who took the risk of writing *L'Homme-Dieu: Traité des deux natures*.[146] All distinction must be inclusive and not exclusive, otherwise many seekers will get lost in futile polemics, while "praying together," "meditating together," or "operating together" install a unifying and silent knowledge, a gnosis.

---

146 Jean-Baptiste Willermoz, *L'Homme-Dieu: Traité des deux natures* (Le Tremblay , Fr: Diffusion Rosicrucienne, 1999).

Louis-Claude de Saint-Martin's approach to the mystery of the Trinity is edifying from this point of view. First of all, he expresses that it is not a mystery but an introductory instruction to Christianity with a comprehensive logic:

> A power alone and infinite in the immensity of nothingness creates nothing. All objects capable of being created exist within it only potentially. For it to set itself to create, it must emanate from itself a will or a love that incites it to give existence to one thing rather than another, and it is this will, this love, this word, this fixed speech, that Christians call God the Son or the second power of the Trinity, distinct from the first, although forming a unity with it, for we know that power is not will, and that the one cannot operate without the other; thus the two, though differently personified, are one being.
>
> Power and will together can create a world composed of a multitude of objects that could form chaos, disorder, destruction of each other, cacophony, and so on. It is necessary, so that a creation answers the aim of the creator, that it emanates from him, by his will and his love, a spirit of wisdom, order, harmony, and the like, which establishes the agreement between created objects, and this is what Christians call the Holy Spirit, from the word "holy," which means ordered, and from the word "spirit," which means goal, end, etc.
>
> God is therefore personified in Christians by power, love, and wisdom.[147]

This commentary by Louis-Claude de Saint-Martin reconciles the approach of Martinez de Pasqually and that of Jean-Baptiste Willermoz. It allows us to orient ourselves from duality to nonduality, from fragmentation to unity, by distinguishing the ternary personifications of God from "The Being of God," undifferentiated and indistinguishable, an observation that had already made Saint Ephrem (†373), so dear to Robert Amadou, prefer poetry rather than dogma to speak of God, which earned him recognition as "the harp of the Holy Spirit."

To understand the interest of the instructions to the Professed and Grand Professed, we must take in the spirit of the scale of the grades and classes of the Rite. The first three grades of the Rectified Scottish Rite are marked by the Old Testament and the Old Covenant and lead to

---

[147] Extract from an unpublished work attributed to Louis-Claude de Saint-Martin, *Dictionnaire mythologique, symbolique et étymologique, contenant l'explication morale des principaux personnages de la Fable, la clef de la Mythologie et un mot sur l'Origine de tous les cultes, par Dupuis,* excerpt published in Willermoz, *L'Homme-Dieu.*

the acquisition of the knowledge necessary for the reconstruction of the Temple of Solomon. This reconstruction can be understood as physical and spiritual. It is very Masonic and symbolic. The degree of Scottish Master of Saint Andrew typifies the transition to the New Covenant and the New Testament. It introduces a reversal that will be fully integrated into the grade of Beneficent Knight of the Holy City. It is no longer a question of a physical and symbolic construction of the Temple but of the updating here and now of an *Imago Templi* that endures from the beginning until the end of time. This point is clearly stated in the instruction for the degree of Scottish Master of Saint Andrew:

> The Order shows you today, without mystery, although still under the light veil of an allegory that is very easily explained, the goal and the general term of its works. Everything you have seen up to now in our lodges has had the Old Testament as its sole basis and the general type of the famous Temple of Solomon in Jerusalem, which was and always will be a universal emblem. But here you see a walled enclosure pierced with twelve gates, such as the enclosure of the New Jerusalem is described by Saint John the Evangelist. You see in the middle of this enclosure the mountain of New Zion and on the summit the Lamb of God triumphant, with the standard of Omnipotence, which He acquired by His voluntary and reparative immolation. This figure represents for Masons the passage from the Old Law, which has ceased, to the New Law, brought to men by Christ which He voluntarily sealed with His Blood, to make it forever indelible and universal.

It is also the passage of Hiram, the architect of the Temple, to Hély, figure of Christ as the "Definitive Temple."[148] It is the passage from one mastery to another. Just as Saint Andrew leaves his first teacher, Saint John the Baptist, for Jesus Christ, the initiate moves from formal mastery to seeking a formless mastery, from external to internal.

It will soon no longer be a question of building the Temple but of "building in the Temple," as the instruction for the rank of Squire-Novice specifies: "If you are constantly building in the Temple of the Lord, you can conceive the hope of attaining a goal so desired."

Christ is the Temple and Christ is the Man, the New Man.

"Christ is the high priest, that is to say, He is the representative of all humanity—and with Him the whole of 'human nature' is definitively introduced into the heavenly Temple. With Him, it is the heavenly

---

148 Jean Daniélou, *Le signe du Temple* (Paris: Gallimard, 1942).

Temple into which Humanity penetrates, that is to say in the pleroma of the spiritual creatures that are the Temple and the Glory, within which dwells the Holy Trinity (…) Henceforth, the place of Humanity is heaven: it is there that it already dwells through Christ, Head of the Mystical Body, and through the glorious Church. This is where the only valid liturgy now takes place: no longer near the springs, nor in the Temple of stone,"[149] suggests Jean Daniélou, evoking the heavenly Temple within his septenary vision of the Temple that perfectly suits the expression of the initiatory process (the cosmic, Mosaic, Christian, ecclesial, prophetic, mystical, and heavenly temples).

In the inner Order, equestrian and chivalric, no longer Masonic, it is no longer a question of building the Temple but of keeping its actualization in the world, its permanence requiring no intervention. It is indeed a chivalric mission that does not concern the formal initiatory orders but the essential Order, the "High and Holy Order," as the instruction to the grade of Squire-Novice recalls, the sole "Place" of integral initiatic knowledge, of which the temporal initiatory orders can only hold and transmit fragments.

The CBCS are therefore "Templars," not Templars of a formal order, but Templars of the essential Order, which will lead Robert Amadou to this formula: "This manner of saying Templar, which would seem to embarrass, has a precise object: to declare that the CBCS are Templars without being so, while being so.'"[150] The initiatory relationship of the CBCS with the Temple is of a formless, timeless, and essential nature.

The inner order of the Beneficent Knights of the Holy City is based on a symbolic class in four grades, the last of which has an operative function of passage and reversal of great importance. The grade of CBCS, often called the 6th degree, brings to a close and completes the system of the Rectified Scottish Rite. "He who receives the sixth learns by the instruction which terminates it that this degree, which is really a very satisfactory conclusion, is the last of the Rite; that he has nothing more to ask of it or to expect from it," said Jean-Baptiste Willermoz.[151]

---

149 Jean Daniélou, *Le signe du Temple*.
150 Amadou, "Martinisme," 30.
151 Pierre Chevallier Louis Mathias de Barral (former bishop of Troyes, Freemason of the Rectified Scottish Rite), *Mémoires de la Société académique d'agriculture, des sciences, des arts et belles-lettres du département de l'Aube*, vol. CIV (Troyes, Fr: 1967).

Why then is there a double secret class called the Profession and the Great Profession? Before returning to the function of secret classes in the European initiatory scene and this one in particular, some points of the temporal history of this class must be recalled.

Robert Amadou, in 1969[152] published, under the name Maharba, an update that is still current and is interesting to read again:

1. The Grand Profession, at the same time as the Profession, of the Metropolitan Colleges was instituted when the Order of the Beneficent Knights of the Holy City was created, at the National Convent of the Gauls held in Lyon in 1778.

   At the Convent of Wilhelmsbad it officially ceased to exist. Half a century was enough to abolish it, in fact, with a few exceptions which were individual.

   Also, on May 29, 1830, Joseph-Antoine Pont, *Eques a Ponte alto*, and in his own words, "General Visitor Trustee of the late *ab Eremo* who was General Custodian and Archivist of the Second Province, having become since his death sole trustee of the Metropolitan College established in Lyon"; noting "the inaction and indefinite suspension of the work of the said Metropolitan College"; considering that he happened to be "the only surviving grand dignitary of the Order of the said College and that it is as important as it is urgent to provide for the erection of a College"; given articles 22, 23, 24, and 25 of the Statutes and Regulations of the Order of the Grand Professed, which provide for such a case and relate to the danger of extinction; granted a charter for the constitution of the College and Provincial Chapter of the Grand Professed in Geneva.

   Switzerland, where the Rectified Scottish Rite and the Order of the Beneficent Knights of the Holy City continue to shelter up to the present day, also became the conservatory of the Grand Profession.

2. The Grand Profession cannot be confused with a Masonic grade nor with a chivalric degree and especially not with those grades and degrees that it oversees.

   A goal is assigned to it: to ensure the integrity and promote the culture of the repository inherent in the primordial Holy Order, which has always existed and that the Order of Beneficent Knights of the Holy City,

---

152 Maharba [Robert Amadou], "A propos du Régime Ecossais Rectifié et de la Grande Profession," *Le Symbolisme* no. 391 (October–December 1969). Now available on several websites.

resulting from a double Masonic and chivalric tradition, now embodies. For the four symbolic grades of the Rectified Scottish Rite (Apprentice, Companion, Master, Master of Saint Andrew) and the two degrees of the Inner Order (Squire-Novice and Beneficent Knight of the Holy City) aim to train and employ custodians of trust, each according to the rank and openness he enjoys. The Grand Professed is a trusted trustee.

3. The Grand Profession of the Rectified Scottish Rite, supreme class of the Order of Beneficent Knights of the Holy City, is the act by which the Knights and Brethren of the lower classes of the same Order who shall be found worthy are initiated, after the required tests, to the knowledge of the mysteries of ancient and primordial Masonry and are found fit to receive the final explanation of the Masonic emblems, symbols, and allegories.

One does not enter this class by any ceremonial initiation or by any new decoration. The simplicity towards which the whole system of the Order of Beneficent Knights of the Holy City tends culminates in pure spirituality.

The Grand Profession enshrines the arcana of Freemasonry and participates in it, although it is not of Masonic essence. Its secrets are inexpressible and it is thus that it forms, of itself, a secret class.

4. The Grand Professed, according to their laws, neither conceal nor flaunt their quality. But could a class or moreso an Order, whose basis is spirituality (or better, is the spirit), popularize itself without falling and without losing its honor along with its manner and reason for being?

The Grand Professed refuse applications, statutorily, and they admit with requisite unanimity. They lack the anonymity of the "Unknown Superiors," in the quasi-mythological sense of the title, since they are all known Beneficent Knights of the Holy City.

5. Of these same "Unknown Superiors," the Grand Professed further lack the kind of superiority that this title implies. Their statutes and regulations exclude intervention in the machinery of the pyramidal Order of which they are the point stone, imperceptible to many.

6. Upon the Grand Professed devolve, by right and duty, and eminently so, the tasks that the care of the Order requires in moderation of all Rectified Scottish Masons and of all Beneficent Knights of the Holy City, Watchers, and Guardians; they also speculate, encouraging research and reflections on the repository whose supporters they encourage.

This action of the Grand Professed, what variety there is in its contingent aspects!

But the Grand Architect of the Universe never let it stop. And there is no case where it was exercised—how could it have been? how could it have without denying itself?—otherwise than in spirit and in truth, for the betterment of the Rectified Scottish Rite and the Order of Beneficent Knights of the Holy City; for the good of Freemasonry; with the help of men everywhere who pray, often unwittingly, for the sun of justice to shine, the only source of light and warmth, where the Lord has pitched his tent and from which his Spirit breathes.

A few comments are in order.

The debates on the interest or the non-interest, the legitimacy or the non-legitimacy, of this-or-that historical expression of the RER to "awaken," "establish," or "restore" the double secret class of the Profession and the Grand Profession, under this name or another, are sterile, even toxic. On the other hand, questioning the function of such a class and its reality is necessary.

The function of secret classes in the initiatory West can be apprehended differently depending on the traditional models, but in any case, it is a question of bringing together individuals in freedom who have gone beyond the need for forms to access this zone of silence or symbols, to give way to Ideas that spring up spontaneously in the *imaginal* in order to install them in the world in the form of a Great Work that can be alchemical, theosophical, metaphysical, or mystical. It is a question in the secret classes of the "terminal ways," the ways of completion, which presupposes that the understanding is acquired, that one knows how to extract from substance the spirit that is energy or power, to extract in turn power, the spirit that is essence, the whole ternary being reintegrated into the Free or Holy Spirit. A secret class brings together individuals, not persons, those who have consciously installed themselves in their indivisible part, God, and who come together in absolutely free companionage.

The Profession and the Grand Profession constitute neither an initiation nor an ordination but the delivery of a doctrinal synthesis, that of Martinez de Pasqually's Doctrine of Reintegration, which Jean-Baptiste

Willermoz studied and implemented at length within the setting of the Order of Knight-Masons Élus Coëns. With the Profession and the Grand Profession, he shifts the doctrine from a theurgic setting to another more internal setting, from a ritual operativity to a silent operativity. The doctrine is approached not as matter on a gradualist operative scale but as an immediate deployment of the unity already achieved but not yet extended in the world.

"In the name of this unity, which will triumph over all divisions of time, love one another, support one another, help one another! This is the true meaning of all our instructions! That's the whole spirit! May we feel it, understand it, and experience it!" wrote Antoine Willermoz, nephew of Jean-Baptiste Willermoz, and Joseph-Antoine Pont (in ordine a Ponte alto) in 1830 to the Grand Profess of Geneva.[153]

This invitation, if not injunction, to let radiate what is realized in the internal (which is non-time) even in the external peripheries (which are the times), evokes the diffusion of the light of nonduality even within duality. We are, we should be, beyond links or causalities, as evidenced by an innovation in rituals that appeared in the 19th century, which sees the initiator with the rank of CBCS release the recipient from all Masonic oaths—a very accurate intuition of the purpose of the rite that frees contingencies and constraints, trusting in the original and ultimate nature of the New Man. This is also evidenced by the qualification of this double secret class sometimes as a "non-ostensible" class.

"The crucial points of the secret initiation of the Grand Professed are the nature of the initiation and that of Freemasonry; a summary of the Martinezist epic in which God, the emanating spirits, the created cosmos, and humanity are articulated; and an interpretation of the symbolism of the Temple of Jerusalem in the light of Martinezism and in relation to Freemasonry," says Robert Amadou.[154] We find the Doctrine of Reintegration in broad outline.

This culture of Reintegration must have remained secret at the time in its most formal expression, even if it permeated the entire rite. However, Jean-Baptiste Willermoz also expected the Professed and Grand Professed to study and clarify these instructions from their own experience in order to reinforce the meaning and efficiency of the grades

---

153 Amadou, "Martinisme," 35.
154 Ibid.

and their respective instructions for the entire Rite.[155] For Jean-Baptiste Willermoz, this culture of Reintegration is understood as dynamic: it must reinforce understanding. Willermoz takes into account the environment, its resistances, and its evolutions. However, in no way should the Professed and Grand Professed take care of or concern themselves with the administration and organization of the rite.

Today, as the instructions of the Professed and Grand Professed have become public, a double secret class may no longer be formally necessary, but its dual function, to watch and to guard, remains relevant. It is just as necessary to shed light on the grade scale of the rite which, while it presents a great coherence, does not any the less require a deep theosophical investigation, close to ascesis. Just as the Réau-Croix of Martinez de Pasqually had to "Know in order to operate," the Grand Professed must "Know in order to integrate." While in the days of Jean-Baptiste Willermoz, the synthesis of the Doctrine of Reintegration, which are the instructions of the double secret class of the Professed and Grand Professed, had to be entrusted in the greatest secrecy to those who had already "recognized" it in the operativity of the rituals and had made it alive in their hearts, thus offering a framework of thought to a powerful spiritual experience, the pedagogy of the Reintegration of the RER is nowadays seen reversed by an unprecedented access to the Martinezist, Martinist, and Willermozist corpus. This also applies to other secret classes on other ancient traditional currents. At each level of the system, the doctrine can nourish the meaning and the operativity of the rite, but a balance must be found between corpus and praxis, intellect having the power to stifle the internal meaning. Experience is always superior to analysis; it alone brings together a "wisdom of the body" and the wisdom of the Spirit. The secret classes in general orient spiritually and operationally the rites that they crown invisibly. If they must remain "inconspicuous," it is to ensure the freedom of this radiance that qualifies the intention of the rite. In the specific case of the Rectified Scottish Rite today, it does not matter whether this class formally exists; at the same time it is essential that the Beneficent Knights of the Holy City who "contemplate" (the word is important) the Light of the Holy City let themselves be penetrated by it without holding onto anything.

---

155 Letter from Jean-Baptiste Willermoz to Frédéric-Rodolphe Salzmann, May 3–12, 1812 (Fonds L.A.), transcribed by Robert Amadou, *Documents martinistes*, no. 2, 36.

THE INSTRUCTION OF THE PROFESSED

This secret instruction of the Professed is taken from manuscript 5475 of the Bibliothèque de la ville de Lyon, part 2.

Although it is the first instruction given in the double secret class, it will not seem to us of major interest. It must be remembered that at the time, those who received instruction were unaware of the text of the *Treatise on the Reintegration of Beings into their First Property, Virtue, and Divine Spiritual Power* by Martinez de Pasqually.

Jean-Baptiste Willermoz succinctly introduces the recipient to the Doctrine of Reintegration and places Christian initiation in an initiatory metahistory.

Since the Fall, man no longer knows himself, and the object of the initiatory quest proceeds through the remembrance of his original, timeless, and unalterable nature, which knows no affections. Since the Fall, human beings have lost their ability to act spiritually and to relate to spiritual beings, to be not separate from them. Being now installed in the duality and opacity of appearance, their action is cut off from the thought of God and therefore degraded, whereas prior to the Fall action is just, that is to say adjusted, to the thought of God.

Jean-Baptiste Willermoz here shows the multiplicity of forms and initiatory paths, the permanence of initiation, but also the obstacles to the initiatory process. If the vocabulary used and the beliefs presented are those of his time, the liberatory character of initiation nevertheless appears clearly.

In this instruction, he plainly attacks Cagliostro and his Egyptian High Masonry, which he rejects, following in the footsteps of Louis-Claude de Saint-Martin. In doing so, he also rejects the initiation of Ancient Egypt or at least what he knows about it. We know today that he is wrong on Egyptian wisdom and initiatory science, which was of high quality, and on the work of Cagliostro, who certainly popularized the inner ways of the Neapolitan Osirian current but in a completely respectable way.

Robert Amadou has well analyzed this opposition, which was a mark of the time:

> Regarding the Egyptian Masonry of Cagliostro, in its ritual for example, as obscure as the succession of forms is, nonetheless the permanence of the doctrinal core shines out, which the Grand Copt exhibited better than anyone: theurgy and the "inner ways"; the science of Egypt, in short.
>
> Louis-Claude de Saint-Martin, however, condemned the Egypt of the Grand Copt. [...] The Egyptians threw themselves into sciences that were linked to the nature and principles of beings, namely those of transformation. The victory of Moses over the magicians of Pharaoh manifests the power of man over the "virtues" of the universe and over the principle of evil. Hadn't Moses learned the same sciences as his adversaries? Saint-Martin rejects the book of Exodus on this point and maintains that the sciences of Moses had not been acquired from the Egyptians, but from Jethro, his father-in-law.
>
> This hostility of the Unknown Philosopher against Egypt, which counts no less against him than against his fascinated contemporaries, his very pessimistic conception of Misraïm, agrees with his contempt for the character of the Grand Copt, whom he reduces to its own character. It is an understatement to say that Saint-Martin was not right.[156]

In reality, the two currents, the "Martinist" current (understood as the theurgy of the Élus Coëns of Martinez de Pasqually, the theosophy of Saint-Martin, and the Rectified Scottish Rite of Willermoz) and the High Masonry of Cagliostro, which tends towards Christianity, are closer than Saint-Martin and Willermoz realize. "I have only one father," Cagliostro will say.

"The 'inner ways,' according to Cagliostro," further notes Robert Amadou, "are subject to a theurgy without ceremonies. Here we find Saint-Martin." And Jean-Baptiste Willermoz. Saint-Martinian theosophy and the Willermozist RER both recognize the "physical" transformation that results from the birth from on high. If Saint-Martin is regrettably discreet about the psycho-physiological or spiritual technology that replaces the theurgy of Martinez de Pasqually or is associated in Cagliostro with theurgy, it finds itself inscribed in the rituals of the Rectified Scottish Rite, as a result of correspondences.

---

156 Robert Amadou, "Le rituel de la Maçonnerie Egyptienne," in *Presenza di Cagliostro. Atti del Convegno Internazionale Presenza di Cagliostro, San Leo, 20, 21, 22 Giugno 1991*, ed. D. Callingani (Florence: Centro Editoriale Toscano, 1994).

Jean-Baptiste Willermoz is partly in the wrong fight when he attacks the Grand Copt, in part because he rightly denounces a Freemasonry that his master Martinez de Pasqually described as apocryphal, only to be wrong again when he opposes an alchemy whose principles and practice he ignores. The misunderstanding dates from his activity within the Élus Coëns.

In a letter addressed to Prince Charles of Hesse-Cassel on October 20, 1780,[157] Jean-Baptiste Willermoz speaks in these terms of the Rose-Croix, who are for him alchemists: "their basis is entirely temporal nature; they operate only on mixed matter, that is to say, a mixture of the spiritual and the material, and consequently they have more apparent results than the Réau-Croix." For Willermoz, the Réau-Croix "operate only on the temporal spiritual." He therefore distinguishes operations according to the degree of duality and temporality in which they are installed. For him, the value of an operation grows with its internality. In this he joins Saint-Martin. The error committed by Willermoz, which is common, is to believe that the alchemist accomplishes externally in order to accomplish internally, whereas it is only when they have accomplished the spiritual Great Work that the alchemist can precipitate it into matter.

Confusions of an era? Yes, and confusion still, because it persists.

Fundamentally, and apart from the epiphenomena of the time, including formal errors, Jean-Baptiste Willermoz speaks of the need to orient oneself towards the Spirit who is both the Intention and the Orient of God in the human, rather than towards matter which replicates, *ad infinitum*, the intention that led to the fall into duality.

Let us look at this instruction.

> Dearest Brother!
>
> When you entered the Masonic career, you were warned that important truths were hidden there under the veil of ceremonies and emblems; however, in spite of your efforts to reveal them, you are still today in uncertainty on the species of science that Masonry presents to your researches; and, dissatisfied with the instructions which have been given to you, you desire to be admitted among us, in the hope of discovering there the true basis of the allegories.
>
> Your doubts and your zeal would be insufficient for us to determine

---

157 Quoted in Catherine and Robert Amadou, *Angéliques*, vol I (Guérigny, Fr: CIREM, 2001).

whether you are disposed to affirm things that profane men force themselves to forget, and which they disdain when they are shown them; but thanks to the fraternal ties that unite us, we have assured ourselves of your respect for religious truths, and of the confidence you have in them. So we don't have to fear that you will reject them when they are presented to you on the road you are about to travel.

It is all the more necessary to admit them, my dear Brother, because it is the almost general aversion of men to these sacred objects which, having been introduced among the Masons, prevented them from rising to the truth of allegories. Then, ignoring the goal to which these mysteries were to lead them, they applied them to artificial and material sciences that never had any relation to Masonic initiation: thus by adopting these arbitrary systems, they no longer conceived that initiation, having man as its object, should lead him to a science worthy of him, and proper to his intellectual nature.

To help you get a fair idea of the kind of science that can be the goal of initiation, it is necessary to give you some notions of the state of man in his origin, and of the catastrophic revolutions that were produced in him and in the universe by the disorderly and arbitrary acts of his will.

Before primordial man had prostituted his faculties in pursuit of material objects, as the religious traditions to which you profess to adhere have indicated to us, he had an intimate feeling and a perfect knowledge of the divine spiritual nature; you will not be able to doubt it when you have learned, if you are still unaware of it, that man belongs by his own essence to the class of divine spiritual Beings, and that by the prerogative of the pure and spiritual Beings, there is ceaselessly between them an action and a reciprocal reaction of all their faculties. It is for this reason that before his crime man knew himself clearly, as he knew the universal creative principle and all the creatures emanating from it.

Now this divine science was by its nature absolutely incompatible with the sensible temporal affections and passions of which man was the prey at the moment of his prevarication, since they had destroyed all his natural means of action and reaction upon spiritual beings. The dark knowledge that he had acquired by his material works having thrown him into absolute divine deprivation, he prostituted his regard to the most unworthy creatures, and his faculties were so obscured that he doubted his own spiritual existence and that of all the agents of the universe.

Indeed, in this state he remained deprived of the perception of these agents and of all the direct dealings he had previously had with them, for he could no longer perceive anything but material, divisible, and compound beings. This, my dear Brother, is what made him completely lose the idea of the Unity and the perfection of the divine spiritual beings, and what finally led him to believe that matter was at the same time the only principle of the universe, and the universe itself.

By the things we have just explained to you, you must conceive a noble idea of the knowledge of man before his crime, since it was from the center of light and truth that he drew action, life, and intelligence; it was thanks to the rays that emanate from it on all beings that none of them escaped his gaze, and that he enjoyed a boundless knowledge, being constantly in view of all acts and of all the faculties of spiritual beings.

You must also conceive of the scope of the darkness cast upon the mind of man by the deeds that he wrought against the law of the Creator; for as soon as, without regard to his glorious rank of pure spiritual being, he had conceived and executed the monstrous project of nourishing himself with material fruits, he was not slow, as the traditions have announced to you, to regard himself as a being of matter.

From then on, he occupied himself only with knowing and strengthening the relations that he had just acquired with sensible and inferior nature; he put all his glory into discovering the apparent faculties and properties of bodies, in order to increase his bodily pleasures; finally, he recognized as true science only temporal physical science, because it was the only one of which he could have evidence. This dark error spread to his posterity, and even today, men who call themselves scholars and philosophers do not admit any other science, and most of them believe only in beings subject to their senses.

You must not doubt, my dear Brother, what we have just told you about the original cause of man's ignorance. This ignorance would have become universal if, from the beginning, there had not been brought into being sages well instructed in the divine spiritual sciences, and who perpetuated them on earth by the way of initiation.

You will perhaps object to us that true science being, as we ourselves have recognized, incompatible with the present state of man, you do not conceive of what the science of the sages and of the initiates could be; to enlighten you on this important question, we will tell you that there is certainly a science proper to man today, to the extent that he strengthens himself in his spiritual virtues; but this science is very inferior to that which he was to enjoy, and this is what we are going to try to make you understand.

In the primordial state of man, his science consisted in a full and perfect knowledge of the acts he had to do to fulfill with precision the law he had received from the Eternal, a law that he could not carry out without knowing at the same time the nature and the prerogatives of all the beings emanating from the Creator. It is therefore quite evident that this ineffable science could not suit man after his crime, since being confined within the narrow limits of a corruptible form, he was deprived of all the faculties he had received to fulfill his primary law. This is why initiation and its mysteries, which can relate only to man in deprivation, were so different from primordial science; for they were reduced to instructing the disciples on the glorious state of divine spiritual purity which had been the prerogative of man, and to teaching them that it was by the impious and dark acts of his will that he had fallen from this primordial splendor, and that the universe had experienced the most dreadful revolutions. Also the first steps of the initiate were made in mourning and tears, exposed to all the harshness of the elements.

When, by the revelation of these mysteries, he had come to conceive of the dignity of his spiritual nature and in feeling his deprivation keenly enough to call for the mercy of the Creator, he was told of the power that was manifested in favor of man in this universe and, to defend him from temporal illusions, he was shown the means of making the acts of this power reversible in himself.

This, my dear Brother, is the extreme difference between the science of initiation and the primordial science of man.

In this short presentation you must have glimpsed that, from the first age of the world, when the guilty man groaned over his crime, the mercy of the Creator granted him powerful and effective relief. Then he indeed had the good fortune to pierce the thick darkness in which he was enveloped; but he could not obtain the direct and immediate enjoyment of his first rights, his prevarication having raised insurmountable obstacles opposing his perfect reconciliation, until the conditions necessary for effecting it have been accomplished. However, he had from that time correct notions of his first estate, as well as of the changes that had taken place to his favor in the temporal order. This is what the sages recounted to their disciples through the ceremonial and the emblems of initiation. But for the first posterity of man these facts were taught without mysteries or allegories, so that there was no initiation in the various families that then inhabited the earth.

So you must not trust that which philosophers, poorly informed of the origin of this universe, dared to advance about this first age, claiming according to their mere conjectures that the men of that time lived like savages and without any knowledge of Divinity. For men were never seen on earth in that deplorable state, except after they had obscured their intelligence by the very abuse of the sublime knowledge that was proper to them.

This abuse having become universal, the scourge launched to destroy it and to preserve future posterity was also universal, as it needed to be.

After the Flood, the science preserved by Noah was transmitted without veil to his children, as the traditions have shown to you, so that it might be perpetuated in its original purity among their posterity; but even then, one of this chosen sage's own sons dared to abuse what he had come to know, repeating the crime that the Flood had erased from the earth.

Profanations having soon multiplied among the children of men, the sages of this second posterity became reserved and circumspect; for the nations abandoning themselves to idolatry and purely material acts, the science which they would have profaned was effaced from their memory, and the truth was a mystery that could no longer be revealed except to those among men who proved themselves worthy.

However, the sages employed all the means at their disposal, and all the aid they could procure, to acquire a more perfect knowledge of it and to make true science prevail among men.

We will not tell you, my dear Brother, what these means and aids were; the zeal for the truth that has brought you into our midst, if you constantly persevere in it, will help you to discover them, but you must not ignore today that the road which was followed by these masters was difficult and absolutely opposed to that which had precipitated man into the terrestrial material region.

These righteous men lavished the fruits of their works abundantly on the human family, never ceasing to oppose the progress of evil among the peoples, but impiety and corruption having become almost universal, they were forced to resort to mysterious emblems to propagate science without exposing it to profanation.

With this in mind they beckoned to upright and simple-hearted men, steadfast and fearless in the way of truth, and capable of making all the sacrifices it demanded of them, once it should be known to them.

Beware then, my dear Brother, of thinking that the disciples of science can reach it by some gentler and less painful route than that which was practiced by the first masters. There is only one path that leads to the truth, and if you thought otherwise, you would have to abjure this error before entering the career that opens before you.

Such was the origin of the initiations: they were necessitated by the ignorance and perversity of men.

However, do not believe that all those that took place among the peoples in the different epochs of human society had been equally recommendable; for there were some of divine institution, and others which were established arbitrarily by masters of greater or lesser enlightenment.

This leads us to tell you that, although there is only one true science for man, the form of initiation can vary infinitely, because the signs and types of truth are innumerable.

Among the ancient peoples, the name of Priests, Kings, Magi, Sages, or Philosophers was given to those to whom the secret of the science was reserved. They acquired by their illumination a sort of sovereignty, because they were enlightened leaders for the nations, and the origin of the primordial union of priesthood with temporal power need not be sought elsewhere.

Those who are instructed in the history of the various initiations know that there is not one that has survived for a long time without being altered little by little, by the forgetting of true principles and by the natural inclination of the human animal to settle upon material and inferior things. Such was the true cause and origin of idolatry, by the abominable mixture which soon arose of the sacred with the profane, and of the emblems of the divine spiritual science, with the superstitious practices of corrupt peoples.

This decadence was the inevitable effect of indiscreet or excessively multiplied initiations, and principally of the empire of errors pervading on earth, which penetrated even into the temples of the initiates.

Although, despite the works of the sages, initiation could not guarantee men from the darkness of idolatry, while among their disciples there were some who dared to equate the powers of nature to Divinity itself and who, after having profaned the mysteries of science, lost sight of the true meaning of the allegories or disguised them through apocryphal applications, nonetheless we owe to the true initiations the preservation on earth of the dogma of the immortality of the soul and that of the existence of a unique and intelligent being, the universal principle of all that exists.

The constant doctrine of the sages of antiquity does not allow us to doubt it, and indeed, the main purpose of initiation has always been to instruct men in the mysteries of religion and primordial science, and to preserve them from the total abandonment they would make of their spiritual faculties, to the influences of corporeal and inferior beings.

The initiations were therefore to be the refuge of truth, since it could there form temples in the hearts of those who knew how to appreciate it and pay homage to it.

The Egyptians, like most of the ancient peoples, had been able to know science in its primordial purity. This science taught, as we have said, the laws of divine and temporal spiritual things. It indicated to Initiates the means of participating in the action of the powers that are charged with operating in this universe in favor of man, and with supporting and defending him in the painful career to which he has been subjected by his degradation, but the sages of Egypt, aware of the diversity of manifestations that can result from the action of these powers, soon fixed all their attention on what most flattered the natural inclination of man for sensible and material things, so that they lost sight of the manifestations of a superior Order, even forgetting them entirely, as has happened since to all those who have imitated them.

Thus their initiation soon had no other object than the knowledge of material nature; and it must be admitted that they made great progress in it, having profited from the enlightenment that their masters had acquired in this kind, by a more luminous and reliable rule. From then on their hieroglyphs and their allegories ceased to rise up to the universal spiritual action that manifests itself in the universe by order of the Creator, and related only to the secondary agents that operate temporally for the production and duration of material beings. Thus it came to be that their mysteries expressed much more the worship which the initiates rendered to the active powers of temporal nature, than that which they should have rendered to the unique principle of all general and particular power.

The characteristic signs of each of these powers, which some have called hieroglyphs, having been presented to the people in public worship, they paid homage to as they would to the Divinity itself, and prostrated themselves before the emblems that science had employed; such was the origin of the material idolatry of vulgar and ignorant men; for the priests and initiates of the Egyptian religion had not gone so far as to confuse the powers of nature with the sensible signs that express them. But they had fallen into a much more disastrous error, since after having assured themselves of the reality and efficacy of the action of the various agents of nature, they had believed that they owed their adoration to all the beings of whose power they could not conceive, and they had been blind enough to erect temples and altars, not only to beneficent beings, but also to wicked and perverse gods. This abominable spiritual idolatry was the sole cause of the idolatry of images, for while the Priests invoked by sacrilegious ceremonies the very powers represented by the hieroglyphs, the people, prostrate before these material representations, addressed their prayers directly to them without raising themselves above the figure. Thus an impious cult spread over the earth, and most of the nations remained exposed to the most terrible scourges, having ceased to make restorative to them, by the purity of the cult, the favorable powers that operate in the universe in favor of man.

These aberrations of the Egyptians, which you must not ignore since they are attested by all the monuments, should keep you on your guard against modern writers, who, in view of certain fragments of the mysterious ceremonies of Egyptian initiation, have attributed to its priests a wisdom and a science that had for a long time no longer existed among this people. The vain efforts of the magicians against the victorious wisdom of Moses furnish you with evident proof that from that very time their initiation had deviated from the true aim of science and that, however great their successes in material works, they could not stand against the powerful efficacy of Divine spiritual science.

Primordial initiation had been corrupted among all ancient peoples, much as among the Egyptians; the diversity and plurality of the Powers, whose action was constantly manifesting itself before their eyes, made them forget the Creator, sole source of all these powers, and instead of paying homage to his eternal Unity, they prostrated themselves before the individual agents who, by decree of the Eternal, are depositories in this universe, partial emanations of the divine power.

However, do not believe, my dear Brother, that these disastrous errors were so universal that among these peoples there was no sage instructed in the truth of primordial initiation; for it is very certain that, since the beginning of time, true worship has not ceased for a moment to be offered among men on altars pleasing to the Divinity. There have always been, in the various regions of the earth, the elect who have presented to the Eternal, in all holiness, an incense pure and worthy of him, as true representatives of the human family in whose name and on whose behalf they implored divine goodness and mercy. And it could have been otherwise, but the earth, that sole asylum preserved to man after his repentance, had been changed into a frightful abyss, to remain forever, with all its inhabitants, in eternal divine privation, since, in this universal depravity, no man could have deserved the regard of the Creator. This is what was announced to you by the traditions, when God demanded to know whether there were at least a few righteous people in Sodom on whom his clemency could rest. Besides, you are not unaware that, to preserve true worship in the universe and on earth, an ineffable power was sent there by a decree of infinite mercy, and that after having regenerated the covenant between God and man, it never ceases to vivify, in human posterity, a worship valuable only because this divine omnipotence is itself the High Priest who presents to the Eternal the pure offerings of Men of Desire.

The corruption of worship, having become almost general among men, gave rise to initiations of divine institution and the election of a particular people charged on earth with the practice of true worship in all its purity.

Moses, legislator of this chosen nation which seems to have been preserved only to compel men to useful reflections, had begun to experience science among the Egyptians but, enlightened by a superior light, he rose above his masters and made known to them his superiority. He restored science among his people in its original purity, because they had forgotten it during a long captivity among a corrupt people. It was at this time that he initiated, in different degrees, the chiefs of the tribes and families, to help him in his functions and to transmit successively what they had received from him. But almost immediately one saw among them deviations and abuses, for which they were always severely punished.

After Moses and his immediate successors, science degenerated again, and for a long interval of time appeared only as passing flashes. The great men who arose in those unfortunate times were persecuted, and that blind nation even grew weary of its mighty leaders, and demanded a king. It was granted to them. Saul was chosen and initiated by Samuel but, unfaithful to the law he had received, he was abandoned. Long before ascending Saul's throne, David was initiated. Having become blameworthy on the throne, David was severely punished, but, having always remained faithful to science, he obtained his pardon and deserved to receive the mysterious plans of the temple that was to be built by his son.

Scarcely had Solomon been elevated to the throne of David, when he received the fullness of knowledge and wisdom which he had so ardently desired and demanded. It was then that he renewed the alliance his father had made with Hiram, King of Tyre, an alliance which procured for him the greatest and most famous of the architects, whose allegorical works still serve as the basis for those of the Masons.

Solomon, having acquired profound knowledge of nature, imparted it by initiation to workmen worthy of executing the plans of the Temple which he was to erect, and on the day of the dedication of this building they received together the prize for their sublime work.

The temple having then acquired all its perfection, the workmen were dismissed with distinctions relating to their particular employments. However, the chiefs of the tribes remained with this prince, and it was by the advice of these wise collaborators that Solomon attained the highest degree of glory that any man can obtain. But then, dazzled by his power and the splendor of his throne, he utterly lost sight of the wisdom that had raised him.

The companions of his labors, terrified by the abuses he made of science, withdrew completely from his court and carried the initiation of the Temple of Jerusalem into other countries, where it spread among different peoples.

This initiation did not differ essentially from the primordial initiation; it was the same science and the same original mysteries, separated from all that was impure or foreign that the ignorance and perversity of men would have added, and presented under the emblems of the temple.

Almost all the kings who succeeded Solomon ignored this science, or abused it. However, it remained specially preserved in the race of Judah, for the Temple of Solomon having been destroyed, Zerubbabel obtained its rebuilding and, having overcome all obstacles, he reestablished initiation in Jerusalem.

Shortly after Zerubbabel, science began to degenerate; the abuses multiplied to such an excess that it finally disappeared from the midst of this people. The temple was destroyed to its very foundations, and the Jews, scattered throughout the earth, came to suffer in the face of the nations the penalty of their extreme blindness. This was because they had misunderstood the universal restorer of all science, who had come to vivify it in the Center and restore its original purity so that, from there, it would spread everywhere, and to everyone.

The Great Archetype of the Masons being accomplished by this event, science was secretly cultivated by a few sages who retained the initiation of the temple, while the general instruction of the peoples took a form that brought the nations closer to the true goal of all primordial mysteries. Indeed, if we examine with a little attention the writings of the sages who enlightened men during the first times of Christianity, we will find multiplied proofs of secret initiation, since they speak and act as initiates.

THE INSTRUCTION OF THE PROFESSED 149

This is the moment, my dear Brother, to remind you that admission to Christianity was a true initiation into sacred and ineffable mysteries. One could only obtain the knowledge and participation of it after having successively undergone long and rigorous tests in the four different grades, known under the names of <u>Auditors</u>, <u>Catechumens</u>, <u>Proficients</u> or <u>Elects</u>, and <u>Neophytes</u> or admitted and baptized Christians.

We are not speaking here of the four superior or priestly grades to which were raised only those who were intended to administer the temples, to celebrate the mysteries, to instruct the initiates, and to confer the character of initiation.

The great number of those who desired to be initiated into the mysteries of Christianity, and the violent persecutions that began to arise, compelled them to protect themselves against the inevitable indiscretion of too great a multitude and the profanations that resulted therefrom. The assemblies were very secret, and true initiations became extremely rare. They confined themselves to admitting the elect of different classes to some part of the doctrine or of the mysterious ceremonial, but without granting them understanding, for they were given only pious, moral, or dogmatic interpretations of it, which sufficed for the greatest number.

It will be easy for you, my dear Brother, to convince yourself of this by the slightest examination of the first facts of Christianity, and of the very rites that have been preserved for us without their original archetype having been transmitted to us.

At that time there existed on earth, as there still exist today, several kinds of initiations: namely, the primordial initiation, more or less corrupted or altered, among various peoples of the East; the initiation of the Gentiles or the Egyptians, which is only a criminal and monstrous abuse of science; and finally the Initiation of the Temple, established by Moses and perfected by Solomon. It is this that has come down to us under the name of Freemasonry. It differs essentially from Christian initiation in that it can represent only figuratively the history of the general man and the universe as well as the relations that unite them, while the latter, much more perfect, presents the effective development of the allegories and the real accomplishment of the mysteries of the primordial and universal religion... Let us stop, my Dear Brother—it is not here that you should be enlightened on such great topics. Legitimate instruction, and your own labors, should alone guide you in this sacred career.

The simple admission to Christian initiation, having been offered to all nations, made the doctrine of the fall of man and his regeneration almost universal. From then on, the perverse initiations were almost annihilated among the peoples, the obstinate agents of idolatry were struck down and confounded, and the Law of the Divine Christ reigned in the universe.

The initiates of the temple hastened to pay homage to the truth that had appeared before their eyes in its greatest brilliance, and having thus convinced themselves that their expectation for the rebuilding of the universal and particular temple was not in vain, they made it their duty to perpetuate the very initiation that had enlightened their minds on the mysteries of man and the universe.

The ceremonial and the emblems which they were careful to transmit have acquired in recent times, under the name of Freemasonry, a kind of publicity that has come from the misguided condescension of poorly instructed masters, and from the indiscreet curiosity of the men of this century.

An ignorant and profane mob has entered the Masonic temples; the Professed, no longer seeing themselves surrounded by their Brothers in accordance with science, kept a profound silence on the secret initiation of Masonry as well as on the true meaning of the allegories of the three grades, so that the Profession, which was the prerogative of the masters, was separated from them by intermediate classes useless in themselves.

It was then that we saw a multitude of Masons, worried about their ignorance but little disposed to the development of the mysteries, take up the task of unveiling our emblems, although among these so-called masters there were some daring enough to erect into dogmas their apocryphal systems, supporting them with artificial and illusory grades. It would be of no benefit to you if we put before your eyes the innumerable and arbitrary interpretations that they were unafraid to propose to candidates.

There is, however, a class of Masons whom we must denounce to you today, because they indeed abandoned themselves to a course absolutely opposed to the divine spiritual science which you are about to profess.

The same error, which diverted primordial man from his spiritual activities to affix him to the dark results of matter, forms the basis of the science of the adepts: it is in the decomposition of material beings and by the manipulations of their art that they hope to discover a true light for man, and to find the life-giving spirit of nature, but he who is enlightened in true science knows that it is not in matter that one must seek either the light or the spirit of life.

To further their success in these vain pursuits, the adepts have been blind enough to borrow from the true science some of its methods, and to address their sacrilegious prayer to the Great Architect of the Universe, as if they could ignore the law that He imposed on men to constantly rise above material acts, in order to build temples worthy of Him.

Thus what should distance you from the art of the adepts is that they employ at the same time the most incompatible methods, believing them equally necessary for the success of their works; with this view, they join to their manipulations the acts of a superior order which one can never, without a blatant profanation, prostitute for material results.

Besides, all that the most stubborn alchemist, the most versed in his art, can hope from his perseverance is to penetrate to the elementary principles of the corporeal beings subjected to his manipulations, and to obtain phenomena from them different from the law of individual temporal action that is specific to them; now this is precisely what demonstrates the vanity of the science of the adepts, since they cannot obtain through these beings of apparent life any fruit truly proper to man.

This, however, is the only term of science of which these blind men speak with any enthusiasm and which in fact separates them from the only object worthy of their researches, that is to say, from this light that every man can perceive when he employs the means which are in himself and in nature.

That, my dear Brother, is what you must not ignore about the Masonry of the adepts. Remember, when you are in the position of giving your vote for the admission of a Professed, that you must rigorously examine those who have been partisans of the art, and that you must never grant it before they have convinced themselves that such work cannot be combined with the profession of the Divine spiritual sciences.

My Dear Brother, the instructions that you have just heard were intended by our teachers to give the Professed a glimpse of the true goal of the ancient initiations. Give it the most serious attention so that the good we wished to do for you does not serve to condemn you.

We beg the Great Architect of the Universe, whatever knowledge you may acquire of Him, to preserve you through His infinite goodness from the misfortune of abusing it.

THE INSTRUCTION OF THE GRAND PROFESSED

This far more interesting secret instruction of the Grand Professed is taken from manuscript FM4 507[158] of the Bibliothèque Nationale de France. This is the second part of the instruction. We find there the Doctrine of Reintegration[159] in a quite remarkable synthesis, very probably produced by Jean-Baptiste Willermoz, and of great initiatory and metaphysical significance.

1. The created Universe, which is philosophically called the Great Universal Temple (of which the temple of Solomon was the figure), began along with time, to subsist throughout its individual eternity. It is there that the spiritual beings, principles of secondary actions, operate with precision and in an invariable order the law which they had received from the origin of temporal things, and that all the corporeal beings contained therein manifest themselves according to their nature throughout the duration prescribed for them.

2. This temple being of a nature absolutely foreign to any infinite divine operation, the Great Architect of the Universe could not conceive it in His mind, and order His agents to make it, without being determined thereto by a cause opposed to His eternal unity; and regarding this incidental cause of the universe, it is certain that man has known it, that he must have known it, and that however obscure it appears, he can still know it.

---

158 The manuscript is now accessible on the Gallica site of the Bibliothèque Nationale de France. This version features modernized spelling and punctuation.

159 It is interesting to study this Willermozian version of the Doctrine of Reintegration, more Trinitarian than that of Martinez de Pasqually, in comparison with the metaphysics of Oskar Władysław de Lubicz Miłosz (1877–1939) as it is inscribed in his book *Les Arcanes* (La Bégude de Mazenc, Fr: Arma Artis, reissued 2016). The text of O.V. de L. Miłosz illuminates in an astonishing way certain obscure passages of the Doctrine of Reintegration, difficult to grasp in the works of Martinez de Pasqually and Jean-Baptiste Willermoz.

3. Thus this Temple and all its parts have been executed and are preserved by secondary agents or causes, responsible for manifesting the glory, justice, and decrees of the Creator, upon all beings contrary to His unity. These divine agents, who by their nature were never to exercise their action except in the very center of perfection and eternity, were therefore subjected to a temporal action, by the revolution that the various epochs of prevaricators produced in spiritual nature; and they lost for a time the perfect profession of unity that was their endowment, without ceasing however to enjoy it by their love and by their will. This state must last for them until the times of divine justice are accomplished, and those guilty beings who wished to profit from the very action of these agents, and from the means of reconciliation that have been granted to them, are reunited with the law of eternal unity.

4. This proves to you the violence that caused the production of the universe and that maintains its existence. It is the perpetual contr'action[160] that we notice there between moral and physical good and evil: a contr'action that announces the existence of two causes constantly opposed. Thus it cannot be the abode of Eternal Unity, which gave it being, which dominates it, vivifies it, and maintains it for the accomplishment of His decrees: thus it is a stranger to His immensity, which has no bounds and which no space can contain; to His eternity, which has neither beginning nor end; to His purity, which allows nothing impure to approach Him; to His omnipotence, which knows neither rivalry nor competition when He wishes to exert Himself; and finally to His own Nature, which being the Good par excellence, cannot dwell with Evil.

5. The two opposed causes that act in this universe are not equal, although by their essence they both have an infinite action, and they seem to manifest their power with a strong degree of equality. We call infinite action that which belongs for eternity to each spiritual creature according to its class. This action, inseparable from their existence, could not be taken away from them without the work of the Divinity itself being annihilated; but the Creator can, by the invincible contr'action of these agents, prevent its effects, and confine it within infinitely narrow bounds, as has happened to any spiritual being who wanted to

---

160 The manuscript uses the spelling *contr'action,* a very interesting writing of the word that evokes both what opposes divine action and what contracts consciousness.

use its faculties against the divine law, and to man in particular, during the prevarication.

6. So for you to make sense of the difference between these two causes, it suffices to tell you that the first, which draws its action from the very bosom of the Creator, deploys the infinity of its power over all that exists: no being can escape its universal and limitless action. For on the one hand it operates in unity and in concert with all the agents and powers of the Creator, on the other it exercises its power without obstruction over all beings who have fallen into divine privation, never ceasing to contain and assail their impious will by its invincible strength. The second, since its degradation, carries—it is true—in itself and outside itself, all the horrors of disorder, confusion, and death. But it cannot penetrate to the pure essence of spiritual beings; and in spite of its efforts, its impure action extends only to beings susceptible of receiving its attacks. Thus, as soon as the Light shows itself, it dispels the darkness; but never has the darkness been able to alter its brilliance.

7. The unhappy being of whom we speak, being deprived of any effective action against pure spiritual beings, his power is always without effect when he wants to oppose the very law that constituted him, that is to say his own nature of divine spiritual power. Thus his perverse action is contained, and he never uses it without experiencing the torment of obstacles, joined to an unbridled will. Thus his force cannot extend beyond the narrow limits that are prescribed to it. For as long as this perverse being and its agents refuse to confess their crime and their inferiority, their power can only serve their own torment, its effects being always prevented or destroyed by those who are appointed in this universe to contain and assail it. However, the duration of this combat is fixed by decree of the Eternal, as well as that of the place where it occurs. When the times of mercy are fulfilled, the higher cause will irresistibly prove its power, forever enchaining the original cause of disorder and confusion. For, as the action of spiritual beings is infinite, it cannot be annihilated, although their will can be changed.

8. This, My Dear Brother, is the difference between the two temporal universal causes. You must therefore regard the universe as a place absolutely foreign to eternal unity, but sanctified by agents charged to manifest therein the goodness and justice of the Creator; since those

who are held there in divine deprivation for having adhered to the cause of evil and disorder find there the penalty for their crime, and at the same time the assured means of Reconciliation. This should suffice, my brother, to give you a glimpse of the causes of moral and physical evil, which act on man from the moment of birth, as well as on all the beings of this created universe.

9. We understand by the created universe, generally, all the bodies, forms and corporeal principles that are contained in the universal space, and all the temporal actions that are sensibly manifested there, and that must cease with it, by which we distinguish them from spiritual and indestructible beings, operating in the Universe and outside the Universe.

10. Religious traditions announce that the creator only ordered the temporal works of the six days; but there is no indication that he operated them himself. He said: Let such a thing be done, and immediately it is done, and these material productions having been presented to him conforming to the idea that he had conceived of them and to his decree, he found them good. But when it is a question of man, the immediate action of the Eternal is clearly expressed, since for this act of divine production he invokes, as it were, his council and all his powers, saying: Let us make man in our image and likeness.

11. If the Being par excellence, the unique principle of life and that which essentially gives it to all productions, had Himself directly operated the making of the universe, it would follow that this universe would be forever eternal, like the Creator, because He who is life itself cannot engender death; because nothing that comes immediately from Him can cease to be.

12. There is therefore no comparison between the nature of the direct productions or emanations of the Divinity and that of the temporal productions or emanations of secondary agents; since the one, from the moment of their individual existence, are forever indestructible like God himself, and enter into the class of eternal beings, whereas the others have only a passing temporal existence: without this, there would be no divine Unity, and the secondary agents would be as powerful as the Creator.

13. However, My Dear Brother, beware of confusing the Eternity and Infinity of God with the eternity and infinity of the spiritual beings emanating from him. For Divine Eternity and Infinity exist by themselves;

they have neither boundaries, nor beginning nor end: whereas spiritual beings hold from the Creator the eternity and infinity that they enjoy; and these began with their individual existence.

14. The Creator, unique and eternal principle of all beings, is the source of life; He is life itself and no being lives except through Him. He has always thought, willed, and operated; and in Him these three indivisible faculties form a perfect unity; His ternary, infinite, and limitless faculties, having always operated to manifest themselves outside of Him, have always necessarily had results of life, for the divine life cannot be for an instant without acting and producing.

15. Therefore, God, as the absolute principle of all beings, is essentially one; as manifesting powers out of Himself by his own faculties, He is three; and by the power that is in Him of divine production or emanation, He manifests the quaternary number of divine perfection, by which He multiplies at will the images around Him. What can prove it to you is that by philosophically adding this divine number four, you will obtain the number ten, which contains within it the sign of the expression of all existence, divine and spiritual, corporeal and temporal-material; and by reducing this same number to the root, you will recognize that all beings come directly or indirectly from Unity.

16. It is therefore by their immediate divine emanation that man and all spiritual beings acquire the eternity and future infinity of their action, although it may be limited in its effects, when these beings cease to remain attached to the Unity of divine action, as we have already remarked.

17. According to these instructions on the difference of the divine and eternal infinity from the created infinity, you will see that man is a particular unity, similar to the divine Unity. Like the latter, he manifests his powers through the three faculties that are innate in him, that constitute him as a true divine image. We will have occasion to say elsewhere what also constitutes the likeness of the Creator.

18. This, My Dear Brother, is why the intelligent Being that constitutes man is spiritual and immortal, and why the body, matter, animals, man himself as animal, and the whole created universe have only a momentary duration. Thus, all these material beings or beings endowed with a passive soul will perish and be totally effaced, being only products of secondary actions, to which the unique Principle of all living action has cooperated only through the will that ordered the acts.

19. The Masons cannot deny this truth, since it has been sensibly traced to them by the construction of the Temple of Jerusalem, the plans for which were given to David by a superior hand. This king did not create it but only prepared its execution by assembling the necessary materials. The construction then ordered by Solomon and presided over by his grand architect was operated by the labor of the workmen whom they had chosen; so that the latter were the true builders, according to the plans they had received. It was the same for the Great Universal Temple as for the Temple of Jerusalem that was its representation. The plans for both were equally formed in the eternal mind of the Creator; but they were operated by secondary agents, and since the material temple erected by the orders of Solomon was destroyed as soon as the glory of the Lord and the virtues which he had attached thereto had been withdrawn from it, so also shall the Universal Temple be, when divine action shall have withdrawn its powers from it, and the term prescribed for its duration is fulfilled.

20. We have just shown you the infinite difference that is between spiritual beings, the work of the Creator Himself, and the Great Universal Temple, which was produced only by his agents. However, man, as a bodily spiritual being, has a powerful connection with the Great Universal Temple and with the Temple in Jerusalem. But, to put you within reach of grasping them, it is necessary to study man, first as an intelligent being, image and likeness of the divine, then as a corporeal animal being, uniting in him two opposite natures. With this in mind, the form must be examined: the divisions and dimensions of his material body. This examination will lead you to recognize that he truly is the image and recapitulation of the general temple and of the Great Universal Temple.

21. Man, a spiritual intellectual being, is a direct and immediate emanation of the Divinity of which he is the image and likeness. Like Him, he thinks, he wants, he acts, and his action produces results. Coming from the divine essence itself, he participates by his nature in all the virtues of the powers that are in it. We say only that he participates in them, because he can only possess them in a degree very inferior to his origin, as simple emanations from the very infinity of these powers. From the Being who is, who was, and who will be, from whom all existence has come, man derives an ever-indestructible life. From the womb of omnipotence and infinite intelligence, he was born powerful,

intelligent, and perfect. We call a being perfect, powerful, and intelligent one who, by his own action of spiritual being, operates and acts voluntarily and in unity with the Creator, according to the full extent of the faculties he has received from Him, so that there can be no imperfection in the spiritual being, except when he ceases to act in unity with the Creator and in accordance with His laws. From then on, he ceases to be perfect, his will being opposed to the immutable law that constitutes him. He also ceases to be powerful, since impenetrable limits separate him from the beings over whom he could exercise his power. Finally, he is no longer intelligent, remaining deprived of all divine spiritual knowledge. This is what we call an imperfect being.

22. This, My Dear Brother, should give you a fair idea of man in his origin, and let you glimpse the cause of the state of temporal deprivation that afflicts him today. However, as imperfect as he may appear to your eyes, he has not lost all the rights of his nature nor the immense privileges attached to it. He could weaken and misunderstand them, but not destroy them, because they belong to his very essence. By these explanations, you will be better able to judge certain deeds attributed to some men who, uniting themselves firmly and with confidence to the superior will, have been worthy to see the acts of their own will vivified, and have experienced the extent of their original rights. If the effects seemed incredible to the multitude, it was because they had no idea of the dignities upon which they were based; and unfortunately for them a blind prejudice increases this fatal ignorance every day.

23. We have said that all spiritual beings, having come from the same divine source, participate more or less, according to their class, in the virtues of the powers of the Creator and that these rights are equally indestructible in them, as constituting their own essence. Thus all are endowed with distinct virtues and faculties relating to the superiority or inferiority of action entrusted to them, for the accomplishment of the immutable decrees of the Eternal. Thus, to know the measure of the virtues and faculties to which man was dedicated in his origin, it would be necessary to know what action he was charged with operating in this universe, what mission he must fulfill there, and finally what were his relations of superiority or inferiority to the various agents who were placed there with him. Because despite the current degradation, this destiny, based on the very decrees of the Creator, has not been changed, and no doubt man still has the means to accomplish it.

24. Man was the last and most perfect act of temporal creation; he was placed there to direct its agents in the name of Him who had given them being; and it was on the seventh day, which has been called the day of rest, that he received the proof of his mission and the extent of his dominion. All the agents who were to operate with him in universal space also received a degree of power relative to their particular mission; but man received his temporal fullness, having been established therein superior over all spiritual nature; and he was clothed with an incorruptible form, in order to be able to manifest his action upon all the beings in deprivation who found themselves there subject to corporeal envelopes and upon all the agents of the universe, responsible for contributing under his orders to the work entrusted to him: for he had come into the universe to be the special instrument of the justice wroth with the guilty, and of the clemency that would reclaim them.

25. The power of man over these beings was so great and so effective that he was dazzled by it to the point of wanting to use it as if he himself had been the creator of his own action. He was great, strong, and powerful; he believed himself greater, stronger, and more powerful still; ultimately, he abused in an impious manner the gifts he had received, and lost the use of them. His impassive form, by which he was to manifest his temporal action, was changed into a material, corruptible body, with which he came to crawl on the earth's surface. This body was an impenetrable barrier that separated him from all spiritual beings upon whom his action could extend: thus he died intellectually, being deprived of his original rights and suspended from the use of his powers.

26. We must, My Dear Brother, explain to you here of what this intellectual death consisted. Man had been destined by the Creator to manifest the divine powers in this universe, in order to glorify the Eternal in the presence of all the divine spiritual agents, and to assail the principle of Evil and all its adherents; thereby, he was also to be for them an effective means of reconciliation and return to the eternal Unity.

27. In that glorious state, man had immediate communication with the Creator; his thought was always in unity with the divine thought, from which he continually drew knowledge. His spiritual life therefore consisted in the virtual action and reaction that took place directly between him and the Divinity. This is why he died intellectually, when a material form had, after his crime, placed impenetrable boundaries between him and all spiritual beings: for this intellectual death consisted in the

deprivation of all immediate divine spiritual reaction, so that he could no longer read the mind of the Creator, nor that of any spiritual agent. So from being active and thinking as he was by nature, he became pensive;[161] and the use of his intellectual faculties was made dependent on the same beings that he had previously ruled.

28. You must not, My Dear Brother, look elsewhere for the proof of these sad truths, other than in yourself. At every moment of your bodily life, you will perceive that your thoughts, good or bad, come to you through foreign channels.

29. It is certain that present-day man does not create his thought: he can neither obtain at will that which he seeks, nor preserve that which he has, nor foresee that which he will have, nor get rid of that which disturbs him. Who is he that can become master of the train and continuation of his thoughts? Who can say why he does not have one and why he is obsessed and tormented by the other? Lastly, who is he who can know the process of his speech and his intelligence? Man is thus in this respect in absolute dependence, and everything proves to him that his thoughts come from an action foreign to his own.

30. It could not be otherwise, since corporeal man no longer communicates with the center of thought and intelligence. Also, he can only be susceptible to two kinds of ideas: some, purely sensible, are excited in him by the perception of material objects subject to his senses; the others, intellectual, also come to him through the senses, although they relate only to his intelligence, which judges them, adopts them, or rejects them. It is also by this way of the senses that he experiences the action of the two opposed causes of which we have spoken. Thus, all the thoughts of present-day man are produced in him by the beings that surround him. That is why all religious and human laws agree to locate crime only within the consent of the will, which is today the only principle of action that remains to him.

31. This was indeed the intellectual death of man after his crime, having become purely passive, in his thinking and intelligent being.

32. He even became subject to bodily death, because all forms of matter must infallibly be destroyed and decompose.

33. This transmutation of the first form of man was demonstrated to you by the universal Repairer, when at his resurrection, having stripped

---

161   Fr.: *pensif,* i.e., the passive recipient of thought, as opposed to the thinking agent.–Trans.

away in the tomb all that corporeally belongs to the bygone man, he manifested himself in the eyes of his disciples in the glorious individual form; giving himself as a model to all those who aspire to return to their primordial rights. For before consummating his expiatory sacrifice in favor of guilty and degraded man and for the punishment of those who had brought about his ruin, he had publicly taught men the means of rebuilding their particular temple as he himself was to rebuild the Universal Temple. But, to these lofty ends, he instructed the multitude by parables, and only developed their mysterious meaning for those whom he had prepared above other men, to guide them after him. Often, he even reproached these beings for their lack of intelligence, which obliged him to reveal to them what they should have discovered themselves in the figurative instructions which he presented to them. Thus, he himself gave the example of the respect due to the Truth, which must never be exposed to the gaze of corrupt man or the slave of animal life.

34. There are commentators who, stopping at the letter of traditional scriptures, have gone to great pains to explain how primordial man could have been protected from death, having been as they supposed clothed in a body of matter; for they were obliged to confess that all material form is, by its nature, subject to corruption. Some, unable to resolve this difficulty, have claimed to oppose it to the truth of the traditions which teach us that man was created immortal. But if the latter had known man better, and the traditions they dared to fight, they would not have been unaware that his original form was of a nature far superior to the coarse envelope which today keeps him in deprivation, since it was intended to rule itself, corruption, and death.

35. Man, My Dear Brother, was clothed with a form only to manifest and perform on bodily beings the acts of his intelligence and will: it is no more than the organ of his intellectual faculties to either react to the beings that surround it, or to receive their reaction. If, according to this, you come to consider on the one hand the activity and the extent of his intelligence and, on the other, the insufficiency and the limits of his material body, you will doubtless be surprised that he could have received from the Creator such great faculties and so few means; and you will agree that in his origin he had to have been clothed in a form fit to manifest all the activity of his spiritual power. Indeed, while this body of man, given over to infirmities and destruction, drags heavily

on the surface of the earth, his intelligence embraces the universe at a glance; it travels at the same time to all the extremities of the world and is irritated at not being able to fathom its depths. Man wants to know everything and submit it to his empire; the immensity of the skies, the chasms of the sea, the depths of the earth, nothing stops his ardor; he analyzes, he anatomizes individuals to penetrate to the principle that animates them, as if he wanted to unite to his power the very action of the agents of nature. But the efforts of this unfortunate man are reckless and without success. To manifest such vast and active faculties, which by their nature alight on all beings, he has only fragile and material organs, with which he cannot penetrate beyond apparent forms. Reduced to knowing nothing except through the senses, he perceives only the surface of corporeal beings, and some results of the action of secondary agents. Thus, the gross body of man cannot be the true organ of such great power, and he had to have had a suitable form to exercise it over all beings.

36. This king of the universe is chained in a dark abode; but he preserves there a striking image of his original greatness, for he is still, by his intelligence and thought, the first and the most powerful of the beings subject to his gaze. He elevates his organs, so to speak, despite their weakness and fragility, to the level of his intellectual faculties, in order to dominate, as much as he is able, the elements and nature, and still more importantly, to manifest his preeminence over all terrestrial individuals: and if today he cannot know either the essence of beings or the motors of the universe, or even his own nature, he at least demonstrates his prerogative by creating the systems that he substitutes for reality.

37. This is what we had to tell you about the primordial form of man. It changed in nature after his crime; but the apparent figure of this form did not change since it had been originally determined, in the designs of the Creator, to be a living image of the Universal Temple. It is for this reason that it was and always will be exclusively distinct from every other form, being man's personal temple, called the Lodge by the Masons, in and through which he must operate according to his destiny.

38. You will perhaps ask how the disordered act of primordial man could influence his posterity and why, by his crime, all men were bound to bodies of matter and subjected to the dreadful consequences of such a union? If you asked this question out of some distrust of divine justice,

you cannot renounce this impious doubt quickly enough, to profess that the Creator is the ineffable source of all good, all peace, and all bliss. For it is in Him alone, in fact, that there is unity, harmony, and the perfect accord of all beings. If there are unfortunate ones, it is because they are distant from Him and dwell in the abode of evil and death; it is because, being corrupted and degraded from their original purity, they are necessarily deprived of this supremely pure and perfect being, whom they cannot approach in this state, and far from whom there can be only pain and confusion. You must therefore avow, My Brother, that God is not the cause of our sufferings; for He had created man pure, perfect, and happy to be, according to His divine decree, leader of a prosperity of spiritual beings.

39. It is from this prerogative of the original man, and by the crime of which he was guilty, that all the evils that afflict us came, as we will try to lead you to understand. You have learned from the traditions that the original man had deviated from the Law and from divine convention, by attacking the happy and peaceful reign of eternal unity, by acts of will contrary to this unity. It was from this sacrilegious contradiction that all his misfortunes were born. For from then on he felt the torment of the violent opposition that manifested itself in himself, between the power of his will and the power of divine Law; He whose seal was forever indelible on his spiritual being. Delivered to the horrible confusion of this inner struggle, he lost the peace and calm of Unity, which constituted his essence as a pure spiritual being.

40. So it was man himself who exiled himself from the center of purity and happiness. Unworthy to inhabit this sanctuary, he was absolutely separated from it by the material form which he has since transmitted to his posterity. It was then that this unfortunate man felt all the horror and all the weight of his crime, finding in himself and around him only conflicts, violence, and heartbreak. It was quite appropriate that, having rejected all rules and all laws, he felt the sorrow of having no guide but his dark and disordered will.

41. To judge the dreadful state to which he was reduced, it will be enough for you to consider that he, whose power extended without obstacle over all temporal nature, saw himself at the same time delivered to the action of the most antagonistic beings. As a spiritual being, he found in his very essence the violent combat between his will and divine law. As a material-animal spiritual being, he felt the opposition of the two

natures. This torment consisted in the fact that his being, simple and indivisible by itself, had become, through its union with the body, capable of feeling all the resulting torments and pains, either from the division and destruction of material parts, or the opposing needs of both natures. Finally, as a temporal passive individual, he was opposed to the clash of the elements and to the universal and particular contr'action of the two causes that act in this created universe. These are the terrible evils to which man has fallen prey.

42. You are not unaware that in the excess of his misfortune, he recognized and confessed his crime, and that by this prompt avowal, he deserved consolations and powerful help; which he in turn transmitted to his posterity. This is why none of the children of man experienced on this earth the terrible torments from which he cried before his repentance. It would be difficult, My Dear Brother, to tell you more about the man's crime: all the wise men who have spoken of it have cast thick veils over the manner of his prevarication. However, this image should suffice to show you why his posterity, born in the pains of his corrupt nature, participates in his degradation: for nothing that results from the acts of an impure and degraded being can enjoy the rights of purity and perfection.

43. In view of the evils with which the human family is constantly afflicted, you might perhaps doubt that the original man had transmitted any help to his posterity. But his powerful ministrations are too evident to those who know the life of the intellect for such a doubt not to be proof of blameworthy heedlessness or impious ingratitude. Your greatest duty, My Dear Brother, the first step that can lead you to the enjoyment of the happiness that belongs to the spiritual being, is to recognize the greatness and efficacy of the means that God has employed in favor of man.

44. You must have seen in what we have said about the prevarications of intelligent beings, that from then on they necessarily became enemies of the divine Unity, by their will contradictory to His immutable and eternal law; that strangers by their crime to this Unity, they could not subsist for a moment in spiritual communication with the Creator. In this absolute deprivation, how could they ever see their Reconciliation operate and be re-established in the bosom of perfection from which they drew life, if infinite mercy did not employ strong and powerful agents to finally make these unhappy beings feel all the horror of their situation and lead them to call for the goodness of the Creator?

45. We have been unafraid to show you that man was charged with this important Mission in favor of the first culprits; for he was the greatest and most powerful of the beings emanated from the Eternal. You have learned from religious traditions that the one who was to be the Reconciler of the perverse yielded to the insinuations of these beings of darkness, and that he himself departed from the law and from divine convention. By this second epoch of prevarication in spiritual nature, all rapport between divine mercy and the guilty had been destroyed; and the present misfortune of man would be inexpressible if that mercy had not then employed an infinitely powerful Repairer to raise man from his fatal fall, and restore him to his first destiny; you know who this Repairer was. Oh! Who indeed but a God and Divine Being could enchain the power of him that had subjugated man?

46. Immediately after the crime of man, this powerful agent came to manifest his victorious action over the culprits in the universal Temple; he manifested it specifically within time, to the favor of the posterity of man and to the shame of his enemy, by unifying the Divinity with humanity: finally, he manifest it unceasingly in all regions of the universe.

47. Here, My Dear Brother, are the divine and effective ministrations that man, through his Repentance, transmits to his posterity and in which no one can participate if he does not act in the name and in unity with this universal reconciling agent. But how can man approach it by himself in the state of corruption in which he finds himself, if he does not fortify himself by the action of the particular agents which the divine mediator employs to vivify the corruption itself?

48. The joining of an intelligent being with a material body, which followed the prevarication of man, was a monstrous phenomenon for all spiritual beings. It showed them the extreme opposition between the will of man and divine law. Indeed, the intellect easily conceives the union of a spiritual and thinking being with a glorious impassible form, such as was that of man before his fall. But it cannot conceive of the junction of an intellectual and immortal being with a body of matter subject to corruption and death. This inconceivable assemblage of two such opposite natures is, however, today the sad prerogative of man. By the one, it brings out his greatness and the nobility of his origin; on the other, reduced to the condition of the vilest animals, he is the slave of sensations and physical needs.

49. To construct for you the idea of a junction so shameful for him, it is necessary to distinguish the intelligent man, image and likeness of the Creator, from the corporeal animal man in similarity to terrestrial animals, and to let you know how the nature of the assemblages of matter is opposed to the unity of spiritual nature.

50. The nature of bodies of apparent matter has been determined by a higher Law. They are formed and made sensible to our eyes by the assembly of three bodily principles, resulting from the concurrence of three invisible and impalpable constituent elements. Each of these constituent elements is itself a ternary mixture, in unequal proportion respectively of number, weight, and measure, of the three fundamental principles of all material temporal embodiment; which explains the mysterious and fundamental numbers of primordial Freemasonry, of 3, 6, and 9, which are, for the initiate, the representative sign of the beginning, the duration, and the end of all things temporal, as you see in his place.

51. Indeed, the number 3 of the first degree designates the three fundamental principles of all corporeality, in their state of simplicity and primordial inaction.

52. The number 6 of the second designates the principle of shared life which has been joined to it by a secondary power, to make these three principles likely to amalgamate and unite in order to produce together a temporal action.

53. The number 9 of the third degree designates the assemblage of the three ternary mixtures of impalpable elements whose union, achieved by a new work of the vital principle that is in them, constitutes matter and the material bodies in the form assigned to each by the Original law that presides over their formation. This number nine designates the end of temporal things because the form of material bodies is preserved only by the presence of this particular and momentary life that sustains their existence for the duration prescribed for each species. For in the universe, everything is life; the smallest grain of sand has its vital principle, without which it would soon cease to exist, and would rejoin the invisible mass of the elements from which it came. This vital principle, as existing separately from the body to which it is united, joins its particular number to the number nine of the material body; it is by this junction alone that the individual exists in its individual form. But as soon as the principle of passive and transient life which held

these parts in union is withdrawn, this body remains delivered to its ninth number, which, in the absence of a bond, tends rapidly to decomposition and final dissolution. Then the elements, the principles, and the mixtures of which it was formed return successively to their source.

54. What is said of particular bodies must apply in the same way to the created universe. When the time prescribed for its apparent duration has been accomplished, all the principles of both general and particular life will be withdrawn from it to be reintegrated into their source of emanation. Bodies and all matter will experience a sudden and absolute decomposition, to then reintegrate into the total mass of the elements, which will in turn be reintegrated into the simple and fundamental principles, as these will be reintegrated into the secondary primordial source, which had received power to produce them outside of itself. This absolute and final reintegration of matter and the life-principles that support and sustain its appearance will be as prompt as was its production; and the whole universe will fade away as soon as the will of the Creator is heard; so that no more vestiges of it will remain than if it had never existed.

55. It is this dissolution of bodies and of matter in general that is designated in the third degree by the corpse of Hiram, whose flesh leaves the bones.

56. You may have been surprised to hear of only three elements instead of the four that are commonly accepted for the formation and composition of bodies. There are actually only three of them, just as there are only three fundamental principles that are philosophically called Sulfur, Salt, and Mercury, or fire, water, and earth. There cannot be more because the ternary and sacred law that presided over their creation imprinted its own number on them to be the indelible seal of its power and its will. Air, which some have placed among the elements, isn't one of them. It is infinitely superior to them by its nature: it is that which, by a salutary reaction, preserves the life of every living being, vegetable or animal, as it accelerates the dissolution of them once they are deprived of their vital principle. Finally, although it penetrates into all bodies, it does not amalgamate with the elements of which they are composed and does not constitute the form of its bodies.

57. From these true notions of the composition of material forms, whose apparent existence rests on such a fragile base, you must sense even more the opposition that lies between the two natures of man: for his

spiritual being having in essence an infinite action which knows neither space nor limits, what restraints can bind it in such a contemptible envelope, without it being dissolved and penetrated by the spirit? We find, My Dear Brother, in matter itself an inconceivable merger by the union which is made in it of the two opposed principles that are called water and fire: a mediator or third principle, called earth, performs this merging; it unites them and amalgamates them into a single individual. So it is with the merging of the two natures of man; it could only have been made by an intermediate power which, inferior to spirit and superior to matter, unites them in their contrary being and maintains, by its presence, this union against nature, until its action ceases and it breaks by its withdrawal these momentary bonds. The middle power of which we speak is nothing other than the passive sensitive soul, called animal, which exists in man as in terrestrial animals and assimilates him like them. In every animal, the seat of the soul is in the blood, or in the fluid that takes its place, the focus of which is in the heart. It was given to man as a means of atonement: its essence is neither bodily nor spiritual; it is superior to the body which it animates, and inferior to the spirit which must regulate and direct the action of the soul. It is an emanation of secondary beings, ordained for the life and maintenance of the body. It is therefore without intelligence and can only have a temporary existence, more or less durable. It is through it that man, subject to matter, is animal. It is the principle of all his sensations and of all his sensible animal affections. It is through this that he suffers and becomes passionate, that he fears and desires, that he seeks enjoyment and feels pleasure. It is by this that he avoids pain and wreaks destruction, that he preserves the memory of what has been advantageous or contrary to him; that he feels, knows, and seeks all that is necessary for conservation and reproduction. Such are the functions of the soul: it can never rise to the prerogatives of intelligence, and it is due to this that all animals are so inferior to man.

58. It is true that in some animals instinct is in certain respects more experienced, more prompt, and more perfect than it is in man. But there are several reasons for this superiority. The man distracted by his intellectual faculties, or removed from the path of nature by education, by social institutions, or by his vicious passions, weakens or neglects the feeling of instinct. Often, too, the animal has a very subtle instinct, but only on objects relating to the greater or lesser activity of one or more

of its senses. This is the true cause of the superiority of instinct that has been observed in some animals.

59. The union of the spiritual being and the animal soul is so intimate in man that it is very rare that his intelligence and his instinct act separately, so that one cannot always distinguish exactly in the acts that he produces what comes from one or the other and, as it usually happens that man, dominated by instinct, leaves his intelligence inactive, some philosophers have failed to recognize in him the action of the spiritual being and have taught that he has no will and is only moved by his passive soul, like other animals. Thus they have denied the higher principle or the spiritual or intelligent being that distinguishes man, and have attributed everything to a purely material organization. Others, also confusing the acts of intelligence and those of instinct, let themselves be dazzled by the industrious and far-sighted course of some animals, to the point of raising the animal soul to the rank of spiritual being, and fell into the opposite error to that of which we have just spoken, for they believed that the passive souls, whether of man or of animals, were immediate productions of the creator, of greater or lesser perfection, but which must have the same fate, having the same origin. These philosophers, having agreed to recognize in man only one living principle and not wanting to make any difference between the nature of this principle and that of the animal principle, were divided on the future state of these principles; some attributing immortality to animals also, others teaching that existence ends at the moment of the bodily death of each individual. And indeed, if they are of the same nature and the soul of the brute must perish and be annihilated, it must be admitted that the spiritual being of man has the same end. For the same reason, those of the philosophers who, after having attributed to the passive soul of man all the faculties of his intelligence, were unable to convince themselves that it could ever cease to be, were indeed obliged to grant the prerogatives of immortality to the souls of animals, which they believe to be of the same nature and come from the same divine source. For it is certain that life cannot engender death. This is why we will not dwell on the superficial idea of those who, supposing the same divine origin in the soul of animals as in that of man, and recognizing no difference in their natures but only in a certain faculty of reason and a more extensive intelligence that they recognized in man, nevertheless attributed immortality exclusively to the latter, as if the least extent of

the faculties of a being could deprive him of the immortality that would belong to his nature.

60. These, My Dear Brother, are the errors that have been occasioned by the difficulty of distinguishing the two natures in man and of envisioning the links that can unite them.

61. However, if these philosophers had kept an attentive eye on themselves, they would have easily distinguished their sensible soul from their intelligence. Some would have recognized that since the acts of the spiritual being have by their nature no relation to animal bodily functions, it was without foundation that they depicted its existence as dependent on the life of the body. Others would likewise have convinced themselves that since the faculties of the passive soul are purely sensible and corporeal, it can have no right to immortality since their action is absent when the body ceases to exist.

62. When the bonds that unite the passive soul with the body, and the spiritual being with the passive soul, finally come to be destroyed, the soul is reintegrated into its particular source: as it had been without intelligence, it is susceptible neither to happiness nor to pain and nothing stops its reintegration. The body or the corpse, to which life was absolutely foreign, remains abandoned to corruption; it dissolves and man gives back to the earth all that he had received from it. From then on, the spirit, freed from the shackles of matter with which it was never directly united, approximates more or less to one or the other of the two opposed causes that manifest themselves in the temporal universe, according to whether, having been more or less purified or corrupted, it has contracted more affinity with them.

63. Thus ends the earthly man, and you frequently see the like of him among sensible objects, for when a body dissolves, its fire, akin to the spirit, rises rapidly in the higher region; water, image of the passive soul, evaporates more slowly and does not rise above the middle region. Material and gross principles, like the corpse of man, remain on earth, reduced to inanimate ashes which have neither action nor virtue.

64. Actual man is therefore a ternary assemblage, composed of the spirit, emanating from the divinity, of which he is the image, and indestructible like it; of the soul or passive and perishable animal life, emanating from secondary agents; and of a material body formed of the three corporeal or elementary principles. The animal or brute is only a binary assemblage formed of the passive soul and a material body, neither of

which bears the indelible character of life and indestructibility, and have only a momentary action.

65. The difference between man and animals, between intelligence and the sensible soul, is furthermore strikingly manifested in the speech and voice of man. Speech is in him the figure of intelligence and of his spiritual faculties; the means by which he communicates with all beings in nature and even to divinity itself through prayer; and finally the means by which he was to be King of the Universe. This speech retains all its strength and energy within him, even though he cannot express himself outwardly. He is the only one among the living beings of the earth who can be endowed with it.

66. Sighs, inarticulate cries, signs or expressions of enjoyment or needs, of pain or pleasure, are with him as with all animals, the language proper to his instinct and to his passive soul. Cast your eyes on man in those moments when extreme passions seize hold of him. Left to his instinct, speech becomes useless to him; it expires on those lips because no thought comes to sustain it: the language of instinct is then the only one he can make heard; and you see him uttering only cries or inarticulate sounds.

67. What must convince you that speech is foreign to the passive soul of man is that it is insufficient to express the kind and degree of sensations he experiences. It is the groans of sadness, the cries and howls of pain, the transports of joy and voluptuousness, which alone can render with energy and truth the impulses of the sensible soul and make known the intensity of its feelings. Thus, speech is the prerogative of the spiritual being. It is through it that he expresses his inner word and all the acts of his intelligence, that he manifests his will, that he commands and makes himself obeyed. How can it be that anyone would attempt to confuse this active and powerful speech with the passive sounds that some have been pleased to call the language of beasts? Is it not obvious that there can be no language or speech for purely sensible and unintelligent beings? Thus, let us refrain from attributing any equivalent of speech to material individuals and from refusing to man, image of God, a prerogative that makes him His most perfect likeness, by which he has the right to be heard by all of nature and ascend to the throne of the Lord.

68. To lead you, My Dear Brother, to the understanding of the emblems of the Temple of Jerusalem, which are the basis of Masonry, it was

necessary to have you glimpse the mysteries of man and of the universe that have been hidden from the gaze of the profane under the veil of its allegories. We must now show you the relationship of this Temple to the truths we have just set before you; and thereby demonstrate to you that Solomon and the teachers of primordial Masonry had no other aim than to lead initiates to the knowledge of man, of the temporal universe, and of the spiritual agents who must exercise their action, by decree of the creator until the end of time.

How to understand this text? Freely. Unlike Martinez de Pasqually's *Treatise*, which contains a number of obscure points and contradictions, this instruction is very clear and much simpler in expression. A detailed commentary is not necessary. We will only mention a few avenues to explore... or not. It is to each that the text intends and is able to speak.

The first point that we can keep in mind in order to freely explore the text is the need to distinguish what is cultural and contextualized from what is essential, that which pertains to inevitably conditioned expression from that which evokes the essence. The Real is impossible to speak. There is therefore no truth in a text, but in this one there is perhaps enough of it to sense.

It is necessary to identify and discard what belongs to the beliefs of the time to liberate the sense of the essence. Martinez de Pasqually, Louis-Claude de Saint-Martin, and Jean-Baptiste Willermoz use a classic vocabulary of their time, sometimes in a slightly oblique sense. This vocabulary necessarily carries a different meaning from the one we give it today. We can perhaps beware of words that carry within them values that make people feel guilty, like *fall, prevarication, fault, condemnation, etc.*, to hear in them only what they can say about the operativity of Reintegration. This current vocabulary of Catholicism or Protestantism directs towards what Spinoza designates as the pole of sadness, which he opposes to the pole of joy. Sadness for Spinoza is the inhibition of the power to act. Joy, on the contrary, is the expansion of the power to act. Spinoza expresses, in the *Tractatus Theologico-Politicus*, that the despot and the priest alike need the sadness of their subjects to keep them under their yoke. Sadness is the marker of the diminished power to act. However, any initiatory path is liberatory: it frees from all the conditioning of the ego, of matter, of duality, and therefore directs towards joy and the power to act. It is not a question of the limited action of the person but of the action of being united to the thought of God.

Operationally, this distinction between the two opposite poles and this orientation towards joy seems relevant to the passage from the old Law to the new Law, from the Old Testament to the New Testament or, for those who are familiar with the ancient doctrine of the two Jesus infants,[162] from Jesus of Nazareth to Jesus of Bethlehem.

The first points addressed by the instruction (1–4) highlight the issue that is the return to unity as opposed to fragmentation. The whole quest for Reintegration is a reorientation towards primary unity, towards our original and ultimate nature, not separate from God. There is in creation this permanent opposition between the Good which unifies and the Evil which separates. This fundamental issue, between union with the non-duality of consciousness (41) or union with duality, permeates the entire text.

Coexisting in this text, as in the *Tractatus*, are two approaches that are not opposed but whose articulation does not go without posing problems of understanding in most traditional currents. It is a path of awakening, of awakening to our own nature, of reintegrating it fully, but also of a path of the body of glory essential to exercising this nature in accordance with the divine plan. On this question of the body of glory and immortality, the instruction takes up on the metaphysical level the criticism, founded or not, of Cagliostro, distinguishing immortality to persist from eternity recovered (48).

An essential question posed is that of man's relationship to the center, of his distance from or his rapprochement with this center from which he has chosen to exile himself (40), this state of exile being what we know today. This question calls for an operative response symbolized by the Middle Chamber, the only passage to the Upper Chamber.

Our plunge into duality is not eternal anyway (7). The universe has a duration. The temple is temporary. The fragmentation will have an end and the return to Unity is inevitable. It is a matter of realizing this return consciously before the deadline — here is the awakening, here is the realization — or ultimately to merge unconsciously into the Unity. We are installed in a tension between fragmentation and Unity that manifests

---

162 Claude Bruley, *Le Grand Œuvre comme fondement d'une spiritualité laïque. Le chemin vers l'individuation* (Cordes-sur-Ciel, Fr: Rafael de Surtis, 2008).

itself in a vain human work that wants to assemble (49) what is scattered in a deceptive appearance (the person) or in the realization of the great work of the Reintegration of our divine nature. Appearance has a limited duration (54). It is itself reintegrated by stasis into the primordial Unity. Reintegration is a return to the simple, a return to the principle, to the One.

The instruction distinguishes the power to act of the Creator, which resides in nondual nature and never separates, from the power to act of the agents within duality (12), which always separates. The infinity of God, which is Unity, differs from the infinity of fragmentation, which is bounded and limited in time. Similarly, spiritual beings had a beginning, unlike God (13), and hold their infinity and eternity only due to their union with the Divine.

We find in this instruction, in a synthetic way, the main axes of the Doctrine of Reintegration. This is the case of the essential function of the Numbers (15 and 50–53) and the elements (56), with perhaps a slight difference concerning the air. We also find, of course, the importance of the symbolism of the Temple of Solomon (19 and 20) as the Temple of Man, whose knowledge allows Reintegration. The function of the Good Companion Spirit, which is not named in the instruction, is found in the treatment of the intellective function and of the thoughts which are proposed to the man, "intellectually dead," who is only pensive since his estrangement from God (27–30).

The distinction made between the body, a separator (25) doomed to destruction (32), the ephemeral (57) soul, and the immortal (64) spirit, is fundamental to grasp the meaning of Reintegration, which passes through a conscious disidentification of the body (55) but also of the soul (33, 61, 62). God created the spirit which created the soul which created the body. By reversing this proposition, we have the process of Reintegration. Part of the instruction (59–67) gives an account of the philosophical debates of the time, still current, in various modalities, debates which led Jean-Baptiste Willermoz to write his *Traité des deux natures*[163] and Louis-Claude de Saint-Martin to engage in his *Controverse avec Garat*.[164]

---

163 Willermoz, *L'Homme-Dieu*.
164 Louis-Claude de Saint-Martin. *Controverse avec Garat, précédée d'autres écrits philosophiques*, Corpus of works of philosophy in the French language (Paris: Fayard, 1990.

The question of exile and the memory of our original royalty (36), which orients us in the highest sense towards our Reintegration, permeates the entirety of the instruction. There is exile as soon as we orient ourselves towards separation, which immediately engenders sadness and unhappiness (40). Exiling from exile, deliberately turning back to our original kingship, we realize that by which we can reclaim our original place, function, and mission, the means the Creator left us within duality itself (43) to rejoin the Unity that appearance conceals from us. This return cannot take place without the mediation of Christ, the Repairer (45) who unites man and the divine (46), the dual and the nondual.

The Instruction of the Grand Professed can say a lot to each of us. It would be a mistake to underestimate it or to dismiss it. It is an essential text in itself but particularly for those who embark on the path of Reintegration within the Rectified Scottish Rite in particular or Martinism in general.

It will speak differently at each stage of the journey but it will speak to the Apprentice just as to the Beneficent Knight of the Holy City and it will be an essential tool of the permanent reorientation towards the spirit that characterizes the initiation by Christ specific to the Rectified Scottish Rite.

TO NEVER END

The Rectified Scottish Rite is a flagship of Illuminist Freemasonry and of the Western initiatory scene. Today it flourishes in its various forms. Even if, at the beginning of this millennium, the Rectified Masonic scene does not escape the agitations characteristic of initiatory societies, it can remain rich in its doctrinal contrasts if those do not prevail over what underlies the rectification. "If the doctrine bothers you, reject the doctrine but pursue the practice."

If we discard the adhesions to the body and to the soul, impulses, and passions, then we leave room for the Spirit, the only rectification that matters.

The beauty of the rite leads to silence. Its symbolism leads to practice. The practice in the silence of being allows the celebration of the permanent Eucharist, the only cult that has existed and remained since the beginning of time, of which all cults are a reflection.

Beauty and grace come only with freedom. It is this that the Beneficent Knights of the Holy City must guard above all else. It is only in freedom that the ethics of Beneficence can manifest. So the following rule can be understood, not as a formal constraint, but in its liberating and Christic essence.

Masonic Rule for the Use of Reunited and Rectified Lodges

Adopted at the General Convent of Wilhelmsbad 1782

PROLOGUE

O you who have just been initiated into the lessons of wisdom! Son of virtue and fellowship! Lend an attentive ear to our discourse, and let your soul open to the vital precepts of truth! We will teach you the path that leads to a happy life; we will teach you to please your Author, and to develop with energy and success all the means that Providence has entrusted to you, to make yourself useful to men, and to taste the warmth of beneficence.

ARTICLE I
DUTIES TO GOD AND RELIGION

§ I

Your first homage belongs to Divinity. Adore the Being full of majesty, who created the universe by an act of His will, who preserves it by an effect of His continuous action, who fills your heart, but which your limited mind can neither conceive of nor define. Pity the sad delirium of him who closes his eyes to the light and walks in the thick darkness of chance: may your heart, tender and grateful for the paternal benefits of your God, reject with contempt these vain sophisms, which prove the degradation of the human spirit when it moves away from its source. Raise your soul frequently above the material beings around you, and gaze longingly into the higher regions, which are your heritage and true homeland. Make to this God the sacrifice of your will and desires; make yourself worthy of His life-giving influences, and fulfill the laws He has wanted you to fulfill as a man in your earthly career. To please your God, that is your happiness: to be reunited forever with Him, that is your entire ambition and the compass of your actions.

§ II

But how would you dare hold His gaze, fragile being! Who at every moment transgresses His laws and offends His holiness, had His paternal goodness had not provided you with an infinite Repairer? Abandoned to the wanderings of your reason, where would you find the certainty of a consoling future? Delivered to the justice of your God, where would your refuge be? So give thanks to your Redeemer; prostrate yourself before the Incarnate Word, and bless Providence which gave birth to you among Christians. Profess everywhere the divine religion of Christ, and never blush to belong to Him. The gospel is the basis of our obligations; if you did not believe in it, you would cease to be a Mason. Announce in all your actions an enlightened and active piety without hypocrisy or fanaticism: Christianity is not limited to truths of speculation: practice all the moral duties it teaches, and you will be happy, your contemporaries will bless you, and you will arrive untroubled before the throne of the Lord.

§ III

Above all, permeate yourself with this principle of charity and love, the basis of this holy religion: pity error without hating it and without persecuting it: leave it to God alone to judge, and be content to love and to tolerate. Masons! Children of one God! United by a common belief in our divine Saviour! May this bond of love unite us closely, and eliminate all prejudice contrary to our fraternal harmony!

ARTICLE II
IMMORTALITY OF THE SOUL

§ I

Man! King of the world! Masterpiece of the creation when God breathed life into it! Meditate on your sublime destiny. All that vegetates around you, and all that has only animal life, perishes with time and is subject to your empire: only your immortal soul, emanating from the bosom of the Divinity, survives material things and will not perish. This is your true title of nobility: feel your happiness keenly, but without the pride that expelled your kind, and would plunge you back into the abyss. Degraded being! Despite your primal and relative greatness, what are you before the Eternal? Worship Him in the dust, and carefully separate this celestial and indestructible principle from foreign mixtures; cultivate your immortal and perfectible soul, and make it susceptible of being reunited with the pure source of good, where it will be freed from the coarse vapors of matter. This is how you will be free in irons, happy in the very midst of misfortune, steadfast in the strongest of storms, and how you will die without fear.

§ II

Mason! If you could ever doubt the immortal nature of your soul and your high destiny, the initiation would be fruitless for you; you would cease to be the adopted son of wisdom, and you would be confounded in the crowd of material and profane beings who grope in the darkness.

ARTICLE III
DUTIES TO SOVEREIGN AND COUNTRY

§ I

The Supreme Being entrusted in a more positive manner His powers on earth to the sovereign; respect and cherish his rightful authority over the corner of the earth you inhabit; your first homage belongs to God, the second to your country.

The man wandering in the woods without culture and fleeing his fellows would be little suited to fulfill the views of Providence and to grasp the whole mass of happiness reserved for him. His being expands in the midst of his fellows; his mind is fortified by the clash of opinions: but, once joined in society, he must combat without ceasing self-interest and disordered passions; else innocence would soon succumb to force or cunning. Laws were therefore needed to guide him, and leaders to maintain them.

§ II

Sensible man! You revere your parents; honor in the same way the fathers of the state, and pray for their preservation: they are the representatives of the Divinity on this earth. If they go astray, they will answer to the judge of kings; but your own feelings can deceive you, and never exempt you from obeying.

If you failed in this sacred duty, if your heart no longer trembled at the sweet name of your fatherland and your sovereign, the Mason would reject you from his bosom as contrary to public order, as unworthy to participate in the advantages of an association that deserves the confidence and esteem of governments, since one of its principal motives is patriotism, and that, intent upon forming the best citizens, it demands that its children fulfill with the greatest distinction and by the purest motives, all the duties of their civic status. The bravest warrior, the most honest judge, the gentlest master, the most faithful servant, the most tender father, the most constant husband, the most submissive son, such must be the Mason, since the ordinary and common obligations of the citizen have been sanctified and reinforced by the Mason's free and voluntary vows, and since by neglecting them he would join weakness to hypocrisy and perjury.

ARTICLE IV
DUTIES TOWARDS HUMANITY IN GENERAL

§ I

But, if the patriotic circle that opens up to you such a fruitful and satisfying career does not yet fulfill all your activity; if your sensible heart wants to cross the bounds of empires, and embrace with this electric fire of humanity all men and all nations; if, going back to the common source, you care to tenderly cherish all those who have the same constitution, the same need to love, the same desire to be useful, and an immortal soul like yours, then come to our temples to offer your homage to holy humanity; the universe is the homeland of the Mason, and nothing that concerns man is foreign to him.

§ II

Behold with reverence this majestic edifice, destined to tighten the slack bonds of morality: cherish a general association of virtuous souls, capable of exalting themselves; widespread in all countries where reason and enlightenment have penetrated; united under the holy banner of humanity; and governed by simple and uniform laws. Feel at last the sublime goal of our Holy Order; devote your activity and your whole life to beneficence; ennoble, purify, and fortify this generous resolution, working tirelessly for your perfection, and reuniting you more intimately with the Divinity.

ARTICLE V
BENEFICENCE

§ I

You who are created in the image of God, who deigned to communicate Himself to men and spread happiness upon them; get closer to this infinite model, by a constant will to pour out unceasingly upon other men all the mass of happiness that is in your power: all that the mind can conceive of as good is the patrimony of the Mason.

§ II

See the helpless misery of childhood, it demands your support; consider the disastrous inexperience of youth, it solicits your advice; place your happiness in preserving them from the errors and seductions which threaten them; excite in them the sparks of the sacred fire of genius, and help them to develop it for the happiness of the world.

§ III

All beings who suffer or cry out have sacred prerogatives over you; take care not to misunderstand them; do not wait for the piercing cry of misery to solicit you; counsel and reassure the timid unfortunate; do not poison, by the ostentation of your gifts, the springs of living water where the unfortunate must quench their thirst; do not seek the reward of your beneficence in the vain applause of the multitude: the Mason finds it in the quiet support of his conscience, and in the fortifying smile of the Divinity, under whose eyes he is constantly placed.

§ IV

If bounteous Providence has granted you something superfluous, beware of making a frivolous and criminal use of it; He wished that, by a free and spontaneous movement of your generous soul, you would make less painful the unequal distribution of goods, which entered into His plans: enjoy this beautiful prerogative. Never let avarice, the most sordid of passions, debase your character, or let the cold and arid calculations it suggests arise in your heart. If ever you were to dry up through its sad and self-interested breath, flee our workshops of charity, for they would be unattractive to you, and we would no longer be able to recognize in you the ancient image of the Divinity.

§ V

Let your beneficence be enlightened by religion, wisdom, and prudence: your heart would encompass the needs of all mankind: but your mind must choose the most pressing and important. Instruct, advise, protect, give, and relieve, in turn: never think you have done enough, and only rest from your works to manifest new energy. By giving yourself up to the impulses of this sublime passion, an inexhaustible source of enjoyment is prepared for you; you will have on this earth the foretaste of heavenly bliss: your soul will expand, and all the moments of your life will be fulfilled.

§ VI

When at last you feel the limits of your finite nature, are unable to suffice on your own for the good you would like to do, and your soul is saddened, come to our temples: see the sacred assemblage of benefits that unites us, and contribute effectively to all your faculties, for the useful plans and establishments that the Masonic association presents, and that it realizes; congratulate yourself on being a citizen of this better world; taste the sweet fruits of our forces combined and concentrated on the same object; then your resources will multiply, you will help to make a thousand people happy instead of one, and your wishes will be crowned.

RULE VI
OTHER MORAL DUTIES TOWARDS MEN

§ I

Love your neighbor as yourself and do not do to others what you would not have them do to you. Make use of the sublime gift of speech, the outward sign of your domination over nature, to anticipate the needs of others and to excite in all hearts the sacred fire of virtue. Be affable and straightforward, edify by your example: share in the happiness of others without jealousy. Never allow envy to rise for a moment in your breast; it would disturb the pure source of your happiness, and your soul would be a prey to the most dismal of furies.

§ II

Forgive your enemy; do not avenge yourself except by kindness; this generous sacrifice, whose sublime precept we owe to religion, will procure for you the purest and most delicious pleasures: you will once again become the living image of the Divinity who forgives, with heavenly goodness and the height of grace, the offenses of man despite his ingratitude. Always remember, then, that this is the finest triumph that reason can obtain over instinct, and that the Mason forgets injuries, but never favors.

RULE VII
MORAL SELF-PERFECTION

§ I

In thus devoting yourself to the good of others, do not forget your own perfection, and do not neglect to satisfy the needs of your immortal soul. Descend often into your heart, to probe its most hidden recesses. Self-knowledge is the great pivot of Masonic precepts. Your soul is the rough stone that must be polished: offer to the Divinity the homage of your regulated affections and your vanquished passions.

§ II

May chaste and strict morals be your inseparable companions, and make you respectable in the eyes of the profane: may your soul be pure, upright, true, and humble. Pride is man's most dangerous enemy; it maintains him in an illusory confidence in his strength. Do not consider your starting-place, it would slow down your course: fix upon the point where you must arrive; the short duration of your passage leaves you with hardly any hope of reaching it: remove from your self-esteem the dangerous food of comparison with those who are behind you: rather feel the sting of a virtuous emulation, in seeing more accomplished models in front of you.

§ III

May your mouth never alter the secret thoughts of your heart, may it always be its true and faithful organ; a Mason who stripped himself of candor, to take on the mask of hypocrisy and artifice, would be unworthy to dwell among us and, sowing mistrust and discord in our peaceful temples, he would soon become their horror and scourge.

§ IV

May the sublime idea of the omnipresence of God strengthen and support you; renew each morning the vow to become better; watch and pray, and when in the evening your satisfied heart reminds you of a good deed, or some victory won over yourself, only then rest quietly in the bosom of Providence, and regain new strength.

§ V

Finally, study the meaning of the hieroglyphs and emblems that the Order presents to you. Nature itself veils most of its secrets; it wants to be observed, compared, and often surprised in its effects. Of all the sciences whose vast field presents the happiest results to the industry of man and to the advantage of society, that which will teach you the relations between God, the universe, and you, will satisfy the desires of your heavenly soul and will teach you to fulfill your duties better.

ARTICLE VIII
DUTIES TOWARDS THE BROTHERS

§ I

In the immense crowd of beings with which this universe is populated, you have chosen by a free will the Masons for your brothers. So never forget that any Mason, of whatever Christian communion, country, or condition he may be, presenting his right hand to you, symbol of fraternal frankness, has sacred rights concerning your assistance and friendship. Faithful to the will of nature, which was equality, the Mason reestablished in his temples the original rights of the human family; he never sacrifices to popular prejudices, and the sacred level here assimilates all estates. Respect in civil society the distances established or tolerated by Providence: though often they were conceived through pride, it would also be prideful to rebel against them, and to wish to disregard them. But beware above all of establishing artificial distinctions among us, which we disavow: leave your profane dignities and decorations at the door, and enter only with the escort of your virtues. Whatever your rank in the world, give way in our lodges to the most virtuous and enlightened.

§ II

Never blush in public for an unclear but honest man, whom in our asylums you embraced as a brother a few moments before; the Order would blush at you in its turn and dismiss you with your pride, so that you can display it in the profane theaters of the world.

If your brother is in danger, fly to his aid, and do not be afraid to risk your life for him. If he is in need, pour your treasures over him, and rejoice that you can make such a satisfying use of them: you have sworn to exercise benevolence towards men in general, you owe it in preference to your brother who moans. If he is in error, and he goes astray, come to him with the lights of feeling, of reason, and of persuasion; restore to virtue those who are tottering, and raise up those who have fallen.

§ III

If your heart, ulcerated by real or imaginary offenses, were to nourish some secret enmity against one of your brothers, dissipate the rising cloud instantly: call to your aid some disinterested arbiter; ask for his fraternal mediation: but never cross the threshold of the temple before having laid down all feelings of hatred and revenge. You would invoke the name of the Eternal in vain, as he will not deign to dwell in our temples if they are not purified by the virtues of the brothers and sanctified by their concord.

ARTICLE IX
DUTIES TO THE ORDER

§ I

When at last you were admitted to share in the advantages resulting from Masonic association, you tacitly gave up in exchange a part of your natural freedom: therefore strictly fulfill the moral obligations which it imposes on you; conform to its wise regulations and respect those whom the public trust has designated to be the guardians of the laws and the interpreters of the general will. Your will in the Order is subject to that of the law and of superiors: you would be a bad brother if you ever disregarded this subordination necessary in any society, and ours would be forced to exclude you from its bosom.

§ II

Above all, there is a law whose scrupulous observance you promised in the face of the heavens: it is that of the most inviolable secrecy over our rituals, ceremonies, signs, and the form of our association. Beware of believing that this commitment is less sacred than the oaths you swore in civil society. You were free in pronouncing it: but you are no longer free to break the secret that binds you. The Lord, whom you called upon as a witness, has confirmed it; fear the penalties attached to perjury: you would never escape the torture of your heart, and you would lose the esteem and confidence of a populous society, which would have the right to declare you without faith or honor.

If the lessons that the Order addresses to you, to facilitate the path of truth and happiness, are deeply engraved in your docile soul and open to the impressions of virtue; if the salutary maxims, which will mark, so to speak, each step you take in the Masonic career, become your own principles, and the invariable rule of your actions: oh my brother! What joy will be ours! You will accomplish your sublime destiny, you will recover this divine resemblance, which was the share of man in his state of innocence, which is the goal of Christianity, and which Masonic initiation holds as its principal object; you will again become the beloved creature of Heaven: its fruitful blessings will rest on you; and deserving the glorious title of wise, ever free, happy, and constant, you will walk on this earth the equal of kings, the benefactor of men, and the model of your brothers.

SELECTED BIBLIOGRAPHY

ORDER OF KNIGHT MASONS ÉLUS COËNS OF THE UNIVERSE

Louis-Claude de Saint-Martin, Jean-Jacques Du Roy D'Hauterive, and Jean-Baptiste Willermoz. *Les leçons de Lyon aux élus coëns: Un cours de martinisme au XVIIIe siècle.* Edited by Robert and Catherine Amadou. Paris: Dervy, 1999. [First complete edition published from the original manuscripts. Published in English as *The Lessons of Lyons.* Translated by M.R. Osborne. Bayonne, NJ: Rose Circle, 2021.]

Martines de Pasqually. *Traité sur la réintégration des êtres dans leur première propriété, vertu et puissance spirituelle divine.* Edited by Robert Amadou. Le Tremblay, Fr.: Diffusion rosicrucienne, 1995. [First authentic edition based on the manuscript of Louis-Claude de Saint-Martin.]

Louis-Claude de Saint-Martin. *Angéliques: images du culte théurgique.* 2 vols. Edited by Catherine and Robert Amadou. Guérigny, Fr.: CIREM, 2001. [First complete edition from the manuscripts of Louis-Claude de Saint-Martin.]

Robert Amadou, ed. *La magie des Élus Coëns: Théurgie. Instruction secrète.* Fonds Z: Les manuscrits réservés du Philosophe inconnu. Paris: Cariscript, 1988.

Michel Taillefer. *Le Temple Cohen de Toulouse (1760–1792): Les disciples toulousains de Martines de Pasqually et de Saint-Martin, suivi de Fragments extraits de diverses lettres ayant en vue les vraies connaissances (1776–1780) colligés par Joseph Du Bourg.* Edited by Robert Amadou. Paris: Cariscript, 1986.

Serge Caillet. *A Course on Martinism.* Les Auberts, Fr.: Institute Eléazar, 1990–2008.

Robert Amadou, Georges Courts, and Gino Sandri, eds. "Le Manuscrit d'Alger." *L'Esprit des Choses,* 1st ser., vol. 5 no. 13–14 to vol. 10 no. 29–30. Guérigny, Fr.: CIREM, 1996–2001. [The first complete serial edition of the facsimile, with partial transcription, of the original from the Bibliothèque nationale de France. Published in English as *The Green Book of the Élus Coëns.* 2 vols. Translated by S.J.A. Clelland. Edited by Josef Wäges. London: Hell Fire Club, 2020.]

Georges Courts. *Le Grand Manuscrit d'Alger.* 3 vols. Marseille: Arqa, 2009–2017.

Serge Caillet. *Martines de Pasqually.* Saint-Martin-de-Castillon, Fr.: Signatura, 2009.

RECTIFIED SCOTTISH RITE

Jean-Baptiste Willermoz. *L'Homme-Dieu. Traité des deux natures.* La Tremblay, Fr.: Diffusion rosicrucienne, 1999. [Includes Louis-Claude de Saint-Martin, *Le mystère de la Trinité.*]

Steel-Maret. *Archives secrètes de la Franc-maçonnerie.* Edited by Robert Amadou. Geneva: Slatkine, 2012.

Robert Amadou. *Martinisme.* 2nd ed. Guérigny, Fr.: CIREM, 1997.

Raymond E. F. Guillaume. *Structure des rituels maçonniques des trois premiers grades du Rite Écossais Rectifié.* 4 vols. Toulouse: University of Toulouse–Le Mirail, Department of Modern History, 1993.

Henry Corbin. *Temple and Contemplation.* Translated by Philip Sherrard. London: KPI, 1986.

Jean-Marc Vivenza. *Les élus coëns et le Régime Écossais Rectifié.* Grenoble, Fr.: Le Mercure Dauphinois, 2010.

Jean-Marc Vivenza. *René Guénon et le Rite Écossais Rectifié.* Paris: Simorgh, 2007.

Jean-François Var. *La Franc-maçonnerie à la lumière du Verbe. Le Régime Écossais Rectifié.* Paris: Dervy, 2013.

Yves Saez. *Présence du Rite Écossais Rectifié.* Paris: Dervy, 2010.

Jean Tourniac. *Principes et problèmes spirituels du Rite Écossais Rectifié.* Paris: Dervy, 1969.

Jean-Claude Sitbon. *L'aventure du Rite Écossais Rectifié.* Vol. 1, *Approche historique.* Vol. 2, *De Tubalcaïn à Phaleg.* Aubagne, Fr.: Éditions de la Tarente, 2015.

Jean-Marc Vivenza. *La Doctrine de la Réintégration des êtres.* Hyères, Fr.: La Pierre Philosophale, 2012.

Camille Savoire. *Regards sur les Temples de la Franc-maçonnerie.* Edited by Jean-Marc Vivenza. Archives and Masonic Documents collection. Hyères, Fr.: La Pierre Philosophale, 2015.

Michel Bédaton and Rémi Boyer. *Chevalerie, Franc-Maçonnerie et Spiritualité – Exercices Spirituels pour les Ours et les Chevaliers.* Guérigny, Fr.: CIREM; Sintra, Pt.: Zefiro and Arcane Zero, 2015. [Bilingual Franco-Portuguese edition. Illustrations by Jean-Michel

Nicollet. Partly translated into English as "Appendix I: Spiritual Exercises for Bears and Knights," in Rémi Boyer, *Mask Cloak Silence: Martinism as a Way of Awakening*, Bayonne, NJ: Rose Circle, 2021, pp. 149-194.]

MARTINISM

Louis-Claude de Saint-Martin. *Œuvres majeures.* Hildesheim, Germany: Georg Olms, 1975–2001. [Facsimiles of the original editions with introduction and notes by Robert Amadou.]
- I—*Des erreurs et de la vérité* (facsimile ed., 1775). [Published in English as *Of Errors and Truth.* Bayonne, NJ: Rose Circle, 2017.]
  + *Ode sur l'origine et la destination de l'homme* (1781)
- II—*Le Tableau naturel des rapports qui existent entre Dieu, l'homme et l'univers* (facsimile of 1782). [Published in English as *Natural Table.* Bayonne, NJ: Rose Circle, 2018.]
  + *Discours sur la meilleure manière de rappeler à la raison les nations livrées aux erreurs et aux superstitions* (1783)
- III—*L'Homme de désir* (facsimile ed., 1802). [To be published in English as *Man of Desire*. Bayonne, NJ: Rose Circle, forthcoming.]
- IV—*Ecce homo* (facsimile edition of 1792).
  + *Le Nouvel Homme* (facsimile ed. An IV, 1792). [To be published in English as *The New Man.* Bayonne, NJ: Rose Circle, forthcoming.]
- V—vol. 1—*De l'esprit des choses*, t. 1 (facsimile ed. An VIII, 1800)
- V—vol. 2—*De l'esprit des choses*, t. 2 (facsimile ed. An VIII, 1800)
  + *Controverse avec Garat* (facsimile of 1801)
- VI—*Le Ministère de l'homme-esprit* (facsimile of 1802). [Published in English as *Man, His True Nature and Ministry.* London: W.H. Allen, 1864.]
- VII—*Poésies, Écrits politiques* (1795-1797).

Louis-Claude de Saint-Martin. *Controverse avec Garat, précédée d'autres écrits philosophiques.* Corpus des œuvres de philosophie en langue française. Paris: Fayard, 1990.

Louis-Claude de Saint-Martin. *Mon livre vert.* Edited by Robert Amadou. Paris: Cariscript, 1991.

Louis-Claude de Saint-Martin. *Le Crocodile ou la guerre du bien et du mal.* Paris: Triades, 1962.

Louis-Claude de Saint-Martin. *Mon portrait historique et philosophique (1789-1803).* Edited by Robert Amadou. Paris: Julliard, 1961.

Louis-Claude de Saint-Martin. *Les nombres.* Edited by Robert Amadou. Nice: Bélisane, 1983. [First authentic edition of the autograph manuscript.]

Louis-Claude de Saint-Martin. *Maximes et pensées.* Paris: André Silvaire, 1963.

Louis-Claude de Saint-Martin. "Instructions aux hommes de désir." Edited by Robert Amadou. *Documents martinistes,* nos. 1, 3–11. Paris: Cariscript, 1979.

Robert Amadou. *Illuminisme et contre-illuminisme.* Paris: Cariscript, 1989.

Robert Amadou. *Occident, Orient, parcours d'une tradition.* Paris: Cariscript, 1987.

Jean-Louis Ricard. *Régénération et création littéraire chez Louis-Claude de Saint-Martin.* Guérigny, Fr.: CIREM, 1996.

Jean-Louis Ricard. *Étude sur Le Crocodile ou la guerre du bien et du mal de Louis-Claude de Saint-Martin.* Guérigny, Fr.: CIREM, 2002.

Jean-Marc Vivenza. *Le Martinisme. L'enseignement secret des Maîtres.* Grenoble, Fr.: Le Mercure Dauphinois, 2006.

Jean-Marc Vivenza. *La Prière du Cœur selon Louis-Claude de Saint-Martin, dit le Philosophe Inconnu.* La Bégude de Mazenc, F.: Arma Artis, 2007.

Serge Caillet and Xavier Cuvelier-Roy. *Les hommes de désir: Entretiens sur le martinisme.* Grenoble, Fr.: Le Mercure Dauphinois, 2012.

L'Esprit des Choses, First series, nos. 1 to 33. Guérigny, Fr.: CIREM, 1992–2002.

www.ingramcontent.com/pod-product-compliance
Lightning Source LLC
Chambersburg PA
CBHW041126110526
44592CB00020B/2702